You Won't Believe Your Eyes!

A Front Row Look at the Sci-Fi/Horror Films of the 1950s

By
Mark Thomas McGee
and R. J. Robertson

Published in the USA by:
BearManor Media
P O Box 71426
Albany, Georgia 31708
www.bearmanormedia.com

ISBN: 978-1-59393-273-2
Printed in the United States of America
Book design by Robbie Adkins

Contents

Acknowledgements

Thanks to all of the people (most of them no longer with us) who made this book possible: Forrest J Ackerman, John Agar, Dave Allen, Morris Ankrum, Samuel Z. Arkoff, Jack Arnold, Denetia Arellanes, Ronnie Ashcroft, William Asher, John Ashley, Albert Band, Edward Bernds, Whit Bissell, Paul Blaisdell, Leon Blender, Ray Bradbury, Bob Burns, Barry Brown, Richard Carlson, Robert Clarke, Herman Cohen, Gene Corman, Roger Corman, Jim Danforth, Beach Dickerson, Arthur Franz, Gerald Fried, Beverly Garland, Alex Gordon, Bert I. Gordon, Coleen Gray, Charles B. Griffith, Brett Halsey, Ray Harryhausen, Susan Hart, Jonathan Haze, Russell Johnson, Nathan Juran, Albert Kallis, Phil Kellison, David Kramarsky, Steve Latshaw, Eugene Lourie, Bernard Luber, Jacques Marquette, Karl Malden, Ace Mask, Kevin McCarthy, Ib Melchior, Dick Miller, Jeff Morrow, Terry Morse, Ted Newsome, Darlyne O'Brien, Wyott Ordung, George Pal, Dorothy Provine, Sherman Rose, Don Siegel, Gary Smith, Herbert L. Strock, Ken Tobey, Les Tremayne, Forrest Tucker, Martin Varno, Yvette Vickers, Bob Villard, Bill Warren, Tom Weaver, Mel Welles, and James Whitmore.

Foreword

Twenty years after *War of the Satellites* was made, I was showing a 16 mm print of it to some friends who shared my affection for the science fiction movies from our childhood. At the time, all but the cream of these movies had disappeared from television, and private screenings were about the only way to see them. My eight-year-old daughter, Danielle, came out of her room to get something from the kitchen. She paused for a few moments to watch the movie. "*This* actually played in theaters?" she asked with some surprise. Yes, we told her, it had. "And you *paid* to see it?" To someone weaned on the likes of *Stars Wars* and *Jaws*, something as impoverished as *War of the Satellites* was completely incomprehensible. Frankly, I'm grateful that she didn't ask us why we were watching it again.

Today, obscene budgets are lavished on sci-fi films, and armies of technicians slave over the special effects. In the fifties, there were one or two guys doing the effects, and the budget for the whole movie was $65,000 or less. They were made in ten days or less, in black and white, by people working outside of the studio system. *War of the Satellites* wasn't the exception, it was the rule. For the most part, sci-fi was a low-rent genre.

Samuel Z. Arkoff, co-founder of American International Pictures, one of the leading purveyors of sci-fi and horror movies, said that he and his partner, Jim Nicholson, made movies for "children and morons." These were the movies that we now call "drive-in movies" because that's where most of them played. "That's where all the money was," said producer Gene Corman—he and his brother, Roger, made movies for AIP. According to Gene, nurturing a relationship with the owners of the drive-in movie theaters was crucial. "There were certain givens, of course. One, that you understood where the market was in terms of subject matter and, two, what audience you were aiming for. If you brought them together and you were spending in the area of fifty thousand, it was almost impossible not to make some money. We couldn't compete with the major studios because, with our money, we wouldn't have the production values or the stars. The major studios weren't making science fiction, so that's what we made."

At one time, horror films were aimed at adult audiences deeply rooted in the traditional superstitions and folklore of their European cultures. When a vague, scientific explanation was offered (as in the Frankenstein series), the dark European setting left no doubt that those explanations were euphemisms for black magic. Most of the so-called science fiction movies of the fifties were really horror movies in disguise.

World War II was the turning point for the horror film genre. Mad doctors and other villains were still engaged in their nefarious activities, but now they were enlisted to aid the Nazi cause. Frankenstein's castle was relocated to a mythical, and neutral, European locale. As the war continued, Frankenstein, Dracula, and the Wolf Man lost their credibility, and ultimately became stooges for comedians Bud Abbott and Lou Costello. An age of innocence came to an end with the explosion of an atomic bomb on the Japanese city of Hiroshima—more concentrated destruction than mankind had ever dreamed of.

"Throughout the fifties, our repressed paranoia visited us reshaped in the basic mythology of science fiction," wrote Andrew Dowdy, in his terrific book, *Movies Are Better Than Ever*. "Each Saturday night, we witnessed the latest hostile surprise created by an environment more capriciously malignant than anything [Joe] McCarthy promised in his most lunatic moments."

Monster-movie lovers couldn't get enough of these "lunatic moments." When we weren't watching monster movies, we were talking about them, and when we weren't talking about them, we were reading about them in Forrest J Ackerman's *Famous Monsters of Filmland* magazine. Ackerman (a.k.a. Forry) was the Pied Piper of Horrordum. Children of all ages came from all over the world to visit him at his little Spanish-style home at 915 S. Sherbourne Drive in Los Angeles, Karloffornia, which was stuffed with posters, stills, props, books, and other horror and sci-fi memorabilia; it was a combination of a museum and a clubhouse. Forry's readers became as much a part of the magazine as he was. Photos from amateur films and would-be makeup artists were featured in a section of the magazine called "Graveyard Examiner." These young hopefuls were just some of the people who would gather at Forry's home and share their work and interests with like-minded fans. Forry did whatever he could to encourage and promote their dreams. Every now and then, acting as their agent, he would find them work. And every now and then, his efforts backfired.

I happened to be at Forry's one afternoon when he was on the phone with Fritz Lang, the director of his favorite movie, *Metropolis* (1927). Forry was singing the praises of an aspiring young actress who was standing in his office, and she was happily embarrassed as he went on and on about her. She couldn't have been more than fifteen or sixteen year of age, and was as cute as she could be. I went into one of the other rooms, but I could hear both sides of the conversation because Forry was using the speakerphone and had left the intercom open. Unaware that he was being broadcast, and after listening to Forry at great length, Lang finally cut him off in mid-sentence. "Never mind all that," he said dully. "Has she sucked your cock yet?" I never laughed so hard in my life.

Television was one of the prime factors that helped create the sudden glut of the sci-fi/horror movies that Forry was writing about. When people stopped going to the movies once a week and stayed home to watch TV instead, the studios cut back on their productions. A lot of small-town theaters changed their programs two or three times a week. Now they had nothing to play. Independent filmmakers stepped in to fill the void with low-budget, tailor-made movies for a new market: teenagers. Teenagers didn't want to stay home with Mom and Dad to watch *Lawrence Welk*. They wanted to see hot rod movies, rock 'n' roll movies, and movies with monsters.

Randy Robertson and I were obsessed with these monster movies. We talked about them all of the time. It's been almost twenty years since Randy died, and to the very end, he and I were still talking about these silly movies. As children, we saw them as they were being released, and we caught up with some of the older ones at Saturday matinees or on television. Sometimes, we would sneak out of bed on school nights to watch some piece of junk on *The Late, Late Show*. We had to see them all—each and every one of them. Randy was one of the people in the audience on the night I ran *War of the Satellites*.

Pauline Kael once said that if you love movies, you have to learn to love the junk. That isn't exactly what she said, but I think that's the essence of it, and she was right. Plenty of the movies in this book are junk, but Randy and I loved them anyway. We even loved the movies we hated. We would threaten each other with them. "All right then, just for that, you have to watch *Phantom from 10,000 Leagues* four times in a row." It didn't matter which one of us said it, as we'd both groan at the thought of it.

I had forgotten that Randy and I had written this book until Denetia Arellanes found it recently while she was cleaning out her garage. I remembered that Randy and I had talked about writing such a book at the same time that Bill Warren was getting ready to write *Keep Watching the Skies!* We talked with Bill about collaborating, but he had a different kind of book in mind than we did. His book (which is fabulous) is like an encyclopedia, being both detailed and comprehensive. What we had in mind, as you will see, was something a little less exhaustive.

Reading the text again, I realized it needed a lot of work. I only wish that Randy had been here to help me with it. It will be obvious when you read it that both Randy and I not only loved the movies but also the decade; the decade that disc jockeys used to call the nifty fifties. This was the decade we grew up in. Some people think we should never have left the fifties. When people say, "We need to go back to a simpler time," aren't they talking about the fifties? And if they are, what exactly do they mean? If they're waxing nostalgic about the Good Humor man, the Helms Bakery man, or the milkman, I'm with them. I miss those guys. I miss the doctors who used make house calls. I miss two-tone cars and gas stations on every corner with guys who wiped your windows and checked your oil. I miss restaurants without televisions, newscasters who delivered the news instead of their opinions, and conversations that weren't interrupted by cell phones. But I wouldn't want to go back to a decade where everyone was scared of their own shadow. The fear of being blown to smithereens by an atomic bomb seemed all too real. In school, they taught us that in the event of an attack, all we had to do was to crawl under our desks and we'd be okay. They even had a movie that showed us how to do it. Duck and cover! The dumbest kid in the school knew better than that. We were scared. Our parents were scared. Some people were so scared they built bomb shelters in their backyards. The sale of tranquilizers was at an all-time high. There was all of this talk about the Cold War, the Iron Curtain, and the Communists. If it weren't for the Communists, everything would be hunky-dory. Or so we were told.

The House on Un-American Activities Committee, a committee whose sole purpose was supposed to be to root out communists, wanted known party members to name other party members. But the FBI already had the names. They knew who and where these people were because it was never illegal to be a party member. The only legality in question was the committee itself. The real business of HUAC was not to collect names, but rather to cast suspicion and distrust on fuzzy thinking liberals, intellectuals, integrationists, dissidents, one world pacifists, atheists, and non-conformists. It was a reaction to Roosevelt's New Deal. The ruling class liked the Old Deal. They didn't like the restrictions that had been placed on the banks. They didn't like labor unions telling them to give their workers a fair wage and a safe working environment. In short, they didn't like anything that prevented them from making as much money as they could possibly make. They didn't like being forced to spread the wealth. They figured that the best way to put a stop to it was to discredit the people behind it, to make enemies of the people who helped create the labor unions. Several of the people who were involved in the making of these sci-fi movies were victims of what came to be known as the Communist witch hunts. It's impossible to write a book about these movies and not touch on the issues that helped to shape them. Paranoia and mind control were prime ingredients in the sci-fi movies of the fifties.

Before writing this book, I felt that it was imperative to talk with the people who actually worked on these pictures. Understandably, after so many years, many of them didn't remember much. Actor Russell Johnson—best-known for his role as the professor on *Gilligan's Island*—was sure he'd never been in a movie called *The Space Children*. I attempted to jog his memory by reminding him of the part he'd played: an abusive, alcoholic stepfather. He thought for a moment, shook his head, and said: "Maybe I was drunk. I can't remember it." Likewise, Whit Bissell was certain he'd never been in a movie called *Monster on the Campus*. Back in 1980, when I asked producer-director Bert Gordon to go back twenty-five years to the time he made *King Dinosaur*, he balked. "Well, it wasn't twenty-five... How many years did you say?" I repeated the tally. "Oh! No! No! In the middle fifties is all." When at last he faced the naked truth, he said: "Oh, my God! Now I need some science fiction to erase the time."

Long before I even thought about writing such a book, I wanted to talk to these people. I was surprised to find how many of them were in the phone book. Once you knew what city they lived in, you could find them. *Famous Monsters* revealed that actor Morris Ankrum lived in La Crescenta, so I went to the library and found his number in the book. I was twelve or thirteen years old and my voice hadn't changed yet. He kept calling me "honey." I told him that I loved all of his science fiction movies. "Yeah," he said dully, "I was in a lot of those." He sure was. He usually played a colonel or a general in the military. He kept a uniform in his closet so that he'd always be ready to go. He said that I could come to his home, but warned me that he could only chat for a half hour or so, as he had a part to learn. At the time, I naively believed that people like Ankrum were as excited to be in these movies as I was to watch them. In one of those classic moments where fantasy collides with reality, the General showed me a stack of scripts. *Zombies of Mora Tau* was at the top. On the cover, he'd written in pencil a list of movies he'd recently appeared in and the salaries he'd made from them. I suddenly understood exactly what the movies meant to him: food and a roof over his head. It took a while, but once that simple fact sunk in, I realized how ridiculous it was to expect someone to remember a week's work on some thirty-year-old movie.

One of the first people I wanted to talk to when Randy and I decided to write this book was Arthur Franz. Arthur was the star of seven sci-fi/horror movies, five episodes of *Science Fiction Theatre*, and his own series *World of Giants*. I don't remember how I got his number, but I do remember he wasn't happy to hear from me. When I told him that I wanted to talk about his sci-fi movies, he said, "Why would you want to do that? They were all crap!" He was right. They mostly were. "What about *Invaders from Mars*? That wasn't crap," I said. "Well, that was Bill Menzies. He was an artist," he replied. Now, he could have said it was crap too, and that would have been the end of our conversation, but he didn't. And because he didn't, I suspected that if I could just keep him talking, he might give in, which he did.

Helena Carter, Arthur Franz, John Eldridge, Morris Ankrum, and Jimmy Hunt from Invaders from Mars *(1953). Photo from the author's collection.*

Not knowing exactly how long it would take to get to his Malibu home and not wanting to be late, I arrived an hour early. I was ushered into the living room, where Franz was engaged in a chess game with a friend. "You're early," he said. "You'll have to wait until we're finished." So I sat quietly in front of a large picture window, looking at the ocean. Out of the corner of my eye, I saw someone come out of the kitchen door and walk across the back lawn to the guest house. He looked familiar. "That's Jason Miller," Franz said. "He was in *The Exorcist.* He's staying with us for a while. Wouldn't you rather talk to him?" "No," I said. "I want to talk to you." At the stroke of the hour, Franz walked his friend to the door and returned with something for both of us to drink. I can't speak for him, but after a few awkward moments, I had a wonderful time. Knowing how he felt about his sci-fi movies, I thought it would be better to start the conversation with a movie that I had every reason to believe he would like—*The Sniper.* "Now you're talking about quality," he said. So we talked about quality for a while. Then, out of the blue, he said, "I may be pissing in the pulpit, but I think Charlton Heston is a terrible actor." We talked about terrible acting for a while. Finally, we hit the topic that had brought me to his door: his sci-fi movies. "If they couldn't get Richard Carlson or Marshall Thompson, they'd settle for me," he remarked. "All you needed to play those roles was a pipe." After a while, he became warm, friendly, and chatty, and we talked until the sun went down. As I was getting ready to leave, he said: "You want to be in this business. That's plain enough. What do you want to do?" I said that I wanted to write, but I was getting frustrated. I couldn't seem to find a way to get my foot in the door. "Well, you're young. You have plenty of time," he assured me. I told him I felt like my time was running out. I was getting older every minute. "It's this interview," he said with a grin. "It's ageing us both terribly."

CHAPTER ONE

RIDERS TO THE STARS

The first country that can use the Moon for the launching of missiles will control the Earth. That, gentlemen, is the most important military fact of this century.

—Destination Moon

Remember Sputnik, the first satellite in space? It was a big deal back in 1958 because it was a Russian satellite. The Soviet Premier, Nikita Khrushchev, said he'd bury us, and a lot of Americans were afraid that he might. Now the Russians were ahead of us in the race for space. We had to show them. We had to launch our own satellite and quick.

Ten... nine... eight... seven... six... five... four... three... Uh oh! *Kaputnik*. That's what the British press called our rocket after it toppled and exploded on the launch pad. The egg was still dripping off our faces when the Soviets put a larger satellite into space with a dog in it. This caused President Dwight Eisenhower to divert more money to our space program and he created the National Aeronautics and Space Administration (NASA) to help spend it. Finally, at the end of January the following year, the U.S. sent its own satellite into orbit. The very next day, Jack Rabin—who owned a company that produced special effects for low budget movies—phoned producer-director Roger Corman and told him they should make a satellite picture while the topic was still hot. The idea sounded good to Corman. He pitched it to Steve Broidy at Allied Artists. He told Broidy that he could deliver the movie in eight weeks. He didn't say it would be good or entertaining, and he didn't even say that it would make sense—just that he'd deliver it. Broidy was lining-up play dates while Corman was making the picture.

War of the Satellites

In *War of the Satellites*, our satellites are being blown out of space, not by the Russians, but by people from another planet who think that we're a danger to the universe. They kill Dr. Van Ponder (Richard Devon), the head of the satellite program, and make it look like an auto accident. News of his death reaches a United Nations meeting and everyone is ready to throw in the towel when Van Ponder miraculously appears, turning the tide in favor of continuing with the program. What nobody knows is that Van Ponder has been replaced by an alien saboteur. But how was this masquerade possible? Somebody must have found Van Ponder's corpse or nobody would have known that he was dead. And if the aliens hadn't sent the phony Van Ponder to the United Nations, their worries would have been over, and the program would have been scrapped. But, like we said, Corman never promised the movie would make sense.

Five-foot-five-inch Dick Miller—a regular in Corman films—was the hero of the piece. "I was playing a young scientist going into space; a part that should have been given to William Lundigan or Richard Carlson," Miller recalled. "And I looked at Dick Devon, who's about six-foot-two, and I said, 'Jesus Christ. I gotta beat him up?'"

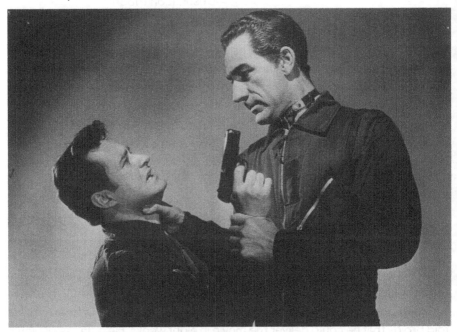

Dick Miller tangles with Richard Devon in Roger Corman's War of the Satellites *(1958). Photo courtesy of Bob Villard.*

Dan Haller was the art director on the picture. It was the first time he'd worked with Corman, and his ability to make the most out of the least made him a valuable addition to the Corman team.

Dan Haller said, "Harry Reif was the set director on that film. [He] brought in these damn lounge chairs and I said, 'Harry, what in the hell are you thinking about? This is supposed to be a spaceship!' Harry said, 'Oh, this is the newest thing.' Well, we were shooting that day, so what could we do?"[1]

Miller said, "You know, we had four arches to make all the hallways in the spaceship. They made 'em long or short, but at the end you always had to make a turn. Four arches. That was the entire ship. Four arches and two lounge chairs."

Exploiting a newspaper headline before the ink had a chance to dry is what low-budget filmmakers did best because the movies were made so quickly. As promised, *War of the Satellites* was in theaters a scant two months after his conversation with Broidy, who was so pleased, he gave Corman $500 to throw a cast party. They're still waiting for that party.

The Flame Barrier

Producers Arthur Gardner and Jules V. Levy also wanted to strike while the headline was hot. Their movie, *The Flame Barrier* (1958), was released the same month as Corman's film. It was written by their production assistant Pat Fielder and George Worthing Yates—the son of Republic Studios prexy, Herbert J. Yates. "I think we were kind of following a pattern of other jungle movies of the time, but there had been the event of a Sputnik going up with a monkey on board," Fielder recalled. "We had fun making *The Flame Barrier*, but we shot it entirely on a sound stage, and we had a very limited budget and schedule."[2]

In Fielder's and Yates's scenario, Kathleen Crowley, Arthur Franz, and Robert Brown take an exhausting trek through the studio-bound jungle to find Crowley's missing husband. They find his corpse covered with globs of radioactive space-stuff spilling out of a satellite. It's up to them to figure out a way to stop this dangerous gunk from covering the entire planet.

Arthur Franz said, "We had a chimp with us in this safari bit. Chimps are a strange animal. If they are anywhere around a lady who happens to be in a certain phase of the moon and they get her scent, they can go bonkers. And this chimp did. He got so excited by our leading lady. . . I can recall to this day him sitting on top of a ladder, eating a banana with one hand and masturbating with the other. I think he bit somebody. Scent or not, he was just mean."

Republic Studios prexy Herbert Yates pulled a fast one by editing two of his old cliffhangers—*Zombies of the Stratosphere* (1952) and *Flying Disc Man from Mars* (1950)—into feature length films with new headline-hot titles: *Satan's Satellites* and *Missile Monsters* (both 1958). Neither movie contained satellites or monsters. The package was still playing in theaters when financial difficulties forced Yates out of business. The following year, he sold his library of films to National Telefilm Associates (NTA), and CBS bought his studio.

By 1955, the era of the cliffhanger had finally reached its end. Republic (once the king of the cliffhangers) and Columbia were the only two studios still making these chapter plays. For the record, the sci-fi serials of the fifties were: *Atom Man vs. Superman, The Invisible Monster* (both 1950), *Mysterious Island* (1951), *Radar Men from the Moon, Zombies of the Stratosphere, Blackhawk, Captain Video* (all 1952), *Commando Cody—Sky Marshall of the Universe, The Lost Planet* (both 1953), and *Panther Girl of the Kongo* (1955).

Satellite in the Sky

Edward and Harry Danziger beat everyone to the punch by making the most expensive of all of the satellite movies before the Sputnik launch. Their movie, *Satellite in the Sky* (1956), was filmed in color and CinemaScope, and was handsomely mounted as well as featuring some decent special effects. Unfortunately, it was a little on the dull side, and the score by Albert Elms was never in tune with the action. The most interesting aspect of the film was the cynical view that writers John Mather, J.T. McIntosh, and Edith Dell had of government officials, whom they depicted as sneaky, dishonest, and ultimately irresponsible. The officials in their script have no interest in the space program until they realize they could use outer space as a testing ground for their bombs; they have a bomb so powerful they don't dare explode it on Earth.

The crew for this mission is virtually hijacked. They think they're on a fact finding mission and aren't told about the bomb until they're well on their way. Donald Wolfit is in charge of launching the thing. He tells the crew there is nothing to worry about. He and the other big brains have covered all of the angles. But the rocket that's supposed to carry the bomb away from the ship doesn't work and Wolfit, who has been pretty smug up to this point, becomes a big crybaby.

Destination Moon

The public's interest in satellites waned as NASA moved on to bigger and better things. The United States' Mercury, Gemini, and Apollo programs culminated in the landing of Apollo's lunar module on the Moon. Neil Armstrong and Edwin Aldrin, Jr., explored the lunar surface, and it was recorded by a television camera. For the first time in history, man walked on a world other than his own. But movie fans had seen it all nearly twenty years before in George Pal's *Destination Moon* (1950).

George Pal got his start in the motion picture business with a series of stop-motion animation shorts called Puppetoons, which earned him an Oscar in 1944. He wanted to make features, but the studio executives at Paramount wouldn't let him, so he cut a deal with Arthur Krim at Eagle-Lion to make two features: *The Great Rupert* and *Destination Moon* (both 1950). Despite some kind reviews, *Rupert* took a box office nosedive, but *Destination Moon* was a hit; the biggest in Eagle-Lion's short history. Robert Heinlein, often called "the Dean of Science Fiction authors," collaborated on the screenplay. Advice from physicists, engineers, rocket experts, and astronomers made the film as scientifically accurate as it could possibly be. All of this technical scrutiny created a very sober film that was more fact than fiction—much to the dismay of the children who hoped the astronauts would find monsters on the Moon.

The astronauts in Pal's film are civilians. Their expedition is financed by a group of rich industrialists, as the Government is being too short-sighted and inflexible to understand the importance of a peacetime space program. The rocket is ready to blast off when government officials rush in with a restraining order. Throwing all caution to the wind, the four astronauts take off, land on the Moon, do what they have to do, and return home.

Dick Wesson, Tom Powers, Warner Anderson, and John Archer from Destination Moon *(1950). Photo courtesy of Bob Villard.*

Audiences were thrilled. The sets and special effects were first rate, and the score by Leith Stevens was subtle and atmospheric. It cost $586,000 to make and it grossed $5.5 million. The big boys over at Paramount were so impressed that they dusted off an old property they'd purchased for Cecil B. DeMille and gave it to Pal for the filming of *When Worlds Collide* (1951)—a multi-million-dollar spectacle with an all-star cast. When the smoke cleared, director Rudolph Mate brought the film in for under a million dollars, and he used a B-movie cast.

When World's Collide

In *When World's Collide*, Dr. Cole Hendron (Larry Keating) warns some top-level officials at a United Nations meeting that a star called Bellus is going to smash into Earth. Other scientists insist it won't come close enough to be dangerous. During the eight months that remain, Hendron hopes to build a rocket ship that will carry forty people to Zyra: an Earth-like planet orbiting Bellus. Sydney Stanton (John Hoyt), a wealthy, crippled business magnate, gives Hendron the money he needs in exchange for a seat on the ship. Hundreds of people

SPECTACLE
NEVER BEFORE
FILMED!

GIANT PLANET
COLLIDES WITH EARTH!

ENORMOUS EARTHQUAKES
SWALLOW WHOLE
CONTINENTS!

TIDAL WAVES FLOOD
ENTIRE COUNTRIES!

SPACE SHIP
LEAVES EARTH!

Paramount presents

In Earth-Shaking Color by TECHNICOLOR

WHEN WORLDS COLLIDE

PRODUCED BY   DIRECTED BY
GEORGE PAL · RUDOLPH MATÉ
SCREENPLAY BY SYDNEY BOEHM

Most Amazing Story That Science Or Fiction Ever
Imagined . . . Based On The Sensational Book By
EDWIN BALMER and PHILIP WYLIE

Magazine ad for When Worlds Collide. *From the author's collection.*

work around the clock with the understanding that only a few of them will benefit from their efforts; lots will be drawn for seats on the rocket. Expecting the worst, Stanton insists that Hendron prepare for the inevitable confrontation with the workers. Hendron doesn't share Stanton's cynical point of view, but it turns out that he's right. The workers revolt and charge the ship. Hendron remains behind and forces Stanton to do the same, knowing that with less weight, the young people on the rocket will stand a better chance of reaching the other planet. The rocket is launched and Earth is destroyed.

Sydney Stanton is the ultimate image of corrupted capitalism. Confined to a wheelchair, crippled both physically and emotionally, his self-serving generosity is in direct opposition to Hendron's selfless concern for mankind. He clumsily rises out of his wheelchair and lurches toward the ship as the rocket takes off, a pathetic symbol of something the passengers are hopefully leaving behind them.

Pal told us he never felt shortchanged on any of his pictures, but he sure was on this one. The effects won an Oscar, and although they're good, some of them were lifted from other movies, and there weren't enough of them. If you look at the very last shot, Zyra's landscape looks like a background plate for one of the studio's Casper cartoons.

"Paramount wanted to sneak the picture, so we had Chesley Bonestell do a painting for the preview," recalled Pal. "It was never supposed to be in the picture. We were going to build this very elaborate set. But nobody complained, so Paramount said, 'That's good enough.'"

When World's Collide opens with a close-up of *The Bible* and the story of Noah and his ark, thus making no pretense of what Hendron and his space ship represent. Religion found its way into a lot of these sci-fi movies. Klaatu, the visitor from space in *The Day the Earth Stood Still* (1951), is a Christ-figure with a message of peace, and Hugh Marlowe is the Judas who betrays him. When the Martians are killed by bacteria at the end of *The War of the Worlds* (1953), narrator Cedric Hardwicke reminds us that it was God, not science, who saved us. A belief in science *and* religion seems incongruous to some people. It's an issue that Walter Brooks wrestles with in Pal's *Conquest of Space* (1955). Brooks, in charge of the first manned expedition to Mars, suffers a nervous breakdown and becomes a religious fanatic. He sees the mission as blasphemy and tries to sabotage the rocket. His son (Eric Fleming) is forced to kill him. This premise could have evolved into a viable, dramatic situation, but James O'Hanlon's screenplay is a concentrated collection of clichés spoken with unrelieved fervor by a crew of simplistic stereotypes. Writers Phillip Yordan, Barre Lyndon, and George Worthing Yates all took a crack at this picture, and it's hard to believe that any of their scripts could have been worse than O'Hanlon's. The film was a flop and ended Pal's career at Paramount. He found a new home at MGM, where he made his best sci-fi film, *The Time Machine* (1960).

"There was a bad feeling toward science fiction in those days, but I didn't care because I'm not a social climber," Pal remarked. "I knew they were good pictures."

Robert Lippert and Rocketship X-M

Around the time that Pal was getting ready to make *Destination Moon*, producer-director Kurt Neumann also wanted to make a movie about an expedition to the Moon and pitched the idea to producer Robert Lippert, but Lippert wasn't interested. He didn't know anything about science fiction; he'd made his money with westerns and cop films. But when he saw all of the publicity Pal's film was generating, he thought it would be criminal not to take advantage of it. He called Neumann back into his office and told him to forget about the Moon. Lippert wanted to avoid any chance of a lawsuit. They'd go to Mars instead. They called their picture *Rocketship X-M* (1950).

Lippert owned sixty theaters in Southern Oregon and California, and like many theater-owners during this period, he started making his own movies. In 1946, he and John J. Jones formed Screen Guild: the embryo of Lippert Pictures, Inc. However, Lippert's troubles with the Screen Actors Guild eventually reached a point where he was forced to close his doors and move his operation to 20th Century-Fox, where he continued to produce low-budget movies under the radar.

"He was a dynamic, self-made man," actress Margia Dean told Mike Fitzgerald, "Short, stocky, and bald, but a nice-looking man in the face. He smoked a cigar and looked like the typical Hollywood-producer type."

Studios would often loan their contract players to other studios for a price that exceeded the actor's salary and pocket the difference. It was a standard practice. Actor Sid Melton was under contract to Lippert when Paramount wanted Melton for a Bob Hope picture. The studio gave Lippert $600 for Melton's services. The actor was given his usual $140 salary, but Lippert wanted Melton to pay the tax on the $600. This was the sort of tomfoolery that made Lippert so popular not only with SAG but also with the IRS.

Kurt Neumann's script for *Rocketship X-M* depicted Mars as a jungle infested with prehistoric animals. The plan was to lift the dinosaur footage from Hal Roach's *One Million B.C.* (1940). According to Bill Warren, blacklisted writer Dalton Trumbo rewrote Neumann's script without credit, and it's likely that Trumbo was the one who threw out the dinosaurs. Instead, the astronauts find the remnants of a highly advanced Martian civilization, reduced to stone-age savagery by atomic warfare. Trumbo's warning about the danger of atomic destruction was echoed so many times by other sci-fi movies, it became a cliché.

Lloyd Bridges and Osa Massen from Rocketship X-M *(1950). Photo courtesy of Bob Villard.*

At the time that *Rocketship X-M* was made, the banks were more likely to give loans to movies that had a little romance in them, so writers were asked to shoehorn women into stories. One afternoon, while Ray Bradbury was working on his script for *Moby Dick* (1956), the film's director, John Huston, came into his office looking like a whipped puppy. When Bradbury asked what was wrong,

Huston told him that he'd just gotten a call from the front office. "They signed Gina Lollobrigida," he sighed, shaking his head gravely. "They want her in the picture. I tried to talk them out of it, but there was no changing their minds. We'll have to work her in somehow." Bradbury shot out of his chair like his pants were on fire. He ranted and raved like a lunatic until he saw the smile on Huston's face and realized that he'd been had.

In the early sci-fi movies, the women were usually the wives of the hero and would be onscreen just long enough to give him a kiss and tell him to be careful. These scenes could later be cut to make room for commercials when the movies were sold to television. Clever writers solved the problem by taking the women out of the kitchen and placing them in occupations that would put them at the center of the action. In *Tarantula* (1955), John Agar expresses a note of irritation when he learns that the lovely Mara Corday is a biologist. "I knew it would happen," he says. "Give women the vote and what do you get... lady scientists." In *Them* (1954), when Joan Weldon insists on going with the men into the tunnels with the giant ants, James Arness expresses a sentiment shared by most of the males in the audience: it's no place for a woman. "There's no time to give you a fast course in insect pathology," she snaps. "So let's stop all the talk and get on with it!" Ken Tobey thinks Faith Domergue should bow out when things get dangerous in *It Came from Beneath the Sea* (1955). Her colleague, Donald Curtis, comes to her rescue. "There's a whole new breed [of women] that feels they're just as smart and courageous as men, and they are. They don't like to be over-protected or have their initiative taken away from them."

"I suppose all you think a woman should do is cook, and sew, and bear children," Osa Mason says to Lloyd Bridges in *Rocketship X-M*. He replies, "Isn't that enough?" Miss Mason plays a physicist, a field she has entered at the cost of her femininity. At one point, there's a problem with the fuel mixture. She and John Emery, the captain of the expedition, go to work on a new formula. When her calculations differ from his, he dismisses them without a second's thought. She diplomatically suggests that they use both of their findings as a base, but he refuses. When she gets upset, he accuses her of being "a woman," which is the real reason he refused to take her seriously in the first place. It turns out that Emery is the one who doesn't know what he's talking about. They don't have enough fuel to make the return trip home and everyone dies. It's a little shocking.

Lloyd Bridges told Tom Weaver, "With *Rocketship X-M*, we did beat our competitor, *Destination Moon* [into the theaters]. And they paid a lot more for their production. We kind of took advantage of the publicity they were putting out—people weren't quite sure whether they were seeing that picture or our picture."

Ironically, because it was more concerned with drama than scientific accuracy, *Rocketship X-M* emerged as the more entertaining of the two films.

We would be remiss if we did not mention the film's wonderful score. Normally, Lippert's resident composer, Albert Glasser, would have been assigned to the project, but Lippert wanted a name that would give his film a little class. He made a deal with Ferde Grofe, the writer of *The Grand Canyon Suite*, to write the music. Director Neumann probably never knew how fortunate he was. Glasser's music was never subtle and it always sounded like his orchestra was still tuning up. After one particularly loud, bombastic, and discordant cue for *The Monster from Green Hell* (1958), a bored technician turned to the composer with his tongue firmly in his cheek and asked, "Is that where he kisses the girl, Al?"

Project Moon Base

Project Moon Base (1953) was an unsold, hour long television pilot written by Robert Heinlein for a proposed series called *The World Beyond*. Unable to make a sale to TV, producer Jack Seaman added six or seven minutes to the front of his pilot and sold it as a feature to Bob Lippert. The story is set in the future, and Donna Martell, Bill Moore, and Larry Johns are sent on a scouting mission to the Moon to find and photograph suitable locations for a military base. Nobody knows that Johns has been replaced by a look-alike enemy agent, but his lack of photographic skills and the fact that he knows nothing about the Brooklyn Dodgers gives him away. Johns and Moore get into a fight, knock the controls, and crash on the Moon. Johns is killed while helping Moore install a communication device. Once they contact Earth, Martell and Moore are told it will be at least a year before they can be rescued. Public opinion being what it is, they are ordered to get married. The ceremony is performed over television and the audience is given a look at the future President of the United States... a woman!

Stranger still, *Project Moon Base* managed to have some effective scenes of the astronauts on the moon. This was something remarkable for a low-budget effort. Costly matte paintings, miniatures, big sets, and optical effects are needed to achieve the look and the feel of being on another planet, which is why, even in George Pal's movies, the characters never stray too far from the ship. Filmmakers working with lower budgets were forced to make other arrangements. Red Rock Canyon, tinted red, became the Martian landscape for *Rocketship X-M*.

King Dinosaur

Producer-director Bert I. Gordon went to Big Bear Mountain and Bronson Canyon to make *King Dinosaur* (1955). "Of course, the locale was supposed to be another planet," Gordon said. "But I got around that by having one of the characters say, 'Strange! This planet is almost identical to Earth!'"[3]

Yes, very strange. Very strange and, one might say, very disappointing. *You might as well go home, you people. There's nothing more to see here.*

There are only four actors *King Dinosaur*—Doug Henderson, Patti Gallagher, Bill Bryant, and Wanda Curtis. For forty minutes, they stroll aimlessly through the pine trees with nothing of interest to say and very little to do. Finally, Doug and Patti paddle off in their rubber raft to explore an island which turns out to be a refuge for dinosaurs! (Did Gordon fish Neumann's old script out of the trash?) Doug opens fire on a giant iguana masquerading as a Tyrannosaurus Rex. He gets so caught up in the moment, he shoves Patti backwards into the hillside between rounds and she smacks her head, leaving her both hurt and angry. Later, the two take refuge in Bronson caves and are trapped when the iguana parks itself in front of the entrance. Doug takes a picture of it. "It's a good likeness," he remarks. (Photographs usually are.) He fires a flare to let Bill and Wanda know that they're in trouble. They arrive just in time to see Doug and Patti sneak past the iguana while it wrestles with an alligator lizard. Bill had the good sense to bring an atomic bomb with him. He sets the timer for thirty minutes, and the four of them have to run like hell to put a safe distance between them and the explosion. One might wonder why he didn't set the timer for sixty or ninety minutes. As a matter of fact, one might question the necessity of blowing up the island in the first place. But then, we shouldn't question art. We should let it wash over us.

Though they were never shown going up a steep mountain slope, the fab four run pell-mell down a steep mountain slope. Poor Wanda slips and falls on her behind. Doug, possibly for dramatic effect, holds his rifle at arm's length above his head as he leaps off the ledge. Predictably, the fool loses his balance, falls on his backside, and smacks into Wanda. Doug is the last one to reach the bottom of the hill and just as he is about to clear the frame, he falls on his backside again. The editor had only to cut a few frames to save Doug from this final embarrassment. It's an editorial decision that would have hurt a better film. Here, it actually enhances something that is, in every respect, a hopeless piece of junk.

Seconds ahead of the explosion, Doug grabs Patti's hand and tries to yank her into a ditch. But Patti wants nothing more to do with the reckless fool. It's difficult to hear above the music and noise, but in a very real and angry ad-lib, you can hear Patti scream, "Let go of me!" The bomb goes off, and as the four astronauts watch the scratchy stock footage of the mushroom cloud, Bill muses, "Well, we've done it." To which Doug replies: "Yeah, we sure have done it. We've brought civilization to planet Nova."

Like we said, let it wash over you.

Flight to Mars *(1951) was so impoverished, Cameron Mitchell told Arthur Franz he was afraid they might be given Mars candy bars in lieu of a salary. The rocket Franz is holding is the miniature used for the special effects sequences. Photo courtesy of Bob Villard.*

Flight to Mars

I was ten years old when I saw *Flight to Mars* (1951). It was a Saturday matinee and the theater was packed with kids. (Randy was there that afternoon, but we didn't know each other yet.) We all wondered what the Martians would look like. Would they have one or two heads, three or four eyes, tentacles or arms, grotesque noses or...?

"BOOOOOOOOOO!"

The Martian leader appeared, wearing one of the colorful spacesuits from *Destination Moon*, and it was just Morris Ankrum. No makeup, no nothin'. The disappointment was overwhelming, and every kid in that audience gave vent. Some of them sought comfort at the snack bar. Others simply settled into their seats, resigned to the bitter truth that they'd been duped.

Ankrum offers to assist the Earth people in the repair of their rocket, but he has ulterior motives. Mars is a dying planet. "Once the rocket is ready," he tells his cronies, "they will become our prisoners. The evacuation of a dead planet will begin; first the army, then the civilians."

Arthur Franz said, "There was one scene where the five of us were supposed to climb this ladder to the spaceship. They'd borrowed it from some other movie [*Rocketship X-M*] and it was too tall for any of the stages. So they cut a hole in the floor. While we were waiting for the director to get a shot of our butts climbing up this ladder, Marguerite Chapman said, 'Well, here we all are, in the cellar at Monogram. Jesus Christ! How low can you get?'"

The film's producer, Walter Mirisch, promised a sequel—*Voyage to Venus*. Fortunately, he never made good on his promise.

Sam Arkoff, vice president of American International Pictures, recalled an afternoon when he and his partner, Jim Nicholson, sat through a movie (he couldn't remember the name) that made *Flight to Mars* look like a masterpiece. "[The producers] built this set inside of this warehouse, which was supposed to be the cockpit of a spaceship. For the first half of the picture, these astronauts talked about what they expected to find on whatever planet it was they were headed for. When they landed, the camera shook a little to give the impression that they'd landed. You never saw the outside of the ship. The astronauts walked out the door and the film faded to black. When it faded in again, the astronauts returned and spent the second half of the film talking about what they'd seen. You never got out of that cockpit."

Fortunately, the movie never saw a release.

Spaceways

Spaceways (1953) was a dull, conventional murder mystery, adapted from an old radio play. It was co-financed by Hammer Films in England and Bob Lippert in America. Outer space was little more than a backdrop for a story that could just as easily have been played out entirely on Earth. The movie might just as well have been called *Hallways*.

"This was really lunacy," said producer Michael Carreras, "as the budget was the same as it would have been if it was about two people in bed—a domestic comedy type of thing."[4]

The whole business is best summed up by a remark made by leading man Howard Duff when he's attempting to describe the sensations of space travel to the people back on Earth, "No sense of speed. No feeling of any kind."

This Island Earth

Unlike *Spaceways* or *Flight to Mars*, Universal-International's lively $800,000 Technicolor sci-fi adventure *This Island Earth* (1955) had everything a kid could ask for—explosions, death rays, flying saucers, and monsters. Director Joseph M. Newman bought the rights to the novel by Raymond F. Jones with the intention of producing the picture himself. He went into partnership with Sabre Productions, but Sabre was unable to raise the money. Newman and the script by Edward G. O'Callaghan

Jeff Morrow as Exeter. Photo from the author's collection.

were sold as a package to Universal. William Alland was assigned to the project and he brought in Franklin Cohen for a rewrite. Universal contract players Rex Reason, Faith Domergue, and Jeff Morrow were chosen as the leads.

Jeff Morrow said, "I read it and liked the basic story, but I felt that the Exeter character was two-dimensional. So Bill Alland and the writer wanted to discuss it with me. I told them what I thought; as it turned out, the writer felt the same way. He had been told to write the script a certain way, but since we agreed down-the-line, the changes were made. The way it was originally written, he was a heavy. When we were through, I think he was more the hero. Even some of the early photographs taken of me tried to make me look like a menace."

The basic plot of *This Island Earth* was that prominent scientists from all over the world are gathered together to bring about world peace, or so they think. Actually, they've been recruited to develop new sources of atomic energy to reinforce the protective shield around the planet Metaluna. In the early part of the film, Exeter, the head of the project, never admits that he's from another planet, but every kid in the audience knew that he was. He had to be with his high-domed forehead and a name like Exeter. Yet the people in the movie don't seem to notice. It's the elephant in the room.

Two of the scientists, Cal Meacham (Rex Reason) and Ruth Adams (Faith Domergue), are hustled off to Metaluna when the project on Earth is abandoned. The planet is in the last stages of devastation when they arrive, and the supreme ruler (Douglas Spencer) doesn't want to waste any time. He orders Exeter to take the Earthlings to the thought-transference chamber. Exeter helps them escape instead. Once they've been safely transported to Earth, Exeter commits suicide rather than continue his existence as an interplanetary expatriate.

The critic for *Variety* wrote, "One of the most thrilling sequences occurs as huge meteors attack the space ship as it is working its way to Metaluna. Ingeniously-constructed props and equipment, together with strange sound effects, also are responsible for furthering interest, which is of the edge-of-the-seat variety. For an added fillip, there's a mutant—half human, half insect—which boards the ship as it escapes from Metaluna."

Riders to the Stars and Gog

Producer Ivan Tors and actor Richard Carlson went into partnership to produce three sci-fi movies in the early fifties, all involving the fictional Office of Scientific Investigation (OSI). Two of these films, *Riders to the Stars* and *Gog* (both 1954), were largely concerned with the training and testing of astronauts for space travel.

The goal of the astronauts in *Riders to the Stars* is to capture a meteor. Herbert Marshall, the head of the project, explains why. Pointing to a meteor fragment, he says, "The iron and steel of which it consists are undamaged, yet it travelled through space an infinite period of time without being destroyed by cosmic rays. Therefore, it must have had some kind of protective outer hull around it. What? Gentlemen, in order to continue with our work, and to win the race of conquering space, we must answer those questions."

The film was written by Curt Siodmak and directed by Richard Carlson, who also played a supporting role. Carlson thought it turned out well for a low-budget picture and the trade magazines agreed. It

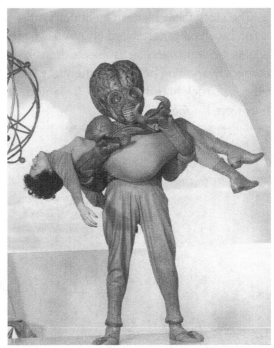

Faith Domergue in the clutches of one of the Metaluna mutants. Photo from the author's collection.

is a serious effort to be sure, but not a very exciting one, largely due to the producer's insistence on realism and scientific accuracy, which more often than not was an impediment to the drama. Never was this more apparent than on Tors's television series, *Science Fiction Theatre* (1955-1957). Each week, host Truman Bradley would say, "Let me show you something interesting." But he never did.

More than likely, Richard Carlson would have been the star of *Gog* if he hadn't been too busy with his television series, *I Led Three Lives* (1953-1956), in which he played real-life double agent Herbert A. Philbrick. The series was produced by Frederick W. Ziv, who was one of the most prolific and successful producers of syndicated television programs.

Frederic Ziv said, "It's very difficult in these times to realize what was going on then. But it was felt that there was a genuine communist threat to undermine the United States, perhaps to take over the United States. The FBI felt that they must have surveillance and the public was entitled to know that that type of surveillance was going on. I feel that we rendered that service to the American public. You may or may not approve of that in today's times."[5]

When Gig Young was offered the lead role in *Gog*, the film's director, Herbert L. Strock, advised him not to take it. "I told him it was going to be lousy and that it wouldn't do his career any good. Gig thanked me and walked away from the project. Richard Egan took the part and he was quite good."

The story takes place in an underground testing center where everything is run by a computer called NOVAC, which has been taken over by enemy agents. Scientists and test subjects drop like flies as their experiments are sabotaged. Everything becomes potentially lethal, including two robots, Gog and Magog. Strock hated them too. "I wanted larger robots," he said. "I thought they were laughable."

John Wengraf is killed by Gog, the Frankenstein of steel. Photo from the author's collection.

In *Gog's* opening sequence (originally a pre-credit sequence), two scientists freeze a monkey and then thaw it out. They want to see if it's possible to freeze the astronauts during space travel and then thaw them out after they've arrived at their destination. To make it appear frozen, the animal was sprayed with white powder and given something to make it sleep, but after two injections, the monkey was very much awake. The people from the Society for the Prevention of Cruelty to Animals wouldn't allow the animal to be injected a third time, so the animal's trainer calmly carried the monkey away from the watchful eyes of the SPCA people and bonked it on the head. "There," he said, returning with the monkey in his arms, "he's asleep now."

Toward the end of the film, after the robots have been neutralized and the enemy spy plane controlling the computer has been blown out of the sky, leading lady Constance Dowling faints and wakes up in a hospital bed. "What happened?" she asks Richard Egan. Nothing to worry about, he tells her, "just a little too much radiation." *Next time get under your desk!*

Ivan Tors stayed active throughout the fifties and sixties. *Sea Hunt* (1958-61) and *Daktari* (1966-69) were among his many television credits. He found his greatest success with animal movies such as *Clarence the Cross-Eyed Lion* (1965), *Namu* (1966), and *Flipper* (1963). He was in Brazil scouting locations for a new series when he died in 1969.

Cat-Women of the Moon

The astronauts in the sci-fi films of the fifties always suffer excruciating pain during blast-offs, the likes of which the real-life astronauts never experienced. Their faces get all contorted and they look like the flesh is going to be ripped from their skulls. There is such a scene in the opening of *Cat-Women of the Moon* (1954), yet each of the five astronauts has a different reaction to the sudden burst of acceleration. Sonny Tufts seems confused, Marie Windsor apprehensive, and Bill Phipps is terrified. Doug Fowley looks like he might be suffering from gas and Victor Jory doesn't react at all. When these same people fasten seat belts on chairs with casters, you know you're in good hands.

Victor Jory and Marie Windsor in the company of the Hollywood Cover Girls. Photo courtesy of Bob Villard.

Before the astronauts in *Cat-Women* land on the Moon, the audience is made aware that Miss Windsor is under the control of the cat-women. With her help, the cat-women hope to steal the ship so they can leave their dying planet. One of the cat-women (Susan Morrow) falls in love with Bill Phipps. She tries to stop her comrades and gets killed for her trouble. As Phipps cradles Miss Morrow in his arms, the camera holds as Jory and Tufts race past him. After some off-stage grunting and groaning, we hear gunshots. Jory yells, "The cat-women are dead and Helen's all right!" Back on the ship, Tufts offers a few words of comfort to the distraught Mr. Phipps: "As for you, young man, what's done is done."

This picture has everything—Sonny Tufts, 3-D, the Hollywood Cover Girls, and a giant spider— but no ending. The spider was rented from Western Costume and it was still there, four years later, in a corner, and gathering dust when Astor Pictures decided to remake the movie.

Hey Ed, come here. Look at this. Am I losing my mind or is that the same damn spider we used in that crappy "Cat-Women" picture we made a few years back? I'll bet you five bucks it is. I can't believe somebody hasn't set fire to it. You know something, though, it looks okay. Dust it off and it'd be good as new. Hell, what are we waiting for? We've got the spider. Let's remake the picture. This time we'll call it "Missile to the Moon" (1958).

Gary Clarke said, "[We] recognized [*Missile to the Moon*] wasn't an A film... Still, we hoped that it was going to do something for our careers! There were people there who took it very serious, particularly if they had money involved. There were a couple of actors who had been around for a while and had done a lot of work, who were just there to get through the day and get their money. They didn't actually say this, but you could feel it."[6]

In one jaw-dropping moment of lunacy, the astronauts are standing in the middle of Red Rock Canyon with four or five rock people coming at them. These rock people look a little like Gumby and don't move fast enough to catch a three-legged turtle and yet, with every possible avenue of escape open to them, one of the astronauts yells, "We're trapped!"

Fire-Maidens of Outer Space

There was no way to see *Fire-Maidens of Outer Space* (1956) when this book was originally written. Randy and I were at the mercy of our memories. We remembered that there was a monster kept at bay by an electrified fence. We remembered that the monster got past the fence (we didn't remember how) just as the leading lady was about to be sacrificed (we didn't remember why) and we remembered that the leading man, Anthony Dexter, showed up in time to save her. So this time around I went to the net, found the movie, and settled back to watch it. For the first five or six minutes, in a master shot, Dexter and some other nudnik talked about a new moon they'd discovered. There wasn't much to say about this new moon, but Dexter had time to light his cigarette twice while they said it. This uninteresting conversation came to a halt when a woman suddenly appeared on the walkway above their heads. She walked *slowly* across the long ramp, came *slowly* down a long flight of stairs, took her sweet time unfastening a latch on this stupid little gate, walked *slowly* to the desk where the two men were standing, grabbed a chair, which she slid slightly to her right for no reason whatsoever, and sat in it. A few words were exchanged, she wrote something down on a notepad, got back up, spent even more time wrestling with the silly latch than she had before, walked *slowly* back up the stairs, and *slowly* back across the ramp.

If Randy had been with me, I could have made it to the end of the movie. Without him, it was impossible. Cy Roth, the man who wrote and directed this vacuum of entertainment, must have been proud of it. His name appeared four times in the credits. So let him watch it. I'd rather eat ground glass.

Forbidden Planet

MGM spent almost two million bucks to make *Forbidden Planet*, one of the best of the fifties sci-fi movies. Directed by Fred McLeod Wilcox, it had a solid cast, an intelligent story, top-drawer special effects, impeccable sets and hardware, the coolest robot anybody had ever seen, and an innovative electronic music score.[7] The studio ran a rough cut of the picture at a sneak preview to see if the score would go over. The audience loved the picture so much that the studio didn't want to tamper with it. They actually released the work print. Because of this incredibly wrong-headed decision, no one will never know how good this picture could have been if the editor had been allowed to fine tune it.

Robby the Robot was designed and built by Robert Kinoshita. Photo from the author's collection.

The story is set in the future. United Planets Cruiser C-57-D, commanded by John J. Adams (Leslie Nielson), is sent to Altair to rescue the crew of the Bellerophon party, which had come to the planet twenty years earlier. There are only two survivors: philologist Dr. Edward Morbius (Walter Pidgeon) and his daughter Altaira (Anne Francis). Morbius explains that the others were killed by some invisible planetary force. It isn't long before a couple of Adams's men are murdered by this mysterious, invisible thing that can't be disintegrated by their ray guns.

For twenty years, Morbius has gathered information about the Krell, a superior race that lived on the planet millions of years before. On the brink of a great discovery, the entire population was wiped out in a single night. Morbius doesn't realize that the Krell had completed their project. They'd built a machine that enabled their minds to project solid matter to any point on the planet. But they forgot one thing: Monsters from the Id! Their subconscious minds had been given access to a machine that could never be shut down and they became the victims of their own secret lust for power and revenge. Morbius must confront his alter-ego, given access to the machine by a freak accident, to save his daughter when his Id-monster comes to punish her for falling in love with the Commander.

Anne Francis and Leslie Nielson. Photo from the author's collection.

Most of the critics were kind to *Forbidden Planet* in a condescending way, but none of them seemed to appreciate how complex and multi-layered it was. If nothing else, it's an extremely well-crafted mystery story with a dilly of a revelation. The story that Irving Block and Allen Adler sold to producer Nicholas Nayfack was pretty simple-minded. An expedition is sent to Mercury to find out what happened to a previous expedition. There are only two survivors, a father and his daughter. The rest were killed by some invisible monster. A device is built to make the monster visible, it's killed, and everyone goes home. Screenwriter Cyril Hume took this routine story—based on Shakespeare's *The Tempest*—and turned it into something remarkable. If Block and Adler had sold their story to Allied Artists, as they'd originally intended, it's safe to assume the film would have been quite ordinary; something along the lines of Edward Bernds's *Queen of Outer Space*, which starred, the Paris Hilton of her day, Zsa Zsa Gabor.

Queen of Outer Space

Edward Bernds said, "Apparently, Zsa Zsa felt she was slumming coming to Allied Artists. At every opportunity, she made demands and threatened to quit if they weren't met. And I don't think she liked all of the competition. How could the crew keep their eyes on Zsa Zsa when Tania Velia, Miss Belgium,* walked by with one of the most gorgeous superstructures man has ever seen? Built like a brick privy, I think the phrase is."

*For the record, she was Miss Yugoslavia.

The genesis of the movie is explained in a letter the director wrote to Leonard Maltin. Here, with the permission of Mr. Bernds, are excerpts from that letter:

> "Walter Wanger, as you know, was sent to jail for shooting an agent in the crotch. Agents being what they are, many people thought Wanger should be given a commendation, but instead was sent to jail for a short time. When he got out, he needed a job and Steve Broidy of Allied Artists gave him one. Wanger brought several properties with him, among them a ten or twelve page outline titled *Queen of the Universe* by Ben Hecht. The Hecht outline wasn't very good—it read as though he had spent at least a half-hour on it and it was mainly a satirical look at a mythical planet ruled, ineptly, by women. It wasn't much of a motion picture at all and about all that Charles Beaumont used was the basic idea of a woman-dominated world. I didn't think Beaumont's screenplay was very good... and decided to lighten it up, spoof it, if you will, and rely on lots of beautiful girls in fetching costumes for commercial appeal."

Bernds didn't have a lot of money to make this picture. Some of the special effects were cribbed from an earlier film of his, and the hardware and some of the costumes were borrowed from *Forbidden Planet*. More than likely, a third of the budget went to Miss Gabor and all of the costumes designed for her by Thomas Pierce. She has a new outfit in every sequence.

Eric Fleming and his infantile crew crash on Venus and become captives of a bunch of women in mini-skirts. Queen Yllana (Laurie Mitchell in a mask), accuses them of plotting to wage war on them and tosses them into the prison chamber while the council decides their fate.

A curious thing happened to this film. Originally, Zsa Zsa goes to the prison chamber to tell the men that their lives are in danger. She explains that she is

Zsa Zsa Gabor is not the Queen of Outer Space. *She is Taleeah, a subversive scientist. Photo courtesy of Bob Villard.*

leading a revolt against the queen and wants them to help. The men are then taken back to the council chamber and the queen gives them a death sentence. They are ushered back to the prison chamber to await their execution. Zsa Zsa returns to say she will help them escape, which she does.

When the film was released to video, the two sequences in the prison chamber were merged into one. A silent close up of Zsa Zsa, looking from left to right, bridges the two. The dialogue doesn't quite work and everyone has shifted positions during her close-up, but nobody seems to have noticed. Why anyone would have bothered to do this is puzzling.

Later, the queen summons Fleming to her chambers, where he clumsily attempts to seduce her. "I understand you better than you do yourself," he tells her. "You're denying man's love, substituting hatred and a passion for this monstrous power you possess! You're not only a queen, you're a woman, too, and a woman needs a man's love. Let me see your face." Before she can stop him, Fleming rips off her mask, revealing her hideous, twisted flesh. "Radiation burns," she snarls. "Men did this to me, men and their wars. You say I need the love of a man. Very well, now that you know, will you give it to me, Captain?" Fleming's self-assured manner is reduced to the stuttering of Porky Pig. Things look grim as the wicked queen makes ready to use her Beta Disintegrator on that last bastion of male superiority: the Earth. But the machine has been sabotaged by the rebels. In a free-for-all that has to be seen to be believed, the rebels subdue the queen's guards as the machine explodes and fries the queen to a crisp.

From the Earth to the Moon

The year before Republic Pictures closed their doors, RKO went belly up, leaving a stack of unreleased films up for grabs. *From the Earth to the Moon* (1958), written by Robert Blees and James Leicester from the novel by Jules Verne, was one of them. Producer Benedict Bogeaus had assembled an impressive cast: Joseph Cotton, George Sanders, and Debra Paget with supporting players Patrick Knowles, Henry Daniell, and Morris Ankrum as Ulysses S. Grant. Warner Brothers bought the picture, giving their advertising department its worst nightmare. Other than the cast, the film had nothing to exploit. There are no special effects to speak of and no action. Desperate for something to put on the posters, the advertising department settled for, "Deadly gas leak almost ends it all!" Milking humor from a remark like that is tantamount to kicking a dead horse. As one critic so aptly put it, the characters talk themselves and the film to death.

It! The Terror from Beyond Space

Short story writer Jerome Bixby, best known for his 1953 story "It's a Good Life," which was turned into a 1961 episode of *The Twilight Zone*, scripted the exciting *It! The Terror from Beyond Space* (1958), which was basically *The Thing from Another World* in outer space. It starred Marshall Thompson as the sole survivor of an expedition to Mars. A rescue ship takes him back to Earth to stand trial for the murder of his crew. Thompson claims they were killed by some creature that struck during a sandstorm. Kim Spalding, the Captain of the rescue ship, thinks he's lying and makes Thompson's life miserable.

Just before blast-off, a blood-drinking Martian sneaks aboard the ship and starts picking off the crew one by one. Spalding is forced to admit that he was wrong about Thompson, and has to suffer the humiliation of watching his girlfriend fall in love with Thompson too—which is what he deserves for being both an insufferable bully and a bad actor.

While Howard Weeks was sculpting the bat-rat-spider-crab, Sid Pink told him that it wasn't exactly what he had in mind. Weeks calmly dropped the thing into the trashcan and said: "What did you have in mind?" Unable to answer his question, Pink walked away and Weeks fished the model out of the trash.

The Martian (Billy Curtis) warns the Earth people to stay off his planet. Photos courtesy of Bob Villard.

The Angry Red Planet

Producer Sidney Pink sent Gerald Mohr, Nora Hayden, Jack Kruschen, and Les Tremayne to *The Angry Red Planet* (1959). Only two of them returned with a rather lengthy taped message from the Martians that basically said, "Yankee go home."

Pink got his start in motion pictures in 1952 as the producer of Arch Obler's 3-D movie *Bwana Devil*. In the hope of repeating the success he had with that film, Pink bought a 1947 PRC movie called *Linda Be Good*, inserted some 3-D scenes of chorus girls, and released it as *I Was a Burlesque Queen* (1953). Six years later, he hired Ib Melchior, a decorated war hero, spy, and gourmet chef to write and direct *The Angry Red Planet* in Cinemagic; a revolutionary new process that seamlessly blended drawings and live objects. Or so it was ballyhooed. The picture went into production a month after Melchior had completed his final draft.

Pink said, "Our portrayal of the unnatural creatures that our crew met on Mars was rendered credible by the results of the new Cinemagic process. Our man-eating plant and our rat-bat-spider-crab lost their comic-relief miniature look in the newly discovered process. They became frightening and real, as did our long-distance view of the Martian city. There was no need to do anything more than let Norman's nimble fingers draw up a landscape, and presto—we were able to go there via Cinemagic."[8]

"The much-ballyhooed 'new' Cinemagic process... it is sad to report, is scarcely anything to shout about—or even talk about," wrote critic S.A. Dick. Variety reported: "While it may take considerable ingenuity to produce this effect, the result isn't really worth it."

Les Tremayne said, "We had a sneak preview and the audience burst into laughter when Nora Hayden ejects my dead body into space. Very solemnly, she says, 'Goodbye, Professor,' and when she pushed the button, it sounded like a toilet flushing. I almost died of embarrassment."

Pink went $50,000 over budget to make his picture, and had to sell it to American International to get the creditors off his back.

Notes:

1. French, Lawrence. "California Gothic: The Corman/Haller Collaboration," *Video Watchdog*, No. 138, pg. 17.
1. Weaver, Tom. *Science Fiction Stars and Horror Heroes*, McFarland, N. Carolina, 1991, pg. 92.
3. Albert, Hollis and Charles Beaumont. "The Horror of It All," *Playboy*, 1958.
4. Klemensen, Richard. "Interview with Michael Carreras," *Little Shop of Horrors*, No. 4, pg. 31.
5. MacDonald, J. Fred. *Television and the Red Menace: The Video Road to Vietnam*, New York, Praeger, 1985, pg. 103.
6. Fultz Jr., Lawrence. "I Was a Teenage Werewolf, Too!" *Filmfax*, No. 128, pg. 35-36.
7. David Rose was supposed to score the film. His main title was released on an M-G-M single with the theme from *The Swan* on the B-side.
8. Pink, Sid. *So You Want to Make Movies*, Florida, Pineapple Press, Inc., 1989, pg. 75.

CHAPTER TWO

Who Goes There?

*No one would have believed in the last years of the
nineteenth century that this world was being watched
keenly and closely by intelligences greater than man's
and yet as mortal as his own... Yet across the gulf of
space, minds that are to our minds as ours are to those
of the beasts that perish, intellects vast and cool and
unsympathetic, regarded this earth with envious eyes,
and slowly and surely drew their plans against us.*
—The War of the Worlds

As we were aiming at the stars, some people wondered if the stars might be aiming at us. It was no coincidence that UFO sightings reached epidemic proportions as we embarked on our space programs. Many historians believe it was the fear of a Soviet invasion that fueled the hysteria about flying saucers, but there were other factors involved.

On June 25, 1947, Kenneth Arnold reported a fleet of flying objects moving through the late afternoon sky over Mt. Rainier, Washington. Arnold's encounter received unprecedented coverage, and before long, everyone was seeing strange objects in the sky. Most people thought flying saucers were a lot of hooey, and the press seemed to agree until a Kentucky pilot died in a crash while pursuing the metallic craft that he had reported. Suddenly, the wind shifted and people wanted to know what was going on. The Government pretended to take the matter seriously by assigning Edward J. Ruppelt and a four-member team to study the flying saucer phenomenon. The fact that his agency, Project Blue Book, was housed in a tiny eighteen foot by thirty foot room indicated the degree to which the Government was committed.

Retired Marine Major Donald E. Keyhoe wrote a piece in the January 1950 issue of *True* magazine accusing the Government of engaging in a cover-up. Filmmaker Mikel Conrad added fuel to the fire by claiming the Air Force had seized footage of flying saucers taking off and landing that he'd shot near Juneau, Alaska. An FBI agent named McKnight confirmed Conrad's story. Some of the footage, vetted by McKnight, was used in *The Flying Saucer* (1950)—a movie that Conrad wrote, produced, directed, and starred in. It's quite possible that the Alaskan Chamber of Commerce helped Conrad finance his vanity production

WHAT ARE THEY? WHERE ARE THEY FROM?
HAVE *YOU* SEEN A FLYING SAUCER?

Starring Mikel Conrad · Pat Garrison · Hantz Von Teuffen
Lester Sharpe · Russell Hicks · Frank Durien
Produced and Directed By MIKEL CONRAD · Associate Producer MORRIS M. WEIN
Original Story by MIKEL CONRAD · *Screen Adaptation by* HOWARD IRVING YOUNG
A COLONIAL PRODUCTIONS PICTURE · *Released by* FILM CLASSICS, INC.

Poster for The Flying Saucer (1950). Photo from the author's collection.

as the story often takes a backseat to endless scenes of the beautiful Alaskan wilderness. You will be shocked to learn that the Air Force knew nothing about Conrad's footage and the FBI agent was really an actor friend of Conrad's.

Howard Hawks made the first real science fiction movie about the flying saucer scare—*The Thing from Another World* (1951). With a decent budget of $1.6 million, an intelligent script, a solid cast, and a great Dimitri Tiomkin score, Hawks set the tone for most of the visitors-from-space films that followed.

A team of scientists at an Arctic base, spots a UFO and radio the military for help. Captain Pat Hendry (Ken Tobey) and his men, fly the scientists to the spot where they believe the UFO crashed, and there they find a flying saucer buried beneath the ice. They accidentally blow up the saucer, but bring the pilot (James Arness) back in a block of ice. An electric blanket placed over the block of ice by a nervous guard (William Phipps) melts the ice and sets the alien free. It is attacked by a team of sled dogs and the alien loses one of its arms in the struggle. A study of the arm reveals that the creature is made of vegetable matter. After the thing slaughters two of the scientists, Hendry and his men work feverishly to discover a way to kill it. Hendry's girlfriend (Margaret Sheridan) is the one who comes up with the solution. She thinks they should handle it like they would any vegetable: boil it!

Margaret Sheridan and Ken Tobey. Photo from the author's collection.

Hawks let Christian Nyby take the credit for directing the picture so that Nyby, who'd edited several of Hawks's movies, could get into the Directors' Guild. Hawks may also have wanted to distance himself from the project because of the disdain the Hollywood community had for sci-fi in those days. The film not only mirrors the widespread, growing fear of science, it perpetuates it. The lead scientist, Dr. Carrington (Robert Cornthwaite), looks like a Russian with his goatee, Cossack hat, and dark blazer. He's a detached, humorless man who is obsessed with communicating with the alien long after it has become apparent to everyone else that such an idea is not only impractical, but suicidal. Carrington is envious of the alien's intellectual superiority, unhampered by emotions. He's not at all concerned that the alien may have come to Earth to use it as a blood bank. As the military men prepare to electrocute the alien, Carrington tries to talk them out of it. "We've thought our way into nature; we've split the atom!" Serving as a spokesman for the audience, one of the soldiers replies, "Yes, and that sure made the world happy, didn't it?" In the first draft of the screenplay, Carrington is decapitated, rather than wounded, when he attempts to communicate with the alien, after which one of the characters remarks, "Now *both* monsters are dead."

The film is both anti-science *and* anti-military. Following standard operating procedure, the military accidentally blows up the saucer. A careless soldier sets the alien free. Hendry's superior officer, General Fogarty (David McMahon), is the biggest fool of the bunch. He keeps sending messages wanting to know why Hendry isn't keeping him abreast of the situation. It never occurs to Fogarty that Hendry might not be able to. Fogarty knows they've got a visitor from space on their hands. If he had any brains, he would have sent some men to investigate. Instead, not having the faintest idea what's going on, he orders Hendry to keep the invader alive at all costs. Hendry isn't much brighter. His crew chief (Dewey Martin) is the one with all of the ideas. They even joke about it.

The Day the Earth Stood Still

The Day the Earth Stood Still (1951), impeccably directed by Academy Award winner Robert Wise, is the antithesis of Hawks's picture. Instead of a blood-drinking bully from outer space, it had a benign, handsome gentleman named Klaatu (Michael Rennie) whose sole purpose is to stop us from waging war. "The universe grows smaller every day," he tells a group of scientists, "and the threat of aggression by any group, anywhere, can no longer be tolerated. Your choice is simple. Join us and live in peace or pursue your present course and face obliteration. The decision rests with you." Before Klaatu can deliver his message, he is shot, hunted, and shot again.

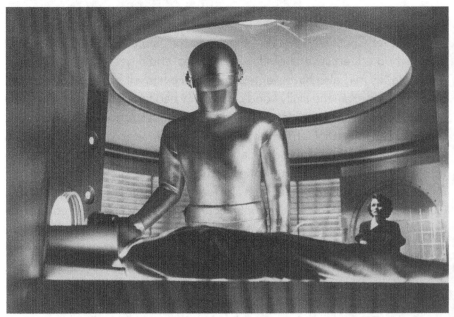

Patricia Neal watches Gort revive Michael Rennie from the dead.

The film received a Golden Globe Award for promoting international understanding, and Bernard Herrmann's terrific score was nominated for an Academy Award, but the box office returns were modest. Most people caught up with the movie when it premiered on NBC's *Saturday Night at the Movies* in 1962. Fox didn't produce another major sci-fi feature for seven years.

There were two dime store versions of Wise's film—*Stranger from Venus* (1955) and *The Cosmic Man* (1959)—neither of them worth a tinker's damn.

While Edmund North was scripting *The Day the Earth Stood Still*, the House on Un-American Activities turned its attention to the movie industry for the second time. The first investigation began in 1947. Ten screenwriters who refused to cooperate were blacklisted and sent to jail. Friendly witnesses assured the committee that it would be easy to sneak subversive content into movies, but nobody could offer an example of it. In a desperate attempt to demonstrate their loyalty, the studios began cranking out silly anti-Communist pictures in which agents and party members were given the worst traits of Adolph Hitler and Al Capone.

The Nazis had been the villains in the films of the 40s. When the war ended, the screenwriters simply transferred all of their malevolent traits to the Commies without so much as missing a beat, which left many people in the dark about the most basic ideological differences between them. Howard Hughes offered *I Married a Communist* (1949) to directors whose political persuasions were in question. *The Red Snow* (1952), *Conspirator* (1949), and *The Red Danube* (1949) presented such horrifically distorted images of communists that anyone who didn't know better would have to assume that all party members were maniacs. In these tiresome propaganda pieces, there was no difference between a communist and a nazi, between socialism and the bubonic plague. Hughes withheld release of *The Man He Found* so that he could shoot new footage: changing Nazi villains to Commie villains. As Otto Waldis is about to scatter bubonic plague over hundreds of miles, he declares: "I am benefiting mankind by ridding the world of all the people who stand in the way of communism." Released as *The Whip Hand* (1951), it became a psychotic mix of director William Cameron Menzie's genius and producer Hughes's delirium.

Red Planet Mars

Peter Graves and Andrea King pick up coded messages from *Red Planet Mars* (1952) and when the world learns that the planet is like a utopia, the free-enterprise system takes a hit. "Our entire civilization is collapsing around our ears like a deck of cards," says Morris Ankrum. (He's not a general this time; he's the Secretary of Defense.) Moscow is delighted, until later messages trigger a religious revival that brings the Communists to their knees, resulting in world peace. A bitter nazi scientist (Herbert Berghof) confronts Graves in his laboratory and tells him that he was the one who sent the early messages. He assumes that Graves was responsible for the religious ones. This malcontent threatens to tell the world that the whole thing was a fraud when a new message from Mars tickles his crazy bone. He shoots the radio, causing an explosion that blows the place to smithereens. Had this movie ever been shown at a children's matinee, it's quite possible the theatre would have suffered the same fate.

When *Red Planet Mars* was made, spiritual broadcasts on radio and television were rampant. There was Billy Graham's *Hour of Decision*, Bishop Fulton Scheen's *Life is Worth Living*, *Crossroads*, and *The Guiding Light*. Sunday mornings were dominated by religious programming. But it wasn't enough for MGM's Dore Schary. He insisted on making *The Next Voice You Hear* (1950) in which God makes a nightly radio broadcast. Schary wasn't foolish enough to spend a lot of money on this silly film, but he felt that the time was right for a movie that offered assurance and comfort.

Albert Zugsmith's *Invasion U.S.A.* (1952) could have been written by Joseph McCarthy. In this piece of propaganda masquerading as entertainment, a TV newscaster (Gerald Mohr) asks some people in a bar how they feel about the Government's fight against communism. None of them seem to care one way or another. A mysterious figure (Dan O'Herlihy) sits at the end of the bar, listening to all of their chatter, and decides to teach the fools a lesson. He picks up his glass and swirls it around, hypnotizing everyone in the joint. They experience a collective nightmare in which every one of them is killed when the Commies take over America. "It's a nightmare; this can't be happening," Peggie Castle says to Gerald Mohr. "It was a cinch to happen," he replies. "The last time I met a girl I really liked, they bombed Pearl Harbor." The implication is clear. If we want peace, we have to curtail Mohr's pursuit of women. At any rate, the nightmare has the effect of a patriotic shot in the arm. Everyone vows to do whatever they can to help the war effort.

The trade publications gave the film a warm reception. *Variety* thought the idea was "...spectacularly presented and Alfred E. Green's direction makes the most of the potential offered in lending credence to the theme." *The Hollywood Reporter* said that it "packs a wallop." Other critics were not so kind. *Time* magazine called it "a shoddy little shocker," while the *New York Times* said, "All the actors in it, especially the leads... are dismal in their roles."

The Man from Planet X

In a decade ruled by fear and distrust, it's no wonder that most of the visitors from space had more in common with the Thing than with Klaatu. There were, however, a few who shared Klaatu's peaceful motives.

The Man from Planet X (1951) was the first of many visitors who came to Earth from a dying planet. At a time when spaceships were shaped like cigars, this little guy arrived in something that looked like a diving bell, predicting the shape

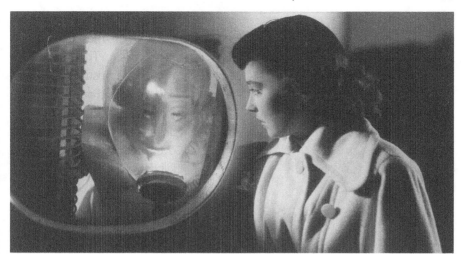

Margaret Field gets her first look at The Man from Planet X *(1951). Photo from the author's collection.*

of satellites some eight years ahead of the game. Toward the end of the film, we learn that the alien intends to pave the way for an invasion of Earth, but the audience is left to wonder if this migration might have been a peaceful one if a power-hungry scientist (William Schallert) hadn't tortured him.

The Man from Planet X was directed by Edgar Ulmer in six days, for $41,000, on sets left over from Walter Wanger's *Joan of Arc*, and proved to be an atmospheric, suspenseful little picture. "We felt fortunate to get into a picture that would be treated as carefully as it could be on that kind of a budget," said the film's star, Robert Clarke.

Clarke was less happy with *The Astounding She-Monster* (1958), which he thought "was kind of a piece of junk," and the critic for *The Monthly Film Bulletin* agreed. "The film is a feeble and ridiculous contribution to the science fiction library, weakly scripted and poorly acted."

The Astounding She-Monster

Ronnie Ashcroft, the *She-Monster*'s producer-director, was a sound-effects editor. He shot his movie in four days at a cost of $18,000 and sold it to American International for $60,000. A surly narrator (Al Avalon) introduces all of the characters and he seems to have a bone to pick with each of them. With a sneer in his voice, he informs us that the rich heroine (Marilyn Harvey) overslept and is late for cocktails—implying that she deserves to be kidnapped. He has little to say about her kidnappers, but he refers to the hero (Robert Clarke) as "the ever-present innocent bystander," whatever that means. He describes the invader (Shirley Kilpatrick) as "evil unto evil." When her sudden appearance causes the kidnappers (Kenne Duncan, Jeanne Tatum, and Ewing Brown) to run their car into a ditch, the ragtag trio and their hostage take refuge in the

A CREATURE
FROM BEYOND
THE STARS
EVIL...
BEAUTIFUL...
DEADLY...!

THE ASTOUNDING
SHE-MONSTER

ROBERT CLARKE · KENNE DUNCAN · MARILYN HARVEY ··· JEANNE TATUM · SHIRLEY KILPATRICK · EWING BROWN
Story and Screenplay by FRANK HALL · Produced and Directed by RONNIE ASHCROFT · A HOLLYWOOD INTERNATIONAL Production

Al Kallis used a photograph of Madeleine Castle to create this poster for The Astounding She-Monster. *Shirley Kilpatrick, the actress who played the She-Monster, couldn't turn her back to the camera. Her costume split up the back on the first day of filming and was held together with safety pins. Photo from the author's collection.*

ever-present hero's mountain cabin, where most of the movie takes place. The kidnappers drink a lot, insult each other, and run in and out of the cabin for one reason or another until all of them are dead. After the ever-present hero manages to kill the evil unto evil she-monster, he finds a medallion with a message from the Tellus galaxy, inviting Earth to become a member of a universal governing body dedicated to the advancement of planetary progress. This "surprise" ending is the final salt in the wound. For sixty minutes, we've watched the she-monster skulk around, smashing windows, killing animals and people, and looking anything but peaceful. The surly narrator even told us she was evil, yet now we're supposed to believe we misinterpreted everything; that she was a messenger of peace.

Phantom from Space

After being chased around the Griffith Park Observatory for twenty minutes, the invisible *Phantom from Space* (1953) falls to his death and evaporates. Scientist Rudolph Anders muses, "So he came here, wherever from, and right before our eyes, his body went through the final stages of life." He says this as if he's saying something profound. It may not be all that important to know where the phantom came from, but it would have been nice to know what he was doing here, yet the screenplay by Bill Raynor and Myles Wilder offers nary a clue.

Willy Lee Wilder produced and directed this doughnut hole. He sold his successful handbag business in New York so he could come to Hollywood to make movies. The fact that he was willing to use his own money proves that he wanted to make movies in the worst way, which is exactly what he did.

It Came from Outer Space

On their way to another planet, a bunch of aliens accidentally crash in the Arizona desert. All they want to do is repair their ship and leave before we kill them. This was the premise of *It Came from Outer Space* (1953), written by Ray Bradbury for Universal-International (U-I).

Ray Bradbury said, "Sometime in the summer of 1952, my agent said Universal was looking for a writer to do a science fiction space project of some sort, did I have any ideas, and would I go over and talk to them? I had several ideas, so I went and had a discussion with the producer, Bill Alland, who had some ideas which, I thought, were not very good. I said, 'Well, I'll go to work on this project for you, but somewhere along the line I will do two versions of it. I'll do one for you, based on your idea, and then I'll do a second outline of some sort based on my ideas. Then at the end of a week or two weeks, whatever, you look at the two versions and decide which one you want to go ahead on, and if you choose the wrong one I'll leave.'… So I brought the outlines back in about a week or ten days, and he said, 'By God, go ahead with your idea. It's a better one, just as you said.' Then I took the outline and did a treatment, which was ridiculous. What I wrote was a screenplay—70, 80, 90 pages, like a fool—I shouldn't have given away so much. I was only being paid $300 a week for five or six weeks. When I turned in the treatment, they promptly fired me and brought in Harry Essex for the screenplay."[1]

William Alland warned Essex not to tamper with Bradbury's material too much. In later years, to his shame, Essex would claim that Bradbury's sole contribution to the project was a three-page short story.

William Alland said, "When we wrote the script, I wanted the monsters to be something that you had to imagine. But after we put [the film] together, Universal said, 'Oh, no, no! You've gotta have *something*, for God's sake!' Bill Goetz was the one who insisted I had to have a monster."[2] Director Jack Arnold returned to the studio to shoot new monster scenes.

Jack Arnold became U-I's number one sci-fi guy, which was hardly an enviable position for a director at the time. Though he directed more westerns and dramas for the studio than he did sci-fi movies, it was the sci-fi movies for which he would be remembered. Arnold may well have been responsible for the infamous hand-on-the-shoulder shot; a directorial device designed to make the audience jump. It works like this: you have a character alone in a dangerous area. In a close shot, a hand suddenly appears and touches the character's shoulder. The character startles. The camera then reveals it's simply a friend trying to get their attention. In *Creature from the Black Lagoon* (1954), another film directed by Arnold, Richard Carlson is searching for the Gill Man when he's startled by Richard Denning.

"Take it easy," Denning tells him. Considering the circumstances, Denning is lucky Carlson didn't spin around and punch him in the nose. In *Tarantula*, Nestor Paiva somehow manages to sneak up on John Agar in the middle of the desert without Agar hearing Paiva's car or the crunch of sand beneath Paiva's feet. "Boy, you've got nerves!" Paiva remarks when Agar jumps at his touch.

Nathan Juran, another director who was fond of using hand-on-the-shoulder shots, told us: "They work every time. I love 'em."

Richard Carlson stands in awe before the spaceship in Ray Bradbury's It Came from Outer Space *(1953). Photo from the author's collection.*

It Came from Outer Space opens with a bang. A fiery ball crashes in the desert near the town of Sand Rock. John Putnam (Richard Carlson) and his fiancée, Ellen Fields (Barbara Rush), enlist the aid of a helicopter pilot to fly them to the crater. Putnam goes down for a closer look and sees what he believes to be a spaceship, jammed into the lower level of an old mine shaft. The door to the craft is half open and Putnam sees something moving inside. As he moves closer, the door slams shut, causing an avalanche that buries the ship. Nobody believes Putnam. The newspapers make fun of him and the sheriff (Charles Drake) thinks he's off his nut until people start disappearing and a lot of electrical equipment is stolen. "Give us time," one of the aliens tells Putnam, "Time or terrible things will happen. Things so terrible you have yet to dream of them." To ensure the cooperation of Putnam and the sheriff, the aliens hold Ellen hostage.

While the sheriff organizes a posse, Putnam races to the mine and convinces the aliens to let his friends go. He then seals the entrance with dynamite so the posse can't get at them. The ship takes off and Putnam tells Ellen, "There'll be other nights, other stars for us to watch. They'll be back."

Although this is a very good picture, it is certainly not without its flaws— some of them caused by the later addition of the monsters. Richard Carlson spends a lot of time wondering what the aliens look like, yet twenty minutes into the film, he and Barbara Rush encounter one of them hovering in the middle of the highway. This shot was added after the film was completed, but there was no attempt to alter the events that followed to accommodate the change.

Richard Carlson and Barbara Rush. Photo from the author's collection.

The aliens, in human form, go to the homes of their kidnapped victims to get a change of clothes. Carlson's closet is cleaned out. Why? Are the aliens planning to open a clothing store in Sand Rock? Actually, they're planning to leave that night, so this is another sequence that doesn't make sense and one that was probably added by Harry Essex.

The terrific score was written by Herman Stein, Henry Mancini, and Irving Gertz. At Universal, a composer had to write 90 percent of a score to get a screen credit. This was the studio's way of keeping their composers anonymous and underpaid. Since Universal always recycled their music, most of the music in their fifties sci-fi films comes from *It Came from Outer Space, This Island Earth*, and *Creature from the Black Lagoon*.

It Came from Outer Space was Universal's first entry into the sci-fi market and they wanted to come out strong. Photographed in 3-D with stereophonic sound, it premiered in two Los Angeles theaters: the Pantages and the RKO Hill Street. Critical reception to the film was lukewarm. By the end of the year, it grossed $1.6 million in domestic rentals alone.

The Space Children

The Space Children (1958) was the last collaboration between producer Alland and director Arnold and it's their worst. Alland's contract with Universal had come to an end, so he went to Paramount, where he thought he could make more money as an independent producer. Oddly enough, after working at Universal for seven years, Alland hadn't learned to ask for a percentage of the gross profits instead of the net. He never saw a dime from either of his Paramount films and ultimately left the business to sell real estate.

In *The Space Children*, a visitor from space—looking very much like a brain soufflé—recruits a bunch of children to sabotage the rocket that their parents have built. Michael Ray is the leader of the pack. Since his father (Adam Williams) is a minor player in the development of the rocket and has nothing to do with the launching, one has to wonder why the devil he and his family have relocated to a trailer park near the launch pad.

Back and forth, the children parade from the trailer park to the cave where the alien is hiding, apparently to no purpose other than to eat up time since the children can communicate with the alien telepathically. Supposedly designed to appeal to children, the film is a bore. The Saturday matinee audience I saw it with grew restless and started playing chase. Good intentions aside, it's easily Arnold's worst sci-fi film.

The 27th Day

One of the most off-beat, naively optimistic, and most outrageous pieces of Commie-bashing ever committed to film was Columbia's *The 27th Day* (1957), written by John Mantley from his novel. An alien (Arnold Moss) from a doomed planet kidnaps five people and gives each of them three capsules in a container that only they can open. By reciting the latitude and longitude of any given area, the capsules will wipe out all human life within a 3,000 mile radius. The capsules are only good for twenty-seven days, hence the title of the movie. In the end, it turns out that the capsules only kill the enemies of freedom, leaving enough room on our planet for the aliens to peacefully relocate. You can guess what happens to the Russians.

The Cosmic Monster

In *The Cosmic Monster* (1958), Alex Mango's experiments with magnetic fields inadvertently rips a hole in the ionosphere, unleashing cosmic rays that turn people into maniacs and insects into giants. Worse still, his experiments interfere with television reception! Martin Benson, a friendly alien from Planet X, stands around observing all of this pandemonium and finally signals one of his flying saucers to blow up Mango and his lab. If only he'd done it sooner, he could have saved us all a lot of grief.

Paul Ruder's screenplay was based on the British television serial *The Strange World of Planet X* by Rene Ray. It was directed by Gilbert Gunn, a writer and director of documentaries. He seems to have been asleep in his chair. The critic for *Variety* called his effort "a gloomy little item... not ingenious enough or sufficiently horrific to add up to anything but a naïve [and] singularly uninspired potboiler." *The Monthly Film Bulletin* noted that the "giant ants, spiders, worms, etc. are all too obviously stock micro-cinematographic material; and the spectacle of the cast running in terror from them is a trifle absurd."

The Giant Claw

Most of the extraterrestrials were not helpful or friendly like Martin Benson. In fact, they weren't friendly at all. We usually had something they wanted and they came to Earth to take it. One exception was *The Giant Claw* (1957), who only wanted a safe place to lay an egg. She did a jolly good job of it.

Flying beast out of prehistoric skies! Big as a battleship! Flies four times faster than the speed of sound! Atomic weapons can't hurt The Giant Claw *(1957). Photo from the author's collection.*

Jeff Morrow said, "I saw [*The Giant Claw*] for the first time at a premiere and when that bird came on, the entire theater began laughing. It was so atrocious. And we were all playing it so straight. It looked like a plucked turkey."

The design of *The Claw* was the brainchild of prolific producer Sam Katzman, who was one of the kings of low budget schlock. Jumping from genre to genre, Katzman went where the money was and made no bones about it. "Lord knows I'll never make an Academy Award movie," Katzman once remarked, "But then I am just as happy to get my achievement plaques from the bank every year."[3] He had his own unit at Columbia, cranking out low budget movies that always turned a profit. One of his favorite directors was Fred Francis Sears, a former actor who often narrated the films he directed. Sears joined Katzman's team in

1952. Five years and thirty-seven movies later, he was found dead in the wash-room adjoining his office at the studio. He was forty-seven years old. Five of his films were still in the can. Officially, he died from a heart attack, but more likely it was from exhaustion. Had he approached his assignments in the perfunctory manner displayed by many of his contemporaries, he might have lived longer. But Sears actually cared about his movies—although it's unlikely that he was able to work up much enthusiasm for *The Claw*.

Writers Samuel Newman and Paul Gangelin wove a couple of current events into their scenario. At the time, there was some talk about the existence of an anti-matter universe, brought about when Emilio Segre, Clyde Wiegard, and Owen Chamberlain discovered a tiny anti-proton at the University of California in 1955. The big bird is from an anti-matter galaxy and can only be killed after a stream of mu mesons penetrates its protective anti-matter shield. A negative mu meson particle acted as the unscathed catalyst in causing a reaction resembling thermonuclear fusion the year this film was made.

When someone writes a script as fast as this one was probably written, the writer can become a little confused. The French-Canadian character, Pierre (who Morrow calls Pepe at one point), almost has a nervous breakdown after seeing the Claw, mistaking it for La Carcagne: a symbol of death from Canadian folklore. According to the legend, anyone who sees it dies. Later, when Pierre is killed by the Claw, Mara Corday remarks with some irony, "Poor Pierre and his La Carcagne. He was right, seeing it did mean his death." Huh?

Mara Corday and Jeff Morrow. Photo from the author's collection.

One of the best sequences occurs about halfway through the picture. With high hopes, Jeff Morrow, Mara Corday, Robert Shayne, and General Morris Ankrum sit around Ankrum's office listening to an Air Force pilot describe his encounter with the Claw. Everyone assumes that the squad will make quick work of the "overgrown buzzard," but they're wrong. The pilot's own bravado quickly melts as he watches his men die. "It's coming after me!" he yells. General Ankrum coldly flips the switch on the broadcast as though it were some radio program he'd grown tired of.

Guns! Cannons! Rockets!

Kronos

Kronos (1957) was a giant robotic storage unit sent from some unidentified planet to drain the Earth of its energy. When scientist Jeff Morrow learns that the Government plans to use an H-bomb against the thing, he's horrified. "Not

only can he withstand any force we're able to throw against him," he tells his superior, John Emery, "but he will actually absorb that energy, become more powerful from it." What Morrow doesn't know is that Emery is under the control of the aliens.

Variety said, "Kronos is a well-made, moderate-budget science-fictioner which boasts quality special effects that would do credit to a much higher-budgeted film."

Kronos, the conqueror of the universe! Photo from the author's collection.

Not of This Earth

The folks on the planet Davanna, ravaged by continuous nuclear wars, want our blood in Roger Corman's *Not of This Earth* (1957). Paul Birch is their scout. Sporting a pair of thick sunglasses to hide his brain-burning, eggshell white eyes, he hires Beverly Garland to give him daily blood transfusions, after which he roams about town in his chauffeur-driven Cadillac, looking for specimens to teleport back to his planet.

"Roger had Paul wearing contact lenses," Paul Blaisdell told Carl Del Vecchio in the *Beverly Garland Fan Club Journal*. "I'm not talking about the ones you slap on your cornea. I'm talking about the full-size ones which can become very painful after a few hours. And Roger just had Paul sitting around between takes, all ready to go. A couple of hours passed and Birch felt like his eyes were burnt holes in a blanket. Then he took the lenses out and his eyes hurt so bad he couldn't see straight."

Birch and Corman got into a fight about it on the front lawn of the house where most of the picture was filmed. "It was a farce and came to nothing really," recalled the film's writer, Charles Griffith. "They took off their glasses and squared off, pushed and shoved and so on." Birch walked off the picture, and Roger replaced him with another actor (Lyle Latell) who had roughly the same build.

Birch's deadpan performance as the alien is right on the money and his encounter with Dick Miller's vacuum cleaner salesman (a role that Griffith had written for himself) is hysterical. It's one of Corman's best and bleakest sci-fi films.

Joseph Tomelty, Patricia Laffan, Adrienne Corri, and Hugh McDermott from Devil Girl from Mars *(1954). Photo courtesy of Bob Villard.*

The Devil Girl from Mars

The Devil Girl from Mars (1954) isn't after our blood; she's after our men. Using an invisible shield, she holds a group of people captive in a small, isolated Scottish inn while she decides which one of them to take home with her. She has to do this before she talks them to death. Writer James Eastwood and director David MacDonald seem to be in a conspiracy to make this Edward and Harry Danziger movie as terrible as it can possibly be. As for the actors, the two to watch are Hugh McDermott and Patricia Laffan. McDermott plays a not-so-bright reporter who hangs around with a not-so-bright scientist (Joseph Tomelty). He's abrasive, tactless, and prone to fits of hysteria. His performance is like nothing you've ever seen. As the Devil Girl, Laffan is funny too, in her dominatrix outfit. She looks like she hasn't had a bowel movement for twenty years. We agree with the *Monthly Film Bulletin* critic, who said. "There is really no fault in this film that one would like to see eliminated. Everything, in its way, is quite perfect."

"I laugh when I think about it," said Hazel Court, the film's leading lady, "but I still get fan mail, and I'm even told Steven Spielberg got some ideas from it. Nearly fifty years later, I wonder if women in leather still rule Mars."[4]

I Married a Monster from Outer Space

The aliens are after our women in *I Married a Monster from Outer Space* (1958), as their own women have been wiped out in a solar explosion. But after a year, these aliens haven't been able to produce children. Gloria Talbott is one of the unlucky brides who discovers that her husband (Tom Tryon) is an alien from outer space. There's no one she can turn to for help; all of the authority figures have been replaced by the aliens. They've got the phones and they've blocked the roads out of town. In a last ditch effort, she tells the family doctor (Ken Lynch), who believes her story and knows who else they can trust—the husbands of the wives who've recently given birth.

Directed by Gene Fowler, the movie is both intelligent and suspenseful. It also mirrors the way the men and women of the fifties looked at marriage. At Tom Tryon's bachelor party, one his buddies tells the waiter to give Tryon a drink because he's about to be married. Another guy says, "Every one of us is married or about to be married, so give us all another drink!" Tryon begs off. He promised Talbott that he'd stop by on his way home. "It's bad luck to see your bride the night before the wedding," someone remarks. "Seeing her at the wedding, that's bad luck," another adds. As Tryon walks away, one of the drunken sots turns to the others and sadly laments, "He's such a nice guy. It's a shame it has to happen to him." They're not joking. It's the most terrifying sequence in the film.

Tom Tryon and Gloria Talbott are menaced by an alien invader in I Married a Monster from Outer Space *(1958). Photo from the author's collection.*

The War of the Worlds

The Martians in George Pal's *The War of the Worlds* (1953) don't want our men, our women, or any other souvenirs; they want the whole damn shebang. Their first act on Earth is to fry three guys who peacefully approach them with a white flag. Later, they kill a priest.

Gene Barry and Ann Robinson from George Pal's The War of the Worlds *(1953). Photo from the author's collection.*

"One of our first decisions," said Pal, "was to move the setting from London... to Southern California. Also influencing our decision were the many stories of flying saucers in the last few years which have emanated from the western part of the United States."[5] Likewise, the decision to set the story in modern times made it more economically practical, yet it still cost Paramount a cool $2 million after all was said and done. The forty days of live action cost $600,000, and the rest was saved for the remarkable special effects. One scene alone—the disintegration of an army colonel—required 144 mattes. Eighty-one-year-old Walter Hoffman simulated an atomic bomb explosion in the studio. "He got his effect by putting a collection of colored explosive powders on top of an air-tight metal drum filled with an explosive gas. Rigged up with an electrical remote control, its second try reached a

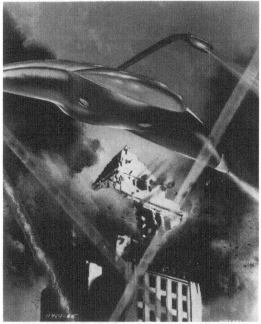

One of the Martian war machines from The War of the Worlds. *Photo from the author's collection.*

height of seventy-five feet with the mushroom top of the real thing."[6] Al Nozaki created the Martian war machines, Charles Gemora created the Martians, and Chesley Bonestell provided the paintings of the planets seen during Sir Cedric Hardwicke's opening narration. Leith Stevens's score brought it all together. It's a very exciting picture.

Veteran actor Les Tremayne played one of the military men trying to stop the Martian invasion. He wanted Pal to give him a death scene since he sort of disappears two-thirds of the way through the picture. During a lunch break one afternoon, he went home to film one.

Les Tremayne said, "I used a hubcap for a flying saucer and water from my hose for the death ray. I had a place out in Sherman Oaks with a big gully that had a drop from the road down about 75 feet, so there was a nice run for me to take while the ray was eating at my footsteps. I doused myself with some catsup and ran and stumbled along the gully until I finally fell into an ash heap which was still burning from that morning. The whole thing was pretty corny. I thought if I could make Pal laugh hard enough, he'd give me what I wanted."

Originally photographed in three-strip Technicolor, an unfortunate thing happened to the movie when it was re-released; Technicolor prints were dropped in favor of cheaper Eastman color prints. Without the intense color saturation, all of the wires supporting the Martian war machines became visible. This has been exacerbated by digitalization, which seems to enhance every flaw in these older movies.

Earth vs. the Flying Saucers

You won't see the wires on the flying saucers in *Earth vs. the Flying Saucers* (1956) because effects wizard Ray Harryhausen put a sheet of glass between the camera and his stop-motion saucers, and he painted the wires out of every frame. "It was not my favorite picture," he said. "There isn't much one can do with an inanimate object."

Producer Charles H. Schneer hired blacklisted writer Bernard Gordon to tailor the script to conform to Harryhausen's production drawings. In Gordon's scenario, the survivors of a disintegrated solar system give Earth 56 days to surrender or be wiped out. When asked what the military intends to do about it, Admiral Tom Browne Henry replies, "When an armed and threatening power lands uninvited in our capital, we don't meet them with tea and cookies." Hugh Marlowe and his men are ready for aliens when they arrive with a new weapon that interrupts the saucers' magnetic fields. One by one, they fall from the sky, but not before they've managed to demolish some of Washington's most famous landmarks. It's an exciting and spectacular finale.

Keep firing at saucers!

The Mysterians

The Mysterians (1959), also from a nuclear ravaged planet, arrive *without* notice. When they're discovered, they pretend to want only the small plot of land that they are presently occupying, and they also express a desire to mate with a few of our women. Without waiting for permission, they expand their parameters and kidnap the women, making their intention to take over the planet pretty obvious.

This showcase for Eiji Tsubaraya and his special effects crew really delivers the goods. There are earthquakes, giant robots, flying saucers, floods, and death rays, and there's a protracted climactic battle that seems to go on forever, supported by Akira Ifukube's enthusiastic, militaristic score. Nothing exceeds like excess and this movie is a prime example of it.

Hillary Brooke wonders why her husband, Leif Erickson, is so cranky while Jimmy Hunt suspiciously eyes police officers Charles Cane and Douglas Kennedy. Photo from the author's collection.

Invaders from Mars

Edward L. Alperson's *Invaders from Mars* (1953) seems to have been designed to scare the hell out of small children. Jimmy Hunt is the little boy who sees a flying saucer land in the field behind his house. He tells his kindly father (Leif Erickson) about it, who goes for a look-see. The ground opens and swallows him. When he returns to the house, he's a son of a bitch. Before the day is up, Jimmy's mother (Hillary Brooke), the chief of police (Bert Freed), two of his officers (Douglas Kennedy and Charles Kane), and a military general (William Forrest) are all under the Martian's control.

The writers knew better than to take things too far. Once Jimmy loses both his father and his mother, he's quickly given two surrogate parents: a pretty psychologist played by Helena Carter and a sympathetic astronomer played by Arthur Franz. These two call in the military and the colonel in charge of wiping out the Martians is none other than our old friend Morris Ankrum.

John Tucker Battle wrote the first two drafts of the screenplay. Richard Blake was called in to streamline what Battle had done, but he turned the whole story into a child's nightmare that caused Battle to withdraw his name from the project. Blake's new ending gave director William Cameron Menzies carte blanche to let his imagination run wild. The imagery in the film is incredible, and the sets are surrealistic and creepy. Jimmy's backyard is an unfriendly, almost barren stretch of sand with leafless trees and a tired picket fence. In the police station, the ceilings are incredibly high, the corridor is the length of a football field, and the front desk is as high as the Empire State Building. Cinematographer John Seitz claimed the sets were designed for 3-D, but as there were no 3-D cameras available at the time, the picture was shot flat.

Jimmy Hunt said, "I don't know if somebody tried to zap this picture right from the start, but [Menzies] had all these storyboards. He had them all blown up and ready to go, and they disappeared. They had to start putting this thing together as we went. You don't know that much about someone when you're in there working, especially as a kid. I never realized just how much of, I guess, a genius he really was. He was very good. He knew what he wanted out of us. He knew the feeling he wanted out of us and I think he did a good job of getting us to portray that."[7]

Robot Monster

Robot Monster (1953) was another child's nightmare. Aliens from another planet, who look like gorillas in diver's helmets, wipe out most of the people on Earth.

"Phil Tucker and I had worked on a picture together and one afternoon, he came to my house with his wife and told me about this picture he wanted me to write about a guy with these big eyes," recalled Wyott Ordung, who wrote the picture. "I don't write comedy and I told him so, but he kept on talking about it. Actually, his wife Francine was the one who kept talking about it because Phil wasn't making a whole lot of sense. She said he wanted to make a movie about the last four people on Earth after the bomb, which didn't sound very funny to me. A couple of days later, we shot some 3-D tests. Phil, me, and a cameraman named Gordon Abel. I wore a fire suit and had a fish bowl on my head with TV rabbit ears. Phil kept blowing his whistle, which was the signal for action and I stumbled around this vacant lot in East Los Angeles shoving my hand at the camera. We used two Arriflex cameras and a mirror box. He thought we had better 3-D than Warner Brothers, but I never saw the footage. I wrote the script and didn't hear another word until I saw Phil walking down the street in Hollywood and I asked him about it. 'You're lucky you weren't there,' he told me and I asked if there'd been any changes in my script. 'No,' he said, 'it's just the way you wrote it.' I found out later that Al Zimbalist, who produced the picture, gave my script to one of his relatives to rewrite. The guy owed him $500 and Zimbalist told him he'd forget about it if he'd rewrite the script. I couldn't believe it when I saw the thing. And it didn't make a dime."

In 1975, StereoVision re-released *House of Wax*, sparking a new interest in 3-D films. Hoping to ride the crest of the wave they'd started, the company purchased *Robot Monster* to reissue with some new scenes and a new "funny" dialogue track. I was briefly involved in this project. I sat in a room with two other writers and someone from StereoVision kicking around ideas. Finally, after about ten or fifteen minutes, the guy from StereoVision, who hadn't said much, suddenly got an inspiration. "What if we have Ro-Man tip over a garbage can?" The three of us waited for the punch line that never came.

Killers from Space

W. Lee Wilder was at it again with *Killers from Space* (1954). These aliens intend to use an army of giant insects to depopulate the Earth, and Peter Graves is the scientist who stops them. In a sequence that seems to last forever, Graves runs endlessly back and forth through Bronson Caves, stopping in front of process screens to look at giant insects. Apparently, the sequence exceeded the editor's ability to care about it; he left a shot of Graves standing in front of a black screen for a few seconds before the projector was turned on with the image of yet another insect.

It Conquered the World

Peter Graves returned to Bronson Caves for Roger Corman's *It Conquered the World* (1956) in which a creature from Venus, with a little help from scientist Lee Van Cleef, hijacks one of Graves's satellites and rides it back to Earth, taking up residence in a cave just outside of Beechwood. Van Cleef gives the creature the names of the people that it'll need to take control of the town, as he believes it has come to save mankind from itself. The creature produces little bats that plant control devices in the necks of its victims. Van Cleef's wife (Beverly Garland) and his best friend (Graves) do their best to convince him that the invader is here to conquer the world, not save it. "How could he care anything about you?" Graves asks. "He doesn't like. He doesn't dislike. He merely reasons, concludes, and uses." Garland gives up trying to reason with her husband and goes to the cave with a shotgun. "You think you're going to make a slave of the world. I'll see you in hell first!" she tells the creature, and blasts it with her shotgun.

Roger Corman was one of the few directors who gave his leading ladies meaty parts in an era when mainstream movies treated women like second class citizens, something for which he's rarely given credit. It was both surprising and refreshing to see Miss Garland taking matters into her own hands. The audience I saw it with burst into applause.

The Venusian from It Conquered the World. *The title is a bit of an exaggeration. The creature couldn't even hold onto the little town of Beechwood for 24 hours Photo courtesy of Gary Smith.*

The monster, nicknamed Beulah by its creator, Paul Blaisdell, was conceived as a kind of cosmic mushroom, built low to the ground. Beverly Garland burst out laughing when she first saw it.

Beverly Garland said, "They were so thrilled with this monster, and he was really tiny and looked very plastic to me. Then I kept thinking he wasn't finished. When he's finished, he will emerge somehow and be much better. Then, when I got into the cave and saw him, he had not done anything. He had not emerged at all."

Blaisdell was asked to make the thing taller. He doubled its size by adding a dome to the top of it, effectively turning his mushroom into a teepee. It remains one of the silliest and most beloved monsters from the decade.

In one of the movie's most memorable sequences, Graves returns home, plops down on his sofa, lights a cigarette, and calmly tells his wife (Sally Fraser) that he saw the Chief of Police kill a man in cold blood and found an army general possessed by the monster. "It's a horrible mess," he says in a manner that one might affect when recounting a bad day at the office. She steps into the room with her hands behind her back, saying she has a present for him. It's one of the bats. She steps out of the house for a breath of fresh air, assuming that when she returns, the bat will have done its duty. But Graves kills the bat and when she returns, he kills his wife too.

The Brain from Planet Arous

While searching for the source of some pulsating radiation, nuclear scientists John Agar and Robert Fuller find *The Brain from Planet Arous* (1957). Agar and Fuller arrive at Bronson Canyon in a jeep, which Agar smacks into a boulder. It was an accident, obviously, but nobody wanted to spring for another take. If director Nathan Juran had had his wits about him, he would have had Fuller jokingly say something like, "What are you trying to do, kill us?" But the actors say nothing, giving the impression that Agar is always crashing into things.

Since they're looking for the source of radiation, one might think these two men would bring protective clothing, but they don't. But they do bring guns and a hair dryer. In a newly formed cave, they find a power-hungry criminal brain named Gor. It kills Fuller and takes possession of Agar. Agar's fiancée, Joyce Meadows, notices the difference in him right away. "You never kissed me like that before," she tells him. "Wow! You should stay away more often." Gor likes Meadows. She gives him "a new elation." Convinced that the answer to Agar's strange behavior lies at Bronson Canyon (called Mystery Mountain here), Meadows and her father (Tom Brown Henry) go to the cave and find Fuller's burned body and another brain: this one is called Vol. Vol explains that he's come to take Gor back to his planet, but there's a problem. So long as Gor is in a transitory state, he's invincible. He can only be captured or killed when he's in his true form, which he has to return to every twenty-four hours in order to breathe.

John Agar said, "They said anyone who wanted to could work for a percentage of the profits. I looked at them and then at that balloon they were using for a monster and told them I'd work for salary and wished them luck."

It's a one-of-a-kind movie, silly but fun and nowhere near the worst film in John Agar's filmography. He entered the business by way of his marriage to Shirley Temple. David O. Selznick signed him to a contract, hoping he and Shirley would make a successful screen couple. But they didn't click, on or off screen. When I caught up with him in 1971, he was selling cars. He was one of the nicest people I've ever met. "You know, I never got a big charge out of doing science fiction pictures," he told me, "Although they were sometimes more difficult to do than straight roles. I mean, when you have to look offstage at something that's supposed to be a big bug and make it believable... that can be hard work."

Invisible Invaders

Agar was back to save us from the *Invisible Invaders* (1959), which was another timecard production from producer Robert E. Kent and director Edward L. Cahn—two gentlemen who often dabbled in the genre.

Cahn began as an editor during Hollywood's silent era. By the time he made this picture, he'd given up any hope of graduating to A-pictures and simply wanted to get the job done with the least possible effort. He planted his camera like a fire hydrant, often in the next zip code, and handled every sequence in the same perfunctory way. His co-conspirator, Robert Kent, once said that making movies was no different than making sausages. *We won't be having breakfast at his house.* In their film, invisible beings enter the bodies of dead people to cause worldwide panic and destruction via stock footage.

To criticize these pictures for their scientific inaccuracy seems as pointless as criticizing the chariot race in *Ben-Hur* (1959) for using the wrong kind of horses. The more you know about any subject, the more you realize how often the people who write these movies are talking through their hats. We decided to take these movies on their own terms, no matter how cockeyed those terms may be. But if the movies don't make sense on their own terms, we feel obliged to lodge a complaint. John Carradine tells Phillip Tonge that we Earthlings will never be able to defeat the invaders *because* they're invisible. So why would they crawl into dead bodies so that everyone can see them? That's a horse that just won't run.

Night of the Blood Beast

Ed Nelson and John Baer track the creature from Galaxy 27 to Bronson Canyon in *Night of the Blood Beast* (1958): a six day, $68,000 movie directed by Bernard Kowalski. Kowalski did his best to keep things lively, but the movie is essentially a talk-fest. His camera setups and staging are imaginative, and the actors give a good account of themselves, but it's all for nothing.

The creature (Ross Sturlin) kills one of the scientists for his vocal chords so that it can communicate with the Earthlings. "Do not be afraid," he tells them. "I'm not here to harm you." The creature explains that centuries ago, the people on his planet discovered the ultimate power, as we are about to. Hatred, greed, and prejudice caused them to misuse that power. The alien has come to save us from a similar fate. "Through me, we will unite our intellects into one body. Within the hour, the first of our new generation will be born." Michael Emmett knows this to be true. He's been impregnated by the creature. "You're imposing your will on us," Emmett says in a burst of revelation. "You're sacrificing our civilization for the resurrection of your own. What you propose is dominance, not salvation!" Emmett, knowing that Baer and Nelson won't toss their Molotov cocktails with him in the way, commits suicide. As the alien dies, engulfed in flames, it still won't shut up. "You're not ready," it says. "But we will still save you. In your path of self-destruction, you will send up more satellites and we will be there, waiting to come again."

Ross Sturlin as the creature from Galaxy 27. *Photo from the author's collection.*

We met the writer of this film, Martin Varno, at Forry Ackerman's house in the early sixties. At that time, Ackerman was his agent. "They tried to cheat me," he told us, referring to Roger Corman and his brother, Gene, the producers of his film. "They kept asking for changes in the script, but they didn't want to pay me." Ackerman took Varno's grievances to the WGA, which ordered the Cormans to pay him $600 in addition to the $900 he'd already received, which they eventually did, kicking and screaming all the way. Uninvited, Varno came to the preview of the movie and sat between Ackerman and his friend Jerry Bixby. Their job, according to Varno, was to keep him from slitting his throat. In the lobby afterwards, he told them he wished he had enough money to buy the negative so that he could burn it.

The Unseen or The Beast with 1,000,000 Eyes

Roger Corman gave $30,000 to two of his assistants, Lou Place and David Kramarsky, and sent them to the desert for ten days to make a non-union movie called *The Unseen*, which was about an invisible alien who takes control of animals and people. With only one day left of location shooting, Kramarsky got a frantic call from Corman.

David Kramarsky said, "He said the union was threatening to shut the picture down. I said 'What are we going to do?' He said: 'Calm them down. We're going to have you join the union. Come in tomorrow.' That's how I got my union card. We had 48 pages of interiors left to shoot. Roger directed those scenes himself. He replaced Everette Baker, who was our photographer, with Floyd Crosby and shot everything at a little studio that Lou had rented on La Cienega. He told Crosby: 'I don't care whether the mike is in the shot or not. Let's just finish this thing.' He did the 48 pages in two days."

Jim Nicholson, the president of ARC, was working on the advertising campaign while the picture was being made. He reasoned that if this invisible monster could see through the eyes of the creatures it controlled, it was like a monster with a million eyes. Unbeknownst to Corman, Nicholson changed the title to *The Beast with 1,000,000 Eyes* (1956) and sent out fliers with an illustration of a multi-orbed monster. When the distributors saw the movie, they were shocked. They wanted to know what happened to the monster. Joe Levine was so angry, he offered to give Nicholson $100,000 to let him burn it.

No monster, no deal. That's what the distributors told Nicholson, and that was what Nicholson told Corman, who was furious. His ten-day, $30,000 trifle had become a real headache. First the union threatened to shut him down, and now he had to come up with a monster. One of the reasons he made the damn thing in the first place was because it didn't have a monster.

This is where Paul Blaisdell came into the picture. Corman phoned Forry Ackerman—Jim Nicholson's high school chum—who was an agent for writers and prop makers. Ackerman told him to get in touch with Blaisdell, who was working as an art director for Jacques Fresco's *Spaceway* magazine. Blaisdell became AIP's go-to guy for bargain basement monsters. In the low-budget arena, he had no rival. His monsters were flashy and unusual. To make *The Beast with 1,000,000 Eyes*, he was paid the whopping sum of $200 plus the cost of the materials.

People often made fun of Blaisdell because he insisted on wearing the costumes he created even though he was a little guy. Everyone thought the monster ought to be taller than the leading lady. They thought Blaisdell's ego was getting in the way of his good sense. Actually, it was a matter of economics. He got more money when he played the monster. Over the years, he became frustrated and bitter because he never understood why everybody had to make these pictures so fast. He didn't understand about the economics of the business. All he knew was that the pictures weren't very good. In the case of *The Beast with 1,000,000 Eyes*, the picture wasn't any good. The performances are all over the place, nothing cuts together, and you could swear you already sat through the scene that you're watching. It was so bad, Lou Place didn't want his name on the thing, so David Kramarsky took the director's credit.

Hitching a Ride

With a lot of these visitors from space, they hitched rides on our satellites and rockets. Besides the films we've already discussed, there was *Space Master X-7* (1958), one of Bob Lippert's Regalscope movies directed by Edward Bernds. The script by Daniel Mainwaring and George Worthington Yates was a sci-fi version of *The Killer That Stalked New York* (1950). A rocket returns from space with something called "Blood Rust" in the nose cone. Some of the spores land on Lynn Bari and she unwittingly spreads the flesh-eating stuff all over the city.

Ray Harryhausen's Ymir from 20 Million Miles to Earth *(1957).Photo from author's collection.*

20 Million Miles to Earth

In *20 Million Miles to Earth* (1957), a rocket ship as big as the Empire State Building, which was crippled by a meteor on its way back from Venus, crashes into the ocean near a fishing village in Sicily. The two survivors—William Hopper and Arthur Space—are rescued by some brave fishermen (George Khoury and Don Orlando) and an obnoxious little boy (Bart Bradley). A sealed metal container, which contains specimen from Venus, is thrown from the ship on impact, and the little boy finds it. He removes the jelly-like egg and sells it to Frank Pegulia, a zoologist living in a trailer with his daughter, Joan Taylor, who is almost a doctor. A cuddly little creature crawls out of the jellied egg and begins doubling in size every twenty-four hours. It's taken to Rome, where it breaks loose and causes quite a lot of damage before it's blasted off the Roman Colosseum.

The special effects by Ray Harryhausen are fabulous. The monster is really cool and it's onscreen a lot. Unfortunately, everything takes a backseat to these effects. The characters are little more than pawns, moving from one effects sequence to the next; they don't seem like real people. When Pegulia and Taylor see the alien for the first time, Pegulia puts it in a cage and immediately walks away from it. Any normal person would have watched the thing until their eyes fell out.

Special effects are supposed to support the story, but in Harryhausen's films, it's the other way around.

The Quatermass Experiment or The Creeping Unknown

Nigel Kneale's six-part television serial, *The Quatermass Experiment*, was turned into a feature film by Robert Lippert and Hammer Films. Lippert had just started working for Fox, but they weren't interested in any movie that wasn't in CinemaScope. Lippert sold it to United Artists, and they changed the title to *The Creeping Unknown* (1956).

Brian Donlevy and Richard Wordsworth from Quatermass Experiment, *aka* The Creeping Unknown *(1956). Photo courtesy of Gary Smith.*

Richard Wordsworth played Victor Caroon, the sole survivor of a three-man expedition into space. The other two astronauts have mysteriously disappeared. Some film developed from a camera inside the cockpit reveals that some invisible force entered the rocket and consumed the other two astronauts. Caroon is now a carrier, and he undergoes a physical metamorphosis that see him eventually becoming a gelatinous mass, absorbing every living thing it touches.

"My part in the film had been over about twenty minutes when the monster attacks Westminster Abbey," Wordsworth recalled. "In that sequence, the monster has become a great round blob of rubber solution draped over everything. A landlady up north said to me, 'Mr. Wordsworth, you were so good. And in the Abbey scene—your makeup! It was marvelous!'"[8]

It's a frightening, tense, and intelligent film with an appropriately nervous score by James Bernard. The sequel, *Quatermass II*, is equally good. Again, adapted from a Nigel Kneale teleplay by director Val Guest, Professor Quatermass (Brian Donlevy) discovers the Government has been taken over by aliens. They've built a top secret plant at Wynerton Flats to produce synthetic food to feed the aliens, who are housed in huge domes. Said Kneale, "It was a time when mysterious establishments were popping up: great radar establishments and nuclear establishments like Harwell and Porton Down germ warfare."[9]

Quatermass II was called *Enemy from Space* (1957) in the U.S. It has a lot in common with Walter Wanger's Invasion of the *Body Snatchers* (1956), which is an even more insidious film.

Invasion of the Body Snatchers

In Wanger's film, the Government isn't responsible for the sinister goings on: it's mainstream America. Daniel Mainwaring's screenplay, based on Jack Finney's three-part *Collier's* magazine serial, is full of deception, secrecy, and people moving about in darkened cellars. All of these conspirators are in a sinister plot to force the inhabitants of a small California town to conform to a new social order.

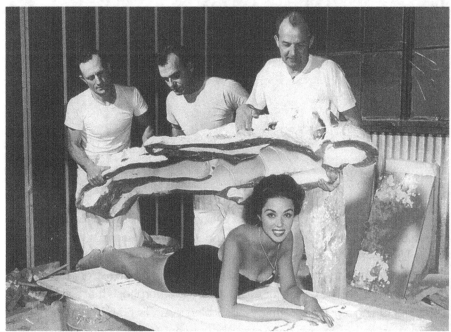

Dana Wynter at Don Post Studios having a body cast made for her pod duplicate. Photo from the author's collection.

Returning home from a two-week medical convention, Dr. Miles Bennell (Kevin McCarthy) finds that the people of Santa Mira have succumbed to what his psychiatrist friend (Larry Gates) calls "an epidemic mass hysteria." They're convinced that their relatives and friends are imposters. They're right. Seeds from space have taken root in a farmer's field, producing pods with the power to duplicate any form of life. While the residents of Santa Mira slept, their minds and memories were sucked into emotionless pod doubles. Before long, Bennell and his lady friend, Becky Driscoll (Dana Wynter), are the only humans left. Eventually, she becomes a pod, too, leaving Bennell alone to warn the world of the danger. The last shot of the film has him standing in the middle of the highway, screaming at the passing cars (and into the camera), "YOU'RE NEXT!"

Allied Artists executives forced director Don Siegel to shoot a new, more comforting and conclusive frame story. In spite of this tampering, the movie remains a chilling allegory of a world in which a retreat from emotions becomes a desirable thing. It grossed over a million dollars and is still one of the scariest movies ever made.

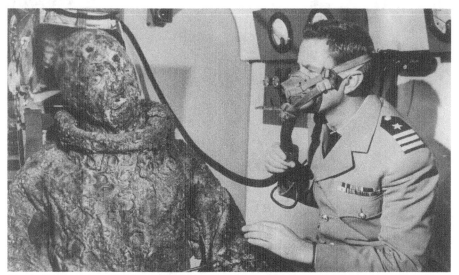

Marshall Thompson and Bill Edwards from The First Man into Space *(1959). Photo courtesy of Bob Villard.*

The First Man into Space

Possibly inspired by the first Quatermass film, *The First Man into Space* (1959) returns to Earth, encrusted with some cosmic gunk that impedes his ability to breathe. Only by drinking blood can he survive. Based on Wyott Ordung's *Satellite of Blood*, it may be the most deceptively advertised movie of the decade. The ads made it look like one of those pseudo-documentary movies like *On the Threshold of Space* (1956). For the first half of the picture, that's exactly what it seems to be. Then, much to the surprise and relief of every little kid in the audience, it turns into a monster movie.

Target Earth!

Herman Cohen's *Target Earth!* (1954) opens strong. Kathleen Crowley wakes up from her suicide attempt and finds Los Angeles has been evacuated, taken over by an army of robots. Once the cat is out of the bag, however, the film all but collapses.

"We had one robot," said director Sherman Rose. "That's all we could afford. It was a very inexpensive movie. We shot in the streets without permits. We had six or seven days to make it, if I remember right. It was okay for what it was."

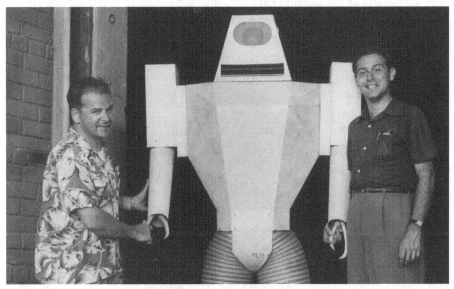

Director Sherman Rose with producer Herman Cohen. Photo from the author's collection.

The Crawling Eye

In *The Crawling Eye* (1958), Forrest Tucker has some concerns about the mysterious, static, radioactive cloud in the mountains above a cozy little Australian resort. Since its arrival, a few dozen mountain climbers have disappeared. A similar thing happened in the Andes three years earlier. One of the casualties at that time was an old psychic woman, an unfortunate recipient of signals from the cloud. A man who'd been dead for twenty-four hours took a meat axe to her. By the time the United Nations sent a team to investigate, it was too late. The cloud had vanished. Tucker is afraid that history will repeat itself. He thinks aliens are hiding in that cloud, waiting to take over the Earth.

This is a Quatermass wannabe written by Jimmy Sangster. It's not nearly as tidy as something Nigel Kneale would write. It raises more questions than it answers, yet it all seems to make sense while you're watching it. It's one of the goriest and most violent sci-fi films of the decade.

"I had a lot of fun making those pictures," Tucker said, referring to The *Crawling Eye, The Cosmic Monster,* and *The Abominable Snowman of the Himalayas* (1957). He was between takes on his short-lived TV show *Ghostbusters*. "I was the good guy for a change." Throughout our conversation, he continued to nurse a glass of scotch between every take. He was the only one that day who never flubbed a line.

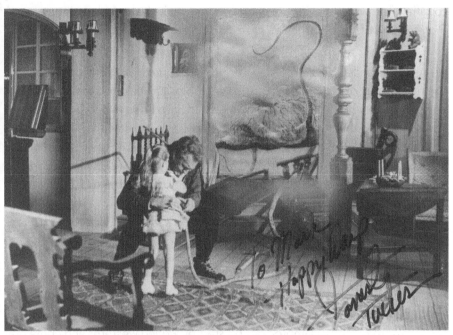

Forrest Tucker rescues Caroline Glaser from The Crawling Eye (1958). *The eye pictured here is not the one used in the movie. Photo from the author's collection.*

Plan 9 from Outer Space

Edward D. Wood's blend of old-fashioned horror and newfangled science fiction, *Plan 9 from Outer Space* (1958), is one of the funniest movies ever made. The inhabitants from another planet want to stop the people of Earth from discovering solarbonite: a means of exploding sunlight, which would endanger the entire galaxy. To this end, the aliens resurrect a couple of dead people who, for some unexplained reason, act like ghouls and vampires.

"This is the most fantastic story I've ever heard," Tom Keene remarks after hearing Mona McKinnon's account of being chased by a vampire. Her husband, Gregory Walcott, assures Keene that every word of her story is true. "That's the fantastic part of it!" Keene adds. Later in the film, irritated by McKinnon's refusal to bow to his authority, a disgruntled cop muses, "Modern women."

"Yeah," says Keene, "They've been like that down through the ages." Only Wood would cast 400-pound Tor Johnson in the role of a police inspector and give him the line, "I'm a big boy now, Johnny."

Criswell, a small-time TV personality and self-professed psychic, caps the whole business, "We once laughed at the horseless carriage, the airplane, the telephone, the electric light, vitamins, radio, and even television. And now, some of us laugh at outer space. God help us in the future."

Some people have called Wood's film the worst movie ever made. We beg to differ. The worst movies are the ones you can't sit through. In its own way, *Plan 9* is one of the *best* movies ever made.

The Atomic Submarine

Arthur Franz and his crew use *The Atomic Submarine* (1959) to investigate the mysterious disappearance of subs and ships around the North Pole. If his navigator knew his business, the movie would have been twenty-minutes long. But we can see that he doesn't because the course is plotted for us, from time to time, by a series of animated arrows on a map. Up and down and around the arrows go, leaving a trail that looks like something out of a Daffy Duck cartoon. Finally, Franz and his crew discover the source of all of the mischief: a flying saucer and its one-eyed occupant. "So, Commander Halloway," the alien says to Franz, "as you Earth inhabitants would express it, we meet face to face." Franz replies, "That's a face?"

Anytime there's a one-eyed monster in a movie, you can bet your life that it will get poked in the eye before the film is over, which is exactly what happens here. It's such a cliché that you would think any writer worth their salt would be ashamed to use it, but in this instance we're talking about Orville H. Hampton, the king of the clichés. Hampton got his start by writing westerns and crime dramas for Bob Lippert. His scripts were routine, dull, and witless. He mostly worked in television, although his one claim to fame was an Academy Award nomination for *One Potato, Two Potato* (1964), which he co-wrote with Raphael Hayes.

Actress Joi Lansing was given a small part in the film as a favor to Frank Sinatra; she was his girlfriend at the time. Her main function (besides being eye candy) is to show what a ladies' man Franz is. Once Franz sets out to sea, we never see her again. If ever a picture could have used a stowaway, it's this one.

"The film was such a disappointment," confessed producer Alex Gordon. "We ran out of money before we could build the interior of the saucer. The art director came up with the idea of having those long ramps against black backdrops. I mean, it wasn't what we wanted, but it worked pretty well, I thought. We hired Jack Rabin and Irving Block to do our monster because they had worked on *The Giant Behemoth* (1959). I didn't know at the time that Willis

O'Brien was the one that was really responsible for the work in that film. Rabin and Block made this little hand puppet and it was awful. I wanted John Agar for the lead, but he was busy at the time, so I had to settle for Arthur Franz and he was a lot of trouble, very neurotic. He kept demanding to see the dailies. You would have thought he was working on a Stanley Kramer picture or something, I mean, this was just a little seven day picture."

The Lost Missile

John McPartland, the bestselling author of *No Down Payment*, co-wrote the screenplay for *The Lost Missile* (1958), which was a unique, if not totally successful, sci-fi thriller. The co-author of the screenplay was Jerome Bixby. Once the two writers agreed on the story, they finished the assignment in a week and a half.

A rocket from somewhere in space locks into an orbit around the Earth and incinerates everything in its path. It's a race against time to see if Robert Logia can stop it before it reaches New York.

This is a champagne disaster film on a Kool-Aid budget. That Lester Berke pulled it off as well as he did, stepping in at the last minute when his father (William Berke) died on the first day of production, merits some respect. The film relies heavily on stock footage to convey the sense of worldwide panic, but it's about the best use of stock footage you're likely to see in one of these movies. For a seven or ten day movie, it has a lot of sets. They aren't great sets, but they're serviceable and it helps to keep the film from looking as small as it is.

"As in every good suspense story, one feels the ticking of a clock through every minute of *The Lost Missile*," wrote Jack Moffitt in *The Hollywood Reporter*.

Notes:
1. Bradley, Matthew R. "Someone Wonderful This Way Came," *Filmfax* No. 131, pg. 52-53.
2. Weaver, Tom. *Monsters, Mutants and Heavenly Creatures*, Midnight Marquee Press, Inc., pg. 26.
3. "Meet Jungle Sam," *Life*, March 23, 1953, pg. 79-81.
4. Court, Hazel. *Hazel Court Horror Queen*, Tomahawk Press, Sheffield, England, 2008, pg. 76.
5. Pal, George. "Filming War of the Worlds," *Astounding Science Fiction*, Vol. LII, No. 2, pg. 102.
6. Ibid, pg. 109.
7. Baumann, Marty. *The Astounding B Monster*, Dinoship, New York, 2004, pg. 141.
8. Brosnan, John. *The Horror People*, St. Martin's Press, New York, NY, pg. 101.
9. *Starburst*, No. 16, Marvel Comics Ltd., the United Kingdom, pg. 16.

CHAPTER THREE
Prehistoric Predators

Of course, the question we are asking ourselves is how
this animal happened to reappear after all these
centuries and so near to the coast of Japan. One
answer could be that some rare phenomenon of nature
allowed this breed from the Jurassic Age to reproduce
itself and for a long span of time it had no reason to
reappear to the world. But now that analysis of
radioactivity of the creature's footprints shows the
existence of Strontium 90, a product of the H-bomb, it
is my belief that Godzilla was resurrected due to
repeated experiments of H-bombs.

—Godzilla

A hopeful young actress named Laurette Luez married a struggling director named Gregory Tallas and got divorced three months later. There were no children from their brief coupling, but they managed to give birth to *Prehistoric Women* (1950), a silly and hopelessly naïve movie about a tribe of Amazons who hate men. These women don't really look like cavewomen because nobody wants to sit through a movie peopled with a bunch of ugly, hairy women, though it seems a bit much to have them to look as if they just stepped out of the beauty parlor.

The movie follows the formula already set in place. Male encroachment is initially met with hostility. This hostile reaction will soften once the men have put to rest the problems that plague the women's world, by virtue of their mental and physical superiority. Implied, but never shown—much to the detriment of these movies in the opinion of your authors—is that some of these women must have resorted to lesbianism. No matter. By the last reel, the men will bring these misguided malcontents back to heterosexual harmony.

The dialogue in *Prehistoric Women* is limited to a few grunts and groans, which sometimes makes it difficult to determine whether the noises are coming from the screen or the audience. The children who came to this movie expecting to see dinosaurs were bitterly disappointed—as were the adult males who came to see a little skin. Never mind that cave people and dinosaurs never co-existed, that's hardly the point. There are plenty of people who don't know that and what they don't know won't hurt them. It didn't stop Hal Roach from making

One Million B.C. (1940) and it didn't stop Hammer from making *When Dinosaurs Ruled the Earth* (1970). If you're going to make a prehistoric movie, you have to have dinosaurs or what's the point?

Two Lost Worlds *and* Untamed Women

Despite the popularity of *The Lost World* (1925) and *King Kong* (1933), prehistoric animals were rarely seen in motion pictures. The explosion of monster movies in the fifties changed all that. Things got off to a decidedly bumpy start with *Two Lost Worlds* (1951) and *Untamed Women* (1952)—footage from *One Million B.C.* was used in both films.

Two Lost Worlds was best described by the reviewer for the *Hollywood Reporter*, who called it "a hastily compiled series of stock and process shots around which a pointless story rambles under the uninspired direction of Norman Dawn." Dale Lee, the owner of the Dream Theatre in Idaho, paired *Two Lost Worlds* with *Prehistoric Women*. "It will open well," Mr. Lee promised his fellow exhibitors, "but with world-of-mouth [business] will fall off."

Untamed Women had pilots Mikel Conrad, Morgan Jones, Mark Lowell, and Richard Monahan survive a plane crash and find themselves on an island populated with a lot of women who don't trust them. A bunch of savages called "the hairy men" murder a lot of the women just before an exploding volcano sinks the island. Everyone but Conrad is killed. If writer George W. Sayre was trying to make some kind of a statement with his apocalyptic climax, it was lost on us. More likely he was following the unstated dictate that all lost worlds must be destroyed once they're discovered. Why this is so, we cannot say. We just know that it seems to be true.

The Lost Continent

When Robert Lippert announced that he was going to make a movie about a group of scientists who, while searching for a runaway rocket, discover an uncharted, tropical plateau full of prehistoric animals, Ray Bradbury and Ray Harryhausen asked him if he would be interested in using stop-motion animation. He was, but when he told them what he was willing to pay, they left his office in disgust. Clearly Bradbury and Harryhausen didn't realize who they were dealing with.

Edward Nassour did the stop-motion work in Lippert's *The Lost Continent* (1951), although his name does not appear in the credits and for good reason: it's some of the worst stop motion animation in screen history. The dinosaurs look like refugees from one of Art Clokey's Gumby shorts. They are simply an embarrassment. "If this was the best you could do," Bradbury told Lippert at the film's premiere, "we're glad that we had nothing to do with it."[1]

Sigmund Neufeld produced the film and his brother, Sam Newfield, directed it. They were both old hands at low-budget moviemaking. The movie was shot

Sid Melton, Whit Bissell, Hugh Beaumont, John Hoyt, Cesar Romero, Acquanetta, and Chick Chandler cower before the battling dinosaurs on The Lost Continent.*(1951) Photo courtesy of Bob Villard.*

in eleven days at the Sam Goldwyn studio. "I think that [Newfield] has gone down on record as being the fastest B-picture director and he was (I think) superb at what he did," Sid Melton told Tom Weaver. Melton, a regular in Lippert movies, played the comedy relief in the movie.

A sixty-foot-high mountain was constructed for all of the actors to climb and boy, oh boy, do they make use of it. It takes Cesar Romero and his buddies about twenty minutes to get to the top. (Even your authors could climb sixty feet faster than that.) There is one effective moment when Whit Bissell is hanging from a ledge, and discovers to his horror that he can't pull himself up. John Hoyt tries to hold him, but it's no use. In a down-angle shot, with Hoyt watching from the ledge at the bottom of the screen, Bissell falls to his death, disappearing into a bank of clouds. It's a great shot, but Bissell's double must have bounced back into the scene when he hit the mattress because there's a dissolve in the middle of the scene and John Hoyt vanishes before your eyes.

Like Sid Melton and actress Margia Dean, Cesar Romero was a regular in Lippert pictures. Screenwriter Richard Landau mentions him by name in his script for *The Lost Continent*. He begs the makeup men not to dye his hair.

Predictably, at the end of the picture, the lost plateau is wiped out by an earthquake caused by an exploding volcano. There's an effects scene of the earth splitting apart that's repeated seven times during the climax; a scene that found its way into every fifties sci-fi movie that had an earthquake.

The Beast from 20,000 Fathoms

When *The Beast from 20,000 Fathoms* (1953) arrived on the scene, there hadn't been anything like it since *King Kong*—Merian C. Cooper's groundbreaking classic about a giant gorilla loose in New York. On its fourth re-release in 1952, Kong made more money than it had back in 1933, a fact that wasn't lost on producers Hal Chester and Jack Dietz. They wanted to make their own monster-on-the-loose movie. And they wanted to use stop-motion animation like Willis O'Brien had used to create Kong. There was only one guy around at the time who was capable of giving Chester and Dietz what they wanted, for a price they could afford to pay: Ray Harryhausen.

Cecil Kellaway, Paula Raymond, and Paul Christian. Photo from the author's collection.

Ray Bradbury said, "[Hal Chester] called me over to the studio and said, 'We have a script here that needs some work and Ray Harryhausen suggested that you might be the proper person to go to work on the screenplay, because it needs editing and changing and what have you. Would you mind going in the next room and reading the script and giving us your opinion and tell us if you'd be willing to work on it?' So I went in the next office and sat there for about an hour and read the script and came back out and sat down and talked to the producer. I said, 'You know, part of this script here resembles a short story of mine... that was in *The Saturday Evening* Post last year.' A look of astonishment and awe and stunned amazement came over his face and I realized that they had borrowed my idea, forgotten where they borrowed it from, and called me in to criticize it. The irony was too much, it was really hilarious."[2]

"I had twelve days to make the picture," said director Eugene Lourie. "I had two location days in New York. I set up everything like a train schedule. I gave myself fifteen minutes for each shot. No more."

Paul Christian is the scientist who sees the prehistoric animal, and who spends the better part of the movie trying to convince people that the creature exists. Everyone thinks he's crazy until the animal marches down Wall Street. This brings into question why we spent so much time with this guy. For all of his efforts, his only accomplishment is to bring about the premature death of Cecil Kellaway. Christian isn't even the one who kills the monster; sharpshooter Lee Van Cleef is called in at the last minute to do that. He and Christian climb to the top of a rollercoaster to fire a radioactive isotope into the monster's gaping wound. It would have been better if the monster had bumped the rollercoaster and sent Van Cleef flying over the edge, forcing Christian to make the shot.

These are tough pictures to write. People go to these movies hoping to see a dress rehearsal for Armageddon, and these scenes cost money. So, the monster is offscreen most of the time. Unless the monster has character, like Kong, the focus of the movie has to be on something else. In this case, writers Lou Morheim and Fred Freiberger chose to focus on Christian. That's okay, but it would have been a more satisfying if his knowledge would have been put to some use. Still, it's a pretty good picture. The director did a fantastic job of making it look like it cost three or four times more than it did, and in that respect, it's a remarkable picture.

The Beast from 20,000 Fathoms *(1953) Photo from the author's collection.*

Without saying anything to his partner, Jack Dietz took this remarkable picture to Warner Brothers, hoping for a distribution partnership, but he was happy to accept their offer of a $400,000 buyout. A few days later, Chester was told by Dietz's attorney that they were selling the film. Chester told the attorney that Dietz could do whatever he wanted with his share, but Chester wanted to hold onto his share because he had faith in the picture. He believed it was going to make a lot of money. The attorney took a gun out of his desk and explained that some of the investors were getting impatient. They wanted their money now. *You gotta nice family, pal. Be a shame if something was to happen to them.*

Generally speaking, the critics were not kind to *The Beast*. An anonymous writer for *Catholic World's* July 1953 issue said, "If this film is widely popular, movie standards have declined alarmingly." *The New Yorker's* John McCarten said he'd "do the actors in this one the small kindness of not mentioning their names." *Variety* came to the rescue. "The sight of the beast stalking through Gotham's downtown streets is awesome... Christian is first-rate as the determined scientist and Kellaway scores as the doubting professor. Miss Raymond appears too stiff and unconvincing as the professor's assistant and Christian's romantic vis-à-vis. Eugene Lourie's direction is excellent, resulting in the proper tension and suspense." An exhibitor in Indiana named James Hardy said it best: "Played this one in extremely hot weather and did better than average business both nights. If your patrons like fantastic stuff, you can't go wrong on this one."

The Giant Behemoth

Five years later, Lourie made a picture in England called *The Giant Behemoth* (1959) starring Gene Evans—an actor who usually played heavies in westerns. Evans was a little uncomfortable with some of the scientific gobbledygook he was given to say, but he's very good in the role. Most of the actors are, but the movie, a pale remake of *The Beast from 20,000 Fathoms*, delivers very little of what the audience paid to see.

Eugene Lourie said, "David Diamond had this script [written by Robert Abel and Allan Adler] about an invisible radioactive substance which floated across the water. But the distributors wanted something they could see... a visible monster. I was given two weeks to come up with something. So I wrote a script about a dinosaur that could project lethal doses of radiation, much in the way a tower transmits radio beams. I assumed, erroneously, that once we had the backing from the distributors, the script would be rewritten."

The script that Lourie co-wrote with Daniel Hyatt[3] is a lot like that old gag about the guy who asked for the time and was told how to make a watch. If Evans has to perform some kind of a test, the audience has to see the entire process. No piece of information is given without a struggle. Once Evans and

The Giant Behemoth *goes on a rampage. Photo courtesy of Bob Villard.*

his buddy, Andre Morrell, have pieced together enough evidence to take their theory about a living radioactive prehistoric monster to the authorities, the audience has to suffer as they work their way up the chain of command until, at last, they find someone with enough authority to take action. The film is about everything but the monster. It's an hour before the behemoth shows itself in a particularly unsatisfying sequence, which was designed and executed by Jack Rabin, Irving Block, and Phil Kellison. The monster attacks a ferry boat, but all we see is its head and neck and the thing is stiff as a board.

Phil Kellison said, "It was a mechanical, rubber puppet. The controls were at the bottom of the neck. The mouth opened and closed, the eyes rolled, and you could raise the lip to make it snarl. Jack Rabin (or maybe it was Louis De-Witt) started playing with it a few minutes before we were ready to shoot the scene and broke it. There was no time to fix it. That was the trouble with all of these pictures. There was never any time or any money to do them properly. There was one scene I was looking forward to where the behemoth causes a huge gasoline storage tank to explode. They ran out of money for that. They couldn't build the model. So Block took a bunch of empty 35 mm film cans, stacked them one on top of another, poured gasoline on them, and set fire to them."

Some of the stop motion animation by Pete Peterson—working under the supervision of Willis O'Brien—is terrific. Peterson didn't seem to share Harryhausen's desire to keep his shots brief. A couple of his scenes run over a minute, and it's some of the smoothest animation you'll ever see. And this was a guy with multiple sclerosis.

Harryhausen's mother (Martha) and Willis O'Brien's widow (Darlyne) were watching *The Giant Behemoth* on television one evening. As the monster paraded through the city, Mrs. Harryhausen sighed and said, "I don't know why Obie bothered with this picture. Ray did all of this in *The Beast from 20,000 Fathoms*." Without looking away from the screen, Mrs. O'Brien replied, "Yes, dear, but Obie did it before that in *The Lost World*."

20,000 Leagues Under the Sea

For his first cartoon-free, full-length feature film, Walt Disney chose *20,000 Leagues Under the Sea* (1954)—Jules Verne's tale of Captain Nemo's vendetta against war ships. Like everything else that Disney tackled, he wanted to go first class. Kirk Douglas was a huge star when he was signed for the lead and James Mason was the perfect choice for Captain Nemo. Location shooting in the Bahamas looked beautiful in Technicolor and CinemaScope, but it was Harper Goff's production design that proved to be the film's greatest asset. His contribution to the film can't be overestimated. It's the look of the film, far more than its content that made it such a hit with its fans. The climax of the film features an attack on Nemo's submarine by a giant squid. We don't know whether or not this giant beast was supposed to be prehistoric, but it's a cinch it wasn't the result of radiation poisoning. The battle between the squid and the crew of the Nautilus was originally shot at sunset on a calm sea, and looked so phony that Disney stopped production. It was either screenwriter Earl Felton or 2nd unit director James Havens who suggested they shoot the scene at night in a storm, which added $200,000 to the budget. The squid still looked phony but it was better, and the film earned an Oscar for its special effects. Peter Lorre complained that the squid got the role that was usually reserved for him.

The Monster from the Ocean Floor

Producer Roger Corman was only 27 years old when he made *The Monster from the Ocean Floor* (1954). It cost a modest $18,000 plus $12,000 deferred. It was an 8 day shoot—6 days at Malibu and 2 days for the underwater photography at Catalina. *The Hollywood Reporter* said the film was being shot in Mexico and that its title was *The Sea Demon*. Corman gave them that misinformation. He didn't want the picture listed in the trade magazines at all knowing that the union would be on his back about not having enough crew people.

When the monster made its first onscreen appearance at a sneak preview, one member of the audience yelled, "It looks like my wife's diaphragm!" Corman turned to marionette maker Bob Baker to save him. Baker made a little puppet that looked like a one-eyed octopus. It was supposed to look like an amoeba, but a one-eyed octopus was better than a diaphragm. Corman sold his $18,000 film to Bob Lippert for $100,000. Whether the monster was supposed to be prehistoric or the result of atomic radiation is never made clear, and it hardly matters. The film has no plot, no characters, and according to the film's photographer, Floyd Crosby, it was made without any direction whatsoever.

The Monster of Piedras Blancas

The Monster of Piedras Blancas (1958) is a mutation of the reptilian family, apparently the only one in existence, and kept alive by a lonely lighthouse keeper (John Harmon). Shortly after the death of his wife, he happened upon the creature one afternoon while exploring some of the caves near the lighthouse. He tells his daughter (Jeanne Carmen) he felt responsible for it and left food for it. "After you left, I was very lonesome, Lucy, and seemed less lonesome knowing there was some living creature nearby," he explains. "I

Pete Dunn played the monster of Piedras Blancas. The claws are from The Mole People *and the feet are from the Metaluna monster from* This Island Earth. *Photo courtesy of Gary Smith.*

know it was stupid, but I never got along with the townspeople. It was something to hang onto." She says she understands, but we sure as hell don't. He knows the thing is dangerous. He warns fishermen to keep away from the area. He sent Lucy to boarding school so she'd be safe from it. Yet when the monster begins slicing off heads and draining bodies dry of blood, he keeps quiet about it. What a jerk!

This lame, independently made effort was shot on location in the little beach town of Point Conception in Northern California, a few miles south of Piedras Blancas. It was produced by Jack Kevan, who was once a member of Bud Westmore's makeup team at Universal. He was one of the many people involved in this movie, along with Joe Lapis, Eddie Keys, and Irvin Berwick, who were let go by the studio during a budget crunch. To help keep them employed, Universal supplied a lot of the vehicles, props, and equipment Kevan needed to make the picture. Too bad somebody didn't give them a decent script.

Godzilla

A broker named Edmund Goldman happened to see a Japanese monster movie called *Gojira* (1954) in a Chinatown theatre one afternoon. He took a five-year lease on it for a modest $25,000 and sold it to producers Edward Barrison, Harry Rybnick, and Richard Kaye. They felt they could make the film more saleable to an American audience if they added some new scenes with an American actor. So they sold a piece of the film, along with the distribution rights, to Boston distributor Joseph E. Levine for $100,000: the money they needed to shoot the new footage. Terrell O. Morse, a former film editor, was hired to direct it.

Terry Morse said, "I've been a doctor of sick pictures for a good many years, ever since I left Warners. We hired Raymond Burr to play a news correspondent named Steve Martin. I invented that character. It was the only way I could think of to work an American into the story, by having this newsman observe everything. We shot the whole thing in five days at a little studio on Vermont."

Morse wrote the new sequences with Al C. Ward who was paid $2,500 for his services. Ward was given the option of working for a piece of the film, but he assumed the thing would bomb, so he took the money. He would later tell the students in his college writing class that it was a decision that probably cost him $5 million in residuals. More likely, creative book-

This scene of Godzilla (Katsumi Tezuka) was used as a reference by the artist who designed the poster. Photo from the author's collection.

keeping would have proved that the film never made a dime.

Morse did an incredible job of integrating Burr into the movie. However, this shift in focus from the characters who actually move the story along, to the one guy who has no effect on anything dramatically hurts the movie. But, for what Morse was trying to accomplish, it worked and most people were fooled.

With the bumper crop of monster movies on the market, Levine wanted his film to stand out. To that end, he launched an advertising blitz that exceeded the production costs. Trailers ran nonstop on television. In Los Angeles, several news programs were sponsored by Godzilla. "Makes King Kong look like a midget!" the advertisements claimed. Kong was 50ft, Godzilla was 150ft! That wasn't enough of an edge. In the American version, Godzilla is 400 feet tall! A guy can do incredible things with dubbing.

In director Ishiro Honda's original version—written by Honda and Takeo Murata—the wholesale slaughter by the fire-breathing dinosaur is an allegory for atomic radiation and American supremacy run amok. Morse eliminated most of the references to the war, but no matter which version of the film you see, it's a pretty grim bit of business. Akira Ifukube's score is depressing, Masao Tamai's photography is dark and gloomy, and a sense of hopelessness permeates the film from beginning to end. Even before Godzilla lays waste to Tokyo, there is no joy in this movie. The lead characters are in turmoil. Emiko Yamane (Momoko Kochi) is supposed to marry Dr. Serizawa (Akihiko Hirata), but she's in love with Hideto Ogata (Akira Takarada). Every time she and Ogata find the courage to tell someone about their dilemma, they're thwarted. Ogata is a heartbeat away from telling Emiko's father, Dr. Yamane (Takashi Shimura), when the two get into an argument over whether Godzilla should be killed or not. Dr. Yamane thinks he should be studied; Dr. Yamane is a nutcase. When Emiko tries to tell Serizawa, he interrupts her to demonstrate his new discovery: the Oxygen Destroyer. (If you destroy the oxygen in water, it's no longer water. What is it?) When Emiko and Ogata plead with Serizawa to use his Oxygen Destroyer to kill Godzilla, the scientist is torn, afraid that his weapon might fall into the wrong hands. He burns his notes, kills Godzilla, tells Ogata to be happy with Emiko, and commits suicide.

Godzilla opened at Loew's State Theatre on Broadway in New York on April 27. Bosley Crowther, the *New York Times* critic, hated it. "The whole thing is in the category of cheap cinematic horror-stuff," he wrote, "and it is too bad that a respectable theater has to lure children and gullible grown-ups with such fare." What did he think he was going to see? *The Country Girl*?

Boxoffice liked it a whole lot better. "Combining most of the frightening features of *King Kong* and the more recent 'Creature' and 'Monster' pictures, this Japanese-made horror melodrama is a natural for sensational exploitation and should attract the hordes of film fans who delight in pictures that will make them shudder... Utterly fantastic, of course, the special photographic effects of this 400-foot creature emerging from the sea to stalk on land and crush the tall buildings of Tokyo should elicit gasps or shrieks from youngsters or from the more susceptible women patrons—even though they really love it."

The film grossed two million dollars in less than a year. A sequel—*Godzilla Raids Again* (1955)—was hurried into production. It's a different Godzilla and he battles another prehistoric animal called the Angurus. These epic monster showdowns kept Eiji Tsuburaya and his special effects team busy for the next three decades. Godzilla continued to take on new challengers, evolving from a walking nightmare into a comic villain and, ultimately, a national hero.

Hoping to repeat the success they'd had with *Godzilla*, Rybnick and Barrison bought the rights to *Godzilla Raids Again*. They would save themselves the hassle of trying to integrate an American character into the mix by simply hiring Ib Melchior and Ed Watson to write an entirely new story around the special effects sequences. A deal was cut with the newly formed AB-PT Productions (a merger of the American Broadcasting Company and United Paramount Theatres) to co-finance and distribute *The Volcano Monster*. Toho shipped the monster suits to the Howard Anderson Company for some additional scenes, and everything was set to go when AB-PT went bankrupt. And that was the end of that.

A few years later, Toho's attorney, Paul Schriebman, bought *Godzilla Raids Again* and changed the title to *Gigantis the Fire Monster* (1959). He hired Hugo Grimaldi to "Americanize" it. Grimaldi added some stock footage and replaced the Japanese score with cues from *Kronos*, *She Devil*, *The Deerslayer*, and *Project Moon Base*. It was sold to Warner Brothers as part of a package with *Teenagers from Outer Space*, another film that Schriebman owned. The package did not perform well. Schriebman might have had better luck if he hadn't concealed the fact that it was a Godzilla movie. The fool had the sequel to a box office hit, but he didn't want anybody to know it. *Yes, my good woman, we do have the sequel to Avatar, but we're calling it The Fuller Brush Man.*

Whoever wrote the English-language script for *Gigantis* must have thought they were writing for the radio. There is no dead air. Narrator Keye Luke never shuts up. Anytime there's a break in the conversation, he steps in to tell the audience what the characters are thinking and feeling. Sometimes, he describes what the audience is looking at.

Dubbing a movie is just about the worst thing you can do to it. The mouths never match the words, but that can't be helped. The real problem is that nobody wants to spend the money to do the job right. The scripts are not translated in any meaningful way: the writers simply make stuff up. Their infantile, sometimes incomprehensible, dialogue is delivered by actors who are apparently hired for their inability to give credible performances.

Top: Baby Rodan makes his first appearance. Bottom: All grown up, Rodan attacks the city. Photos courtesy of Bob Villard.

Rodan, the Flying Monster

In Toho's *Rodan, the Flying Monster* (1956), some military guy is looking out of a window at the devastation caused by the monsters. Hundreds of people have been killed, buildings toppled, and the city is in flames. The military guy is dubbed by Paul Frees, who plays so many roles in this picture that he often asks and answers his own questions. Surrounded by people, the military guy bitterly says, "The Rodans did this!" Well, of course they did. He watched them do it. Everybody in the room watched them do it. *We* watched them do it. That simply can't be what he really said, unless he was supposed to be a simpleton. David Duncan wrote the American dialog, and he said it was the most boring job he ever had.

Rodan made more money than *Godzilla*.

Donald Curtis, Faith Domergue, and Ken Tobey from It Came from Beneath the Sea. *Photo from the author's collection.*

It Came from Beneath the Sea

It Came from Beneath the Sea was another remake of *The Beast from 20,000 Fathoms*. This time, the prehistoric monster is a giant octopus, which is again animated by Ray Harryhausen. It was produced by Charles H. Schneer with Sam Katzman acting as an executive producer. Ken Tobey, who'd been a supporting player in The Beast, had the lead role.

Ken Tobey said, "It was the last day of the picture. The director [Robert Gordon] told Sam Katzman he needed another day. He had too many pages left to do. Katzman asked to see the pages. The director gave him the script and Katzman tore them out. 'As I said, we finish today.' That was a helluva way to end a picture."

Shot in seven days, at a cost of $150,000, *It Came from Beneath the Sea* made a lot of money: enough money to promote producer Charles H. Schneer out of Sam Katzman's unit at Columbia. The profits put his picture in the same competitive bracket as movies that had been made for three or four times the cost. William Alland was impressed. We wish we could report that he wanted to hire

The giant octopus attacks San Francisco. Photo from the author's collection.

Ray Harryhausen for his next picture, but, alas, it was the stock footage used in the film that impressed him. His next offering *The Deadly Mantis* (1957), was crammed full of stock footage.

The Deadly Mantis

The Deadly Mantis opens with seven minutes of stock footage where tractors and snow plows pave the way for the Distant Early Warning Line: a Cold War system of radar stations in the far northern Arctic region of Canada. There's a glimpse of the film's star, Craig Stevens, climbing out of an airplane, after which the movie quickly retreats into more stock footage. It's only a taste of what's to come.

The script was written by Martin Berkeley, who had the distinction of giving HUAC more names than any other friendly witness, which earned him the dubious honor of being the Motion Picture Alliance's chief authority on communism. Berkeley brings absolutely nothing new to the table. His script simply follows the formula set down by *Them!* in 1954. (see Chapter Four.)

The formula: In an isolated location, a series of unexplainable incidents occur. Animals or people are missing or murdered. Their bodies are pumped full of something, drained, eaten, or otherwise mutilated. The clues are puzzling—mysterious footprints, radioactivity, puddles of gooey guck, and loud, grating noises often attributed to the wind. One of the characters might evoke a legend or curse peculiar to the area to explain things. The hero is usually a scientist or a doctor, the heroine is a scientist herself, the daughter of a scientist, or both. She never wears anything provocative and usually has a name that can be shortened to something that sounds masculine. A third of the way through the story, the perpetrator of the mysterious events turns out to be a mutated bug or animal, unearthed by atomic explosions or the result of exposure to radiation, either accidentally or deliberately. The hero is the first one to realize the truth, and he has a devil of a time convincing the local authorities of the danger that's headed their way. By the time he does, the monster is already headed for town. For one reason or another—and sometimes for no reason—it cannot be killed by conventional weapons. The hero must discover some new and/or ingenious method to dispose of it.

The formula had been used on so many occasions by the time Berkeley and director Nathan Juran got around to it, even they seemed bored with it, and so do the actors. At one point, Craig Stevens, thoroughly unprovoked, plants a kiss on Alex Talton while the two are sitting in a parked car. He seems to be doing it out of obligation rather than desire, and Talton looks like she wishes he hadn't. It is an antipassionate moment that could well have been concocted by the pod people. If anyone involved in this fourteen-day clunker was actually trying to make a piece of entertainment, it certainly doesn't show.

The Monster That Challenged the World

Life magazine ran an article about the discovery of some shrimp eggs buried in a salty pond for millions of years that were still fertile. This provoked Jules V. Levy, Arthur Gardner, and Arnold Laven to make a movie about giant sea slugs in Japan called *The Monster That Challenged the World* (1957). David Duncan wrote a script, but the deal with Japan fell through and the script had to be rewritten for a local setting. Levy and Gardner let their production assistant, Pat Fielder, write it.

Levy, Gardner, and Laven met during World War II, while serving in the Air Force's Motion Picture Unit, making training films at Hal Roach Studios. They struck a deal with United Artists and began making modestly budgeted, quality crime films. Their biggest success came in television with *The Rifleman* and *The Big Valley*. Their first feature, *Without Warning* (1952), is still a chilly little item. Of the four sci-fi films they made, *The Monster That Challenged the World* was the best and the most expensive ($254,000) and the only one that Laven directed. He was reluctant to do it, knowing the negative feeling toward sci-fi films at the time, but he felt he owed it to the company. It may well have cost him a directing gig on a far more prestigious film, *The Dark at the Top of the*

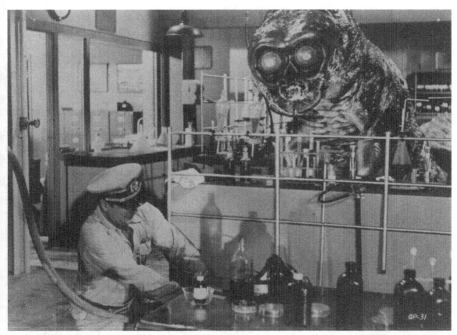

Tim Holt is about to give The Monster That Challenged the World *(1957) a blast of hot steam. Photo from the author's collection.*

Stairs (1960), at Warner Bros.

Tim Holt is excellent as the short-tempered, by-the-book naval commander who falls for Hans Conried's widowed secretary, Audrey Dalton. Holt is a little overweight, and somehow that adds to his appeal. He's a refreshing change from the conventional, stalwart sci-fi hero. He sweats like a pig when he's trying to kill the monster and nobody ever looked more terrified. Incidentally, for a big old mechanical thing, the monster is pretty cool. The work of Augie Loman, it cost $15,000 and weighed 1,500 pounds. For a brief time, it was housed in the underwater ride at Pacific Ocean Park: a short-lived amusement park in Santa Monica, California.

The Black Scorpion

Earthquakes were responsible for *The Black Scorpion* (1957), which was another formula film written by David Duncan. There is one dilly of a sequence that looks and plays like an extended version of the proposed spider-pit sequence for the original *King Kong*. Richard Denning and Carlos Rivas are lowered into a huge cavern filled with giant scorpions and other creepy crawly things animated by Pete Peterson. It's very exciting.

By shooting the film in Mexico, producers Frank Melford and Jack Dietz could afford to hire enough extras to populate a Cecil B. DeMille movie. Peterson and O'Brien set up shop at a Mexican studio where Ralph Hammeras was working on *The Giant Claw*. He helped O'Brien and Peterson with some of the model work. When money got tight, Obie and Peterson came home and finished the film in Peterson's garage.

Phil Kellison said, "I did a lot of the optical work on *The Black Scorpion*. I was working on the climax when the producers ran out of money. We had the hold-out mattes generated from the animated figure, but we hadn't laid the image of the scorpion on top of it. That's what you see in the picture, the hold-out matte. People don't realize how cheap these movies were. We were asked to create these incredible images for practically no money."

The Black Scorpion *(1957). From the author's collection.*

Edward Lugwig's direction is less than stimulating, but the movie is okay; any movie with Mara Corday is okay. The worst thing about the picture is Wah Chang's drooling, lethargic scorpion head, seen in close-ups that are randomly cut into the film whether it matches the action or not. It was the only image on the posters and the only thing featured in the television spot. The TV spot was funny. A woman screams off camera, then the terrible drooling scorpion head appears and the announcer says, "What's the matter, lady, chicken? *The Black Scorpion* is only a movie. What if it is the roughest, toughest horror picture ever made?"

What if it isn't?

The Beast of Hollow Mountain

The Beast of Hollow Mountain (1956), based on a story by Willis O'Brien, was also filmed in Mexico and pitted a Tyrannosaurus Rex against Guy Madison— TV's *Wild Bill Hickok*. It was the first stop-motion movie in CinemaScope and the first movie in Regiscope, which, according to the press release, was "an electrical, remote control system bringing flexible, life-like action to miniature characters." What we're talking about, is a series of replacement figures, like the replacement heads on George Pal's Puppetoons, each sculpted in a slightly different position. It does not require electricity or remote controls.

The advantage that replacement puppets have over a stop-motion puppet is that the sculptor can factor in muscle movement and other subtleties. The colors might shift from puppet to puppet, but in every other respect, it is a surprisingly effective technique. Most of the time, however, the dinosaur in this movie *is* a stop-motion puppet, seen in close-ups from the waist up and poorly animated in front of the worst process screen photography ever. As a curiosity, this film may be worth seeing, but it shouldn't go to the top of the list of films to be preserved. And for the record—too much fiesta!

The Animal World *(1956). Photo from the author's collection.*

The Animal World

Hoping to repeat the success of his Academy Award winning documentary *The Sea Around Us* (1953), producer Irwin Allen made *The Animal World* (1956). Allen had something that Disney's "True Life Adventures" didn't have: dinosaurs!

Ray Harryhausen and Willis O'Brien generated some new dinosaur footage, in color and done as cheaply as possible. No optical work, no process photography, just table-top animation and a couple of matte paintings. Their work sold the picture. The music by Paul Sawtell was used again in *The Black Scorpion* and *The Cosmic Man*.

The Land Unknown

While flying through a storm, a Navy helicopter gets smacked by a pterodactyl and is forced to make an unscheduled stop in *The Land Unknown* (1957). When the fog clears, the pilot (William Reynolds) and his passengers (Jock

Mahoney, Shawn Smith, and Phil Harvey) find themselves in a warm-water oasis that's populated by dinosaurs and carnivorous plants.

This was going to be an epic by Universal's standards, in color and CinemaScope with an all-star cast. Just before the picture went into production, the studio pulled the plug. It would be a black-and-white

Top: Reynold Brown poster for The Land Unknown (1957).
Bottom: The Tyrannosaurus Rex attacks the helicopter, or tries to. Photos courtesy of Bob Villard.

movie with some of their second-string contract players. Jack Arnold, who'd been working on the storyboards with Virgil Vogel, walked away from the project and Vogel took over. Supposedly, they'd spent more money on the sets and the dinosaurs than they'd planned and that's what caused the studio to change its mind. Maybe, but does it seem logical that the studio would have allowed Laszlo Gorog—a man whose only credit was *The Mole People* (1956)—to write the script for this so-called A-movie?

Journey to the Center of the Earth

James Mason, Arlene Dahl, Pat Boone, and Gertrude the Goose *Journey to the Center of the Earth* (1959) and find dinosaurs, landslides, and huge sets that are better suited to one of Walt Disney's amusement park rides. 20th Century-Fox spent almost $3.5 million to make this big-budgeted thrill ride, and took home over $5 million in profits for their trouble. American critics called it "glorious nonsense." Foreign critics were not so kind, leaving leading man James Mason to muse, "Producer Charles Brackett supplied a good script and the technicians could not be faulted, so I guess it must have been the actors and the director [Henry Levin] who so let down the English critics."[4]

Monster on the Campus

Arthur Franz became the *Monster on the Campus* (1958) after accidentally being exposed to the radioactive blood of a prehistoric fish. This variation on the Jekyll and Hyde theme was inspired by the discovery of a Coelacanth living off the Comoro Islands near Madagascar in 1952. Unchanged since the Devonian period, the species was believed to have been extinct for 70 million years. In the script by David Duncan, gamma rays are used to preserve the fish. Troy Donahue's friendly dog drinks some of the bloody water dripping from the container and reverts to a vicious, long-toothed throwback. A dragonfly makes a meal on the fish and becomes a prehistoric giant. In two unlikely accidents, Franz ingests the Coelacanth's blood and turns into a caveman.

Joanna Moore in the arms of the Monster on the Campus *(1958). Photo courtesy of Gary Smith.*

Jack Arnold thought the script was badly written and claimed he did the picture as a favor for Joe Gershenson, who was Universal's full-time music supervisor and part-time film producer. More likely, Arnold did it because the studio told him to do it. The film's star, Arthur Franz, shared Arnold's disdain for the movie. "I think Universal was on uppers at the time," he said. "I remember there was grass growing in the streets and I'm not talking about turf."

Many people think this is Arnold's worst sci-fi film. It is silly and contrived, but it's a lot more exciting and entertaining than either *Revenge of the Creature* (1955) or *The Space Children* and it had a shorter shooting schedule and a smaller budget than either of those pictures. It benefits from Russell Metty's moody photography and it has several stand-out moments. The scene of Helen Westcott's corpse, hanging by her hair from a tree branch, is shocking. Joanna Moore's struggle with the caveman is effective and terrifying. And the Saturday matinee audience I saw this with went wild when the caveman's axe split Richard Cutting's skull.

Creature from the Black Lagoon, Revenge of the Creature, and The Creature Walks Among Us

It seems disproportionate, that in a decade inundated with mutants, scientific misfires, and monsters of all shapes and sizes, only two of these monsters would take their place in the Horror Hall of Fame—Toho's *Godzilla* and U-I's *Creature from the Black Lagoon* (1954).

Richard Carlson, Julie Adams, Richard Denning and Whit Bissell examine the skeleton of the Gill Man in Creature from the Black Lagoon *(1954). Photo from the author's collection.*

In their book, *The Westmores of Hollywood*, authors Frank Westmore and Muriel Davidson credit producer William Alland, Universal's special effects department, and Bud Westmore—who was then in charge of the studio's makeup department—for the design of the famous Gill Man. Westmore was more than happy to pose with the monster as it was being constructed, and he was eager to perpetuate the myth that it was his baby, but there's one thing you can take to the bank: the head of any studio department rarely does any of the work. Dennis Saleh's *Science Fiction Gold* correctly identifies Milicent Patrick—the first woman animator at Disney studios—as being the one responsible for the design of the creature. Chris Mueller and Jack Kevan sculpted it. The costume was worn by two people: Ben Chapman on land and Ricou Browning underwater. Browning was hired for his ability to hold his breath for long stretches of time, and he compared the experience to swimming in an overcoat.

One of the icons of 1950s sci-fi, The Creature from the Black Lagoon. (1954) Photo from the author's collection.

It Came from Outer Space had been such a big money-maker for U-I, the studio wanted a 3-D follow-up and *Creature from the Black Lagoon* was it. Richard Carlson comes to the Black Lagoon hoping to find more fossils of the legendary Gill Man: the missing link between mammals and fish. The expedition is headed by Richard Denning, who's another 50s sci-fi stalwart. The two spend a lot of time in their swim trunks, sucking in their tummies while they argue about everything. Carlson is in love with Julie Adams and Denning doesn't seem to like it much, though he shows no indication of wanting her for himself. Writing in the *Journal of Popular Film*, Frank D. McConnell finds great significance in this supposed love triangle. "It is in terms of this triangle, [Adam's] instincts, [Denning's] possessive jealousy, and [Carlson's] uncertainty and self-doubt, that the action will develop," he writes. McConnell believes it's a better and more important film than either *Invasion of the Body Snatchers* or *The Thing*, and he discusses the lagoon as a return to the primal sink. Commenting on the design of the Creature, McConnell thought the reason the costume was so effective was because it was "exactly in tune with his deep-structure function in the plot: simply, his now-famous head looks like a penis."

Carlson said, "That suit was so frightening and so real that I'd forget we were play acting. We'd be shooting at midnight in freezing cold water and suddenly this thing would swim toward me. It took all my discipline to hold my position and let it come near me."[5]

For a while, the battle of wits between the humans and the Gill Man seems to favor the latter. By placing a barricade of wood at the exit to the lagoon, the Gill Man succeeds in distracting the scientists long enough for him to quietly slip aboard and kidnap Miss Adams. What exactly he intends to do with her is open for discussion. He takes her to his lair, which becomes a sort of O.K. Corral—the place for the showdown between the Gill Man and what's left of the crew.

The best sequence in the film, and the one most often discussed, is the water ballet. Julie Adams goes for a swim in the lagoon, arousing the interest of the Gill Man, who is mesmerized by her. He follows her, keeping a safe distance until he simply can't resist touching her foot.

"It surprised us and went beyond our wildest expectations," said Agha Rafique Ahmed, a Pakistan exhibitor. "Patron comments were very good. Did outstanding business." Mr. Ahmed thought he would have done even better business if he'd shown the 3-D version.

The Gill Man was back the following year in *Revenge of the Creature*, again directed by Arnold. Like its predecessor, it's a little thin on story. Reprising his role as Lucas, the Captain of the Rita, Nestor Paiva returns to the Black Lagoon with John Bromfield, who in ten minutes manages to do what Carlson and Denning couldn't do in eighty. He captures the Gill Man and puts him on display in Marineland. Naturally, the Gill Man breaks loose and spends the rest of the film searching for Lori Nelson.

Jack Arnold said, "I asked if they'd do us a favor and put a net to divide the dangerous fish from the fish that looked bad. They said they would. When I got there the day we were ready to shoot, I went up to look at the tank and there was no net. I said, 'Fellas, I gotta get actors in there.' They said not to worry, that they fed the fish every hour on the hour and that the divers go down all of the time. I said that it was a diver's job, but these were actors. To get them to walk up a three-foot hill is a stunt! They said they couldn't use a net. Ricou Browning put on the suit and dove right in. He didn't care. I looked at the cameraman and he looked at me and said, 'If you want to get those actors in there, you'd better go in yourself.' So I put on the mask and jumped in, but I kept my eyes closed. Then I slowly opened one eye and I was looking down the gaping mouth of a shark. I wondered, 'What do you do? Do you move or not move?'

And he just went by me. It felt like sandpaper as he rubbed against me. I shot out of the water and said, 'There's nothing to it, kids.'"

The third and last entry in the series, *The Creature Walks Among Us* (1956), was considered the weakest of the three by producer Alland, who never wanted to make it, and director Arnold, who turned it down. The studio gave it to one of their assistant directors, John Sherwood. His film is the best of the bunch as far as we're concerned. It actually has a story.

Ad art for The Creature Walks Among Us *(1956). Photo from the author's collection.*

The Gill Man is captured by a group of scientists who surgically attempt to accelerate his evolution after the poor guy is burned from head to toe. They find human skin beneath his charred gills, as well as a set of lungs, which they activate. He's taken to Sausalito, California, and imprisoned behind an electrically charged fence outside the home of his captor, Jeff Morrow. Although confused and disoriented, the Gill Man becomes more human. Morrow insists that the change is biological, but Rex Reason believes it's because they've treated him with kindness. "You mean he returns kindness with kindness?" Morrow asks. "You think that's always true, doctor? Imagine how often love is returned with hate and loyalty is returned with infidelity. How long does it take before something has to be done about it?" Reason is no fool. He realizes they're no longer talking about the Gill Man, but about Morrow's relationship with his wife. He reminds Morrow that in the animal kingdom, when one animal kills another it's called the law of the jungle, but between men it's murder. Morrow thinks his wife (Leigh Snowden) is cheating on him with handyman Greg Palmer. She isn't, but she can't convince Morrow of that. He kills Palmer and attempts to put the blame on the Gill Man. The outraged Gill Man breaks free and destroys half of the house before he gets his hands on Morrow. In the final scene, the Gill Man— no longer a fish—lumbers toward the ocean and certain death.

Julie Adams said, "These days, hardly a week goes by that someone doesn't call or write to ask me about the Creature, whether it be giving interviews to film magazines about my experiences on the movie, or meeting brilliant visual effects supervisors who were inspired by the iconic half-man, half-fish. In one way or another, this film has touched the lives of many, many people."[6]

After completing the first "Creature" movie, William Alland was summoned by HUAC to answer a few questions about his prior involvement with the Communist Party. Behind closed doors at the Federal Courthouse in Los Angeles, Alland didn't just buckle under the committee's grilling, he caved. To save his

own neck—much like his buddy Martin Berkeley—he threw as many people under the bus as he could. He made the outrageous statement that ninety-five percent of the party membership was emotionally disturbed and should be on a psychiatrist's couch. No one knows what they would do in a situation like this, but it's too bad that Alland and the rest of the Hollywood community didn't collectively tell the committee to go to Hell instead of aiding and abetting a blacklist that was not only illegal, but morally reprehensible.

Leigh Snowden is the object of the Gill Man's affection in The Creature Walks Among Us *(1956). Photo from the author's collection.*

Notes:

1. Hankin, Mike. *Ray Harryhausen Master of the Majicks*, Vol. 2, Archive Editions, LLC, Los Angeles, California, pg. 69.
2. Bradley, Matthew R. "Someone Wonderful This Way Came," *Filmfax*, No. 131, pg. 51.
3. Hyatt was one of the pseudonyms used by blacklisted author Daniel Lewis James. For twenty years, he and his wife, Lilith, worked as volunteers in Hispanic neighborhoods, giving him the background to write (as Danny Santiago) his best-known novel, *Famous All Over Town*, for which he received the Richard and Hinda Rosenthal Foundation Award from the American Academy and Institute of Arts and Letters.
4. Hirshenhorn, Clive. *The Films of James Mason*, The Citidel Press.
5. Westmore, Frank and Muriel Davidson. *The Westmores of Hollywood*, Berkley Medallion Books, New York, NY, pg. 183.
6. Adams, Julie and Mitchell Danton. *The Lucky Southern Star*, Hollywood Adventures Publishing, USA, pg. 65.

CHAPTER FOUR
The Monster That Devoured Cleveland

*When man entered the Atomic Age he opened a door
to a new world. What we'll eventually find in that new
world nobody can predict.*

—Them!

Scott Carey's pants don't fit. Too big, he says, just like his shirt. He thinks the cleaners are responsible. Old Andy Anderson claims that something has been eating his cattle during the night. Of course, he had sunstroke a few years back, maybe he... No. He had a stack of bones to show the sheriff. Then there's that doctor, Gil McKenna. Every time he gets a little too much sun, he turns into a lizard or something. His neighbors are complaining. And what's with that scientist over in England; the one who answers questions before they're asked? Is he some kind of psychic or what?

All of these seemingly unrelated events will eventually be traced to a single cause: radiation. It's making Scott Carey shrink, it created the giant spider that's eating old Andy Anderson's cattle, it turned Gil McKenna into the sun demon, and it caused that English scientist to slip ahead in time. Radiation was a magic word in fifties sci-fi, and it could do anything and everything.

Since the first atomic bomb was exploded in a stretch of desert between Albuquerque and the Mexican border (known as Jornada de Muerto), there was a growing concern over the potential dangers of radiation poisoning. Following the thirtieth A-bomb explosion, which was televised to 35 million viewers, Dr. Robert Oppenheimer—a prime mover in the Los Alamos A-bomb development—warned that the U.S. and the U.S.S.R. were like two scorpions in a bottle: each capable of killing the other, but only at the risk of his own life. For this accurate analogy, Oppenheimer's loyalty was questioned and he was stripped of his security clearance. Likewise, Albert Einstein warned that a nuclear war could end in mutual annihilation.

Following each nuclear test, there were various reports of distress. People complained that New York City's dust had become radioactive, others were certain the nation's water supply was being poisoned, and there was film fogging in Boston. Radioactivity became as much of a threat as the bomb. Newspapers reported that exposure to it could cause harmful changes in somatic cells, possibly resulting in cancer; many of the Hiroshima survivors suffered from leukemia. The U.S. Navy began experimenting with large doses of x-rays, attempting to duplicate the effect that hydrogen bomb radiation would have on test animals. A rat grew an extra set of teeth. That piece of information was probably all that writer George Worthing Yates needed to conjure up a story about giant ants in the Los Angeles sewer system.

Them!

Them! was Warners Brothers' follow-up to *The Beast from 20,000 Fathoms*, originally slated for color and 3-D, but the studio got cold feet and the picture was shot flat in black and white, directed by the underrated Gordon Douglas. It was the first and the best of the big bug movies, being both crisp and exciting.

Edmund Gwenn is about to bring Sandy Descher out of her coma with a little formic acid. Photo from the author's collection.

A child (Sandy Descher) is found wandering in the Arizona desert in a state of shock by policemen James Whitmore and Chris Drake. Down the road, they find a trailer that's been torn apart. While a plaster cast is made of a strange print near the trailer, Whitmore and Drake stop at the general store and find the place in shambles, and the owner is dead. An autopsy reveals that his neck and back were broken and his chest was crushed. "And here's one for Sherlock Holmes," the doctor says, "There was enough formic acid in him to kill twenty men." The FBI sends James Arness to help with the investigation. The trailer belonged to one of their agents. Everyone assumes that some lunatic is at large until myrmecologist Edmund Gwynn identifies the strange print as belonging to a giant ant. They locate the nest and flood the tunnels with cyanide gas, but they're too late. Two queens had taken flight with their mates. A new nest is unhappily discovered by the crew aboard a freighter. The ship is sunk. Another colony is forming in a Los Angeles sewer system and two children are trapped. Whitmore rescues them at the cost of his own life. The colony is wiped out by flamethrowers.

James Whitmore said, "They had two full-sized ants that were operated by pulleys and wires and the rest were, shall we say, less sophisticated. I didn't think they were very believable, but I thought the picture was pretty good. Of course, in real life, my character wouldn't have been involved in the story once the FBI took over, but those kinds of liberties are taken in movies all of the time. I thought my death was pointless."

We don't agree. Right after Whitmore is killed, one of the tunnels collapses behind Jim

Joan Weldon and James Arness are cornered by Them! (1954) Photo from the author's collection.

Arness, leaving him alone to fight off a swarm of ants. Having just seen the star of the picture bite the dust, the audience has every reason to believe Arness may share his fate. Whitmore's death added a sense of urgency to the sequence that wouldn't have been there otherwise.

When she read the script, Joan Weldon didn't think much of *Them!* She said Gordon Douglas couldn't take it seriously and that he thought they should get Martin and Lewis to star in it. Jack Warner hated it. After the preview, he said that if anyone else wanted to make a giant ant movie, they could do it at some other studio. But the critics liked it. *The New York Times* called it "taut science fiction." *The Hollywood Reporter* thought it was "one of the scariest pictures to hit the screen." *Variety* said it was "well-plotted... expertly directed and acted." *The Saturday Review* called it "a crisply satisfying pseudo-scientific thriller." Audiences agreed. It was Warner Brothers' biggest hit that year and imitations were quick to follow.

Tarantula

Robert M. Fresco wrote "No Food for Thought" for TV's *Science Fiction Theatre*, and Jack Arnold directed it. Arnold told Fresco that if they added a monster to this story about scientists trying to create an artificial nutrient, they could make a movie out of it. The result: *Tarantula!* The film's producer, William Alland, told Fresco he thought the story was terrible and was angry that he'd been assigned to the project. Years later, Alland claimed the movie was his idea. He also claimed that he'd never heard of *Them!*

Fresco believed that Alland and Martin Berkeley (who shares a writing credit on *Tarantula*) were kept on Universal's payroll because they'd both been friendly HUAC witnesses. The studio felt that their presence might keep Red Channels off their backs. *Red Channels* was a pamphlet published by *Counterattack*, which was a right-wing newsletter funded by Alfred Kohlberg—one of the founding directors of the John Birch Society. *Red Channels* listed the names of anyone working in the entertainment industry suspected of being a subversive.

Reynold Brown's poster art for Tarantula! *(1955). Photo from the author's collection.*

At the time *Tarantula* was made, roughly two-thirds of the world's population didn't have enough to eat and 60,000 people were born every day. The scientist in the film, Dr. Gerald Deemer (Leo G. Carroll) is working on a non-organic, inexpensive nutrient to feed this rapidly expanding population. A radioactive isotope binds and triggers his nutrient, but it also makes it unstable. Animals become giants, and humans develop an accelerated case of acromegaly. A few years before this movie was made, experiments on rats had proven that radioactive iodine enlarged the pituitary gland.

A precredit sequence shows one of Deemer's assistants wandering alone on the desert in his pajamas, his face looking very much like the monster from *Abbott and Costello Meet Dr. Jekyll and Mr. Hyde* (1953). He falls dead and the sheriff (Nestor Paiva) wants Deemer and the local country doctor, Matt Hastings (John Agar), to identify the body. Deemer says it's his assistant all right: a victim of acromegaly. Hastings knows that it takes more than a week for acromegaly to show itself. He suspects Deemer of foul play.

Deemer returns to his lab, where he is attacked by his other assistant, Paul Lund. During the struggle, a tarantula the size of a police dog escapes from the lab. Deemer is knocked unconscious, Lund injects Deemer with the nutrient, and then Lund drops dead. Much later, we learn that both Lund and Jacobs had injected themselves with the nutrient one afternoon while Deemer was in town, knowing that he would have objected.

In a better film, after Deemer returned from the sheriff's office, he would have checked on Lund before going back to work. A little concern and conversation would have been nice, even touching. And it could have foreshadowed and explained Lund's action against Deemer. But the film has no heart as the emphasis is on horror, not drama. The acromegaly victims are treated like monsters. In the end, Deemer meets the same fate as the maddest of the

John Agar and Mara Corday. Photo from the author's collection.

mad scientists. First, he suffers the agonies of acromegaly and, just before he dies, he is consumed by the giant spider.

At the end of the film, as everyone watches the spider burn to a crisp, the script called for Hastings to say, "Evil is goodness turned upside down. Someone else will go on from where [Deemer] left off—and it'll work next time." The line was cut, leaving the viewer to believe that Deemer got what he deserved for tampering in God's domain.

Tarantula proved to be a big moneymaker for Universal and, much to his dismay, John Agar became the studio's resident sci-fi hero. His performance in the film is adequate, but he isn't given much to do other than to cast suspicion on Deemer while pitching woo to Deemer's new assistant, the beautiful, charming, and underrated Mara Corday. No stranger to cheesecake (she was *Playboy's* October centerfold in 1958), Miss Corday expressed her disappointment when she was told to wear pajamas and a robe instead of a flimsy nightgown when the spider parks itself outside of her window and becomes a peeping Tom. She wasn't the only one who was disappointed.

The Saturday matinee audience I saw this picture with laughed when Leo G. Carroll came on the screen. They knew him from his role as *Topper* on the popular TV show. No matter. His performance as the doomed professor is intelligent and sympathetic. He was an unusual choice, but the role fits him like a glove, and he effortlessly runs rings around everyone else in the cast.

Universal had intended to use a goofy-looking puppet—like the God-awful rod puppet in *The Deadly Mantis*—but saner heads prevailed and the puppet is seen only in close-ups. A real spider was used for the rest of the film. Once in a while, Stan Horsley and Clifford Stine get their horizon lines wrong and the spider seems to be walking on air, but it's minimal. The scene where it attacks a corral full of horses is chilling. But there's one scene that's so terrible, one wonders why it wasn't cut. The spider is making its way across the mountains when one of its legs disappears behind what was supposed to be a hill, but the hill isn't there. It's something you would expect to see in a Bert Gordon movie. For the most part, the scenes with the spider are quite effective. This is the one and only department where this film trumps *Them!* In every other respect, it comes up short. Jack Arnold's direction is flat and the script is rather pedestrian. Even the climax is a gyp. The posters show the spider in the middle of the city with dozens of people at its feet, but such a moment never happens. The town has been evacuated by the time the spider shows up and it's killed just outside of the city limits. It's like waiting for the big showdown between Will Kane and Frank Miller at the end of *High Noon* only to discover that Miller took the wrong train. With a little more thought, *Tarantula* could have been a much better film. As it stands, it's just okay, which is still better than most of the big bug films that followed it.

Beginning of the End

In Bert Gordon's *Beginning of the End*, entomologist Peter Graves is also trying to solve the food shortage problem, only his solution is to grow giant vegetables. Locusts feeding on his radioactive crop grow into giants and march on

Chicago. General Ankrum wants to drop an A-bomb on the city, but Graves saves the day by electronically simulating the locusts' mating call. He lures the pesky critters into Lake Michigan. In five quick cuts that total maybe nine or ten seconds of film, the locusts meet their death in what looks like a small bowl of water. It couldn't be a more unconvincing or unsatisfying finale.

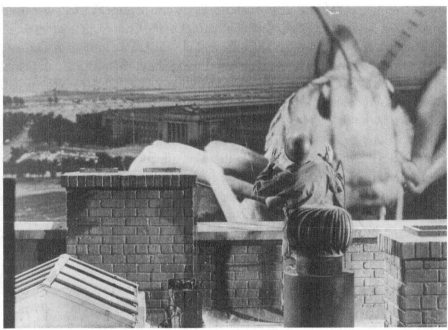

A giant grasshopper attacks a soldier in Bert Gordon's Beginning of the End *(1957). Photo courtesy of Bob Villard.*

The critic for *Variety* felt that if *Beginning of the End* was really the answer to the industry's sagging output, as AB-PT Pictures had claimed, it was time for the industry to close its doors. He's a little harsh as it's certainly not the worst movie ever made. It's not even the worst Bert Gordon movie. But, it isn't very good, and almost every sequence runs longer than it should. When Peter Graves leads a squad of soldiers into the woods to search for the grasshoppers, the truck full of soldiers comes slowly up the road and turns into an empty field. The driver pulls to a stop. The soldiers should jump out, but they don't because the driver isn't finished yet. He throws the truck into reverse, backs up five or six feet in this empty field in the middle of nowhere, and stops again.

Attack of the Crab Monsters

When Allied Artists sold a package of their fifties sci-fi films to television in the early sixties, Herb Strock was hired to make sure all of the films hit the 70-minute mark. His standard operating procedure was to reprint a sequence from somewhere in the film to use as a teaser before the credits. After the credits, he added a little crawl telling the audience what they were about to see. At the end of the film, he added a crawl of the cast and the characters they played. If the film had a chase sequence, it was repeated. Just before the chase reached its conclusion, Strock would cut and return the chase to its beginning. Sometimes he lifted footage from other movies. And if the picture was still too short, every twenty-fourth frame was repeated. Every one of Strock's tricks was used to add nine minutes to Roger Corman's *Attack of the Crab Monsters* (1957).

The picture was shot in ten days at a cost of $70,000. According to Corman, it grossed over a million bucks. The worst thing about the picture is the crab, made by the Dice Company for $400. When they brought the thing to the set, everyone burst out laughing.

There are holes in Chuck Griffith's script big enough for a giant crab to crawl through, but it moves so fast that you may not care. The monsters in Griffith's tale absorb the minds of the people they eat, effectively raising their IQ with every meal. They've already polished off one scientific research team, and when their colleagues arrive to continue their work, the crab uses their voices to lure them to their deaths. Pamela Duncan wonders why their former colleagues have turned against them. "Preservation of the species," Richard Garland tells her. "Once they were men, now they're land crabs."

One scene that struck me funny as a kid was the scene where Duncan and Russ Johnson risk their necks to plant an electronic device to paralyze the crab. It's unusual for a woman to take this sort of a risk in a fifties film and even more unusual to see boyfriend Garland watch her do it. Chuck Griffith loaned me a copy of the script. There was a sequence where Garland was supposed to have injured his leg, but the sequence was cut when Corman ran behind schedule.

The giant crab makes a meal of Leslie Bradley. Photo from the author's collection.

The Monster from Green Hell

Louis Vittes and Endre Bohem fashioned a big bug story around the footage that producer Al Zimbalist purchased from *Stanley and Livingston* (1939). Jim Davis played the scientist dressed just like Spencer Tracy. Davis goes to Africa in search of his runaway rocket. "I discovered that a safari was a simple matter of putting one foot in front of the other and then repeating the process," Davis tells the audience. He has every reason to believe that the wasps that were inside of the nose cone of his rocket have mutated into giants after being exposed to cosmic radiation. Only after director Kenneth Crane has exhausted all of Zimbalist's stock footage will Davis and his cohorts find *The Monster from Green Hell* (1958). Actually, there's more than one of these monsters, but no matter. Davis and his bunch haven't brought enough firepower to kill them. They might just as well have stayed home. The same could be said of the audience.

Jack Rabin, Irving Block, and Louis DeWitt were in charge of the special effects, or rather what little there were of them. There are some stop-motion wasps animated by Gene Warren, but they're not very exciting. Phil Kellison and Irving Block shot the film's climax where the wasps are covered in lava.

Phil Kellison said, "The producer wanted the climax to be in color because he had some color footage of a volcano exploding. We shot the sequence in two store fronts on Santa Monica Boulevard with two high speed cameras. We had to steal electricity from four other buildings. We had this large set with a bunch of wasp puppets in all of these little nooks and crannies. The cameras were crammed in the corners. We had to get the thing in one take because the fake lava would ruin everything. The cameras were rolling and we poured our fake lava and in the middle of it all, Block gets into a panic. 'It doesn't look hot enough!' he screamed and he started flinging chunks of dry ice on the set. When we got the film back, there was so much smoke, you couldn't see an image on one of the rolls. On the other roll, you could see Block's hands tossing the dry ice. We didn't have the money to do it again."

Attack of the Giant Leeches

Sexy Yvette Vickers was the object of desire of a degenerate pack of Florida swamp folk in the Corman brothers' dreary *Attack of the Giant Leeches* (1959), written by Leo Gordon. Better known for his acting, Gordon manages to add some nice character touches to his script, but his story runs out of gas about a third of the way through and the film becomes a tedious bore. It was directed by Bernard Kowalski in eight days for $65,000.

The leeches were created in a little back room at the Chaplin Studios by Ed Nelson and Ross Sturlin by stretching pieces of old raincoats over chicken wire skeletons. "There was no ventilation in that room," Sturlin recalled, "and at times,

CRAWLING HORROR...
RISING FROM THE
DEPTHS OF HELL...
TO KILL AND CONQUER!

THE
GIANT
LEECHES

KEN CLARK·YVETTE VICKERS·JAN SHEPARD·MICHAEL EMMET

3-sheet poster for The Giant Leeches *(1959).
Photo from the author's collection.*

Nelson and I (and probably everyone else nearby) were high as a kite from the strong odor of the glue. They must have been made in a week's time at the most. When we would run out of glue or other materials, either Ed or I would run over to the hardware store nearby and pick up what we needed and pay for it out of our own pockets. It was just the way you did things when you were a part of working on these films with Roger."[1]

Nelson was saved from having to play one of the leeches when Corman decided to cast him as the lead in *The Devil's Partner*, which was made in 1958, but not released until 1962. Guy Buccola, a UCLA basketball player, took his place.

Sturlin said, "We both worked our tails off doing our shots. Moving and swimming in those things was perhaps the worst thing we could have done. They would start splitting in spots and repairing them often included sewing them up and shooting shots brief and quick. Shooting out at the Arboretum wasn't fun either. The water was cold and filthy with moss and surface debris. The shots at the end of the movie where the leeches swim out of the cave were done in a private swimming pool."[2]

Everything's Going Atomic

Whenever advertising people get hold of a word, they huckster the sense right out of it. Look what happened to the word "classic." It used to mean something that stood the test of time, and something that was exceptional; now it's just something that's old. In the fifties, Madison Avenue took the word "atomic" and ran with it. There were atomic golf balls, atomic coffeemakers, and believe or not, a book called *Atomic Power in Christ*. Children could play with atomic energy kits and atomic robot men while sucking on atomic fireballs. At the movies, you could see *Canadian Mounties vs. Atomic Invaders* (1953), *The Atomic City* (1952), *The Atomic Kid* (1954), and the British-made *Timeslip*, released in America as *The Atomic Man* (1956).

Mickey Rooney was thirty-four years old when he played *The Atomic Kid*. Caught in an atomic blast, Rooney glows in the dark, interferes with radio reception, and causes a lot of slot machines to pay off. The movie makes fun of flying saucers, capitalism, communists, and, above all, radiation poisoning. But it has a major problem for a comedy: it isn't funny.

The Atomic Man (Peter Arne) is fished out of the water with a bullet in him. For ten years, he's been working with radioactive isotopes to produce synthetic tungsten. As a result, his brain has become radioactive and now, after being clinically dead for seven and a half seconds, he lives seven and a half seconds ahead in time. Everyone thinks he's talking gibberish until Faith Domergue realizes the atomic man is answering questions *before* they're asked. The movie is as exciting as it sounds. The time slip factor serves no purpose other than to eat up time.

On March 1, 1954, at 6:45 in the morning, the United States dropped an H-bomb on the island of Bikini. For almost three hours, sandy ash rained down on The Lucky Dragon, a Japanese fishing boat 100 miles from the test site, twenty miles outside of the supposed danger zone. The crew, suffering from nausea, pain, and skin inflammation, had to be hospitalized. One of them died. Although a general warning had been issued, the U.S. had kept the exact location and time of the test a secret. To the people of Japan, America seemed more concerned about developing weapons of mass destruction than it did them. Although the U.S. paid $2 million dollars to the Japanese Government to compensate for the damage it caused to the people and the tuna industry, "The Lucky Dragon Incident" sparked a new wave of anti-American sentiment in Japan and served as the inspiration for Toho's *The H-Man* (1959), written by Takeshi Kimura—the man responsible for *Rodan* and *The Mysterians*. In his scenario, radiation turns the crew of an ocean steamer into deadly globs of green slime. They ooze about the city, dissolving people and interfering with police efforts to bust a drug ring. It's a creepy, gruesome, and colorful surprise that reunites actors Akihiko Hirata, Yumi Shirakawa, and Kenji Sahara from *The Mysterians* under the direction of Ishiro Honda. The discovery of the H-men on the steamer, told in a flashback, is a standout.

The Hideous Sun Demon

Suffering from a hangover, Robert Clarke gets a little careless with a new type of radioactive isotope he's working with and becomes *The Hideous Sun Demon* (1959). Clarke used his own money to make this picture, and he shot it on weekends using film students for his crew. He couldn't afford to rent a sound stage, so he approached a woman who owned a house that had been used in an episode of *I Led Three Lives*. Guardedly, the woman said she'd rent it to him, but only if he paid what ZIV had paid: a whopping $25 a day.

Robert Clarke said, "Here we were getting a three-floor house, complete with furniture. In those days you couldn't get onto a sound stage for less than $150 a day. We quickly rewrote the script to make use of the house.

"My brother knew someone who owned a drive-in theater in Texas who agreed to show *The Sun Demon* and back it with a lot of publicity. We made close to $1000 a night. That gave me some leverage when I started shopping the film. I took it to Universal and Warner Brothers, but they didn't want it. AIP said they'd distribute it, but I wanted another picture out of the deal. Besides, it was fairly common knowledge that they kept two sets of books. So I went with a new company, Miller Consolidated, but they went bankrupt and I lost my shirt. I know the picture is no classic, but I thought it compared favorably with some of Roger Corman's early works like *Attack of the Crab Monsters* or something along that line."

The Cyclops

Dean Parkin gets lost in Mexico somewhere and his fiancée, Gloria Talbott, comes looking for him, unaware that radiation has turned him into *The Cyclops* (1957). Parkin's friend, James Craig, who is also in love with Talbott, comes with

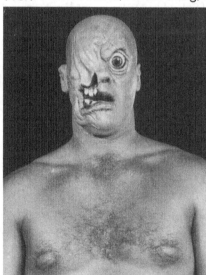

Dean (Duncan) Parkyn played The Cyclops (1957) and would later play another one-eyed giant in War of the Colossal Beast *(1958). Photo from the author's collection.*

her. Tom Drake is the pilot who takes them there and Lon Chaney tags along in the hope of finding uranium. They discover a valley full of giant lizards and insects. Craig believes there must be some sort of radioactive substance in the soil or water that's causing them to grow. "Well, if what you say is true," Chaney says, "we might grow bigger and bigger." How right he is. Talbott is kidnapped by a thirty-foot-tall inarticulate madman with half of his face covered with melted flesh. "There's something about his face," she tells Craig, "that left side that's not completely mutilated, makes me feel sorry for him." They find parts of Parkin's plane and some of his old clothes, yet Craig is the only one who realizes the one-eyed giant is the man they've been searching for, which makes these people dumber than the smallest child in the audience.

The only thing that the film has going for it is a scene-chewing performance by Chaney. And, yes, the monster gets his eye poked out.

Bert Gordon

Born in 1922 to Charles and Sadeline Gordon, Bert Ira Gordon was bitten by the movie bug when his aunt gave him a 16 mm camera for his thirteenth birthday. He dropped out of college to join the Air Corps at the outbreak of World War II, and after his discharge he married Flora Lang. The two began making 16 mm documentaries and commercials for local TV stations in Minnesota. Their daughter, Susan, appeared in one of their candy commercials when she was two years old. She recalled that they "sat me down on a carpet in a pretty white frock and put some chocolates in front of me, and I was soon covered with the stuff!"[3] When asked if that was the moment when she was bitten by the movie bug, Susan said that she was only interested in the candy.

Bert came to Hollywood with his wife and two children and pounded on a lot of doors before landing a gig on a short-lived TV show called *Cowboy G-Men*. He was also production assistant (a.k.a. go-for) on *Racket Squad*. In 1954, he photographed *Serpent Island*, which was one of the most delightfully inept "adventure" movies ever made. When Bert started making his own films, he did everything *but* photograph them.

The president of American International Pictures, James H. Nicholson, loved science fiction. For several years, Nicholson had wanted to make a film based on a short story he'd read in *Amazing Stories* about a two-mile tall giant called "The Nth Man," written in 1928 by Homer Eon Flint. Nicholson gave the project to Roger Corman to develop. Corman hired Chuck Griffith to write it. He turned it into a comedy for Dick Miller. When the project was taken away from Corman and given to Bert Gordon—probably because of his expertise in special effects—Griffith was told to write a serious treatment.

Chuck Griffith said, "I spent one day with [Bert] hanging over my shoulder, telling me what words to write and I quit. He wanted to dictate, demanding bad dialogue, horrible clichés. I said, 'I'm sorry. I can't work this way.' We both got mad and that was the end of that."

Mark Hanna (Griffith's writing partner at the time) took over and the result was a more conventional script titled *The Amazing Colossal Man* (1957).

The Amazing Colossal Man

Former 20th Century-Fox contract players Glenn Langan and Cathy Downs were signed for the leads. Langan was married to Adele Jergens, an actress in several of Alex Gordon's movies for the company. Alex Gordon, who often cast

AIP movies other than his own, hired Langan as a favor to his wife. His performance is the glue that holds the picture together.

A plane crashes in the middle of an atomic test site and in his attempt to rescue the pilot, Colonel Glenn Manning (Langan) gets caught in the blast of a plutonium bomb. He's burned to a crisp and isn't expected to live through the night, but the next morning, he's grown new skin. By the time he regains consciousness, he's eighteen-feet tall. "What sin could a man commit in a single lifetime to bring this on himself?" he asks his fianceé, Carol Forrest (Downs). "What's making him grow?" Carol asks Dr. Coulter (Larry Thor). "Glenn Manning is growing from eight to ten feet a day. At the moment, he's eighteen feet tall.

Glenn Langan on a rampage in Las Vegas. Photo courtesy of Bob Villard.

Tomorrow he'll be twenty-six feet, the next thirty-five, maybe forty, and the next day..." Realizing the doctor will never answer her question, Carol cuts him off. If she hadn't, there's no telling how long the fool would have gone on. The film is loaded with goofy moments like this.

Reminiscing with Carol about the old days, Glenn recalls that his college classmates voted him the man most likely to reach the top. Al Glasser's score punctuates this line with a musical horselaugh. "I don't want to grow anymore," Manning bellows as he storms off. Dr. Lindstrom (William Hudson)—who's been eavesdropping—approaches Carol, and in a masterpiece of understatement says, "Things aren't going very well, are they?"

We believe that part of the appeal of Bert Gordon's movies *is* his terrible special effects. Sometimes his rear screen shots are passable, his split screens are always obvious, but it's his matte shots that torpedo him. Apparently, travelling mattes were not in Bert's budget as so many of his giant effects are basically double exposures. Langan was photographed against a black background and flooded with light to wipe out shadows. Backgrounds bleed through anything that's black, which is why his giants are always bald. The result is a milky white, almost ghostly image, a signal to the most untrained eye in the audience that some-

thing is definitely askew. Langan wears something that looks like a diaper which, of course, has to be white and with his bald head, he looks a like a big baby. However, we must give credit where credit is due. The scene of Langan being seared by the blast of the bomb is quite effective.

Bert Gordon said, "It was done solely with makeup, from scratch, with absolutely no appliances, which are ready-made noses, ears, scars and the like. [Langan] wore no mask. It was all put on him, piece by piece, with latex, wrinkling chemicals, grease paint and about everything else you can think of!"

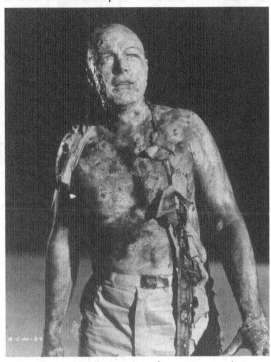

Glenn Langan is all messed up after getting caught in an atomic blast. Photo from the author's collection.

The Colossal Man was a colossal hit; the first AIP movie to play one of New York's Broadway theaters, and it earned $848,000 in six months. The sequel, *War of the Colossal Beast* (1958), written by George Worthing Yates, was a rehash of *The Cyclops*. Dean Parkin took over the role of Colonel Manning, and although we were told in the first film that Manning had no relatives, a sister named Joyce (Sally Fraser) is searching for him. She believes that her brother is alive and well in Mexico and raiding trucks for food. She's half right; he's alive, but not so well. Half his face has been ripped off, one of his eyes is missing, and he's suffering from amnesia. Joyce persuades a skeptical army Major (Roger Pace) and a doctor (Russ Bender) to search for him. They find a giant footprint near the spot where one of the trucks disappeared. "The foot that made that print is about ten times the size of a normal man. That would make him sixty feet tall," the doctor concludes. Joyce turns to the Major and drives the point

Uh-oh! The amazing colossal man has become the amazing transparent man in this scene from War of the Colossal Beast. *Photo from the author's collection.*

home. "Glenn was sixty feet tall!" The Major isn't convinced. For all he knows, the print could have been made by one of the local giants. Eventually they find Manning, drug him, and fly him back to the States. He's kept in an airplane hangar at Los Angeles International Airport while the military decides what to do with him. He breaks loose and somehow manages to get from the airport to the Griffith Park Observatory, across twenty-five miles of a populated city, without being seen. He grabs a school bus full of children and while everyone stands around helpless, Joyce hops into a jeep and races to the rescue. She begs her brother to put the bus down. In a moment of lucidity, he does, then commits suicide by grabbing some high tension wires. The film switches from black and white to color. As the sparks fly, Manning inexplicably vanishes. It's something that could only happen in a Bert Gordon movie.

The Monthly Film Bulletin: "The trick photography of these Further Adventures of the Amazing Colossal Man is ludicrously unconvincing... The dialogue strikes an oddly hieratic note, the charm school heroine reacts to every plot development with a winsome smile, while the rest of the players apparently prefer not to react at all."

The critics' chair is the most comfortable seat in the house, and we've had a lot of fun at Bert Gordon's expense throughout this book, so it's only fair to mention that Bert did care about his movies. He wasn't one of those cynical filmmakers just trying to make a buck. He did the best he could and gave the audience more for their money than a lot of the people working at his level.

Gordon said, "In those days, sci-fi was put in the category of exploitation. It was a dirty word. I remember when Allied Artists made *Invasion of the Body Snatchers*, they didn't realize that they really had something. They thought it was a piece of crap. I always hoped that the pictures could rise above that feeling. It was a challenge. Making imaginative films is what I enjoy."

And nobody ever said you had to be good at what you did.

Attack of the 50 Foot Woman

For our money, *Attack of the 50 Foot Woman* (1958) was the most entertaining, and certainly the most notorious, of these giant-people movies—a zany mix of science fiction, soap opera, and film noir written by Mark Hanna. It is the only fifties sci-fi film with two sexy women—Allison Hayes and Yvette Vickers—and they never looked better. And they don't dress like librarians.

Miss Hayes plays Nancy Archer, a wealthy socialite with low self-esteem. She's hopelessly in love with her husband, Harry (William Hudson), whose two-timing ways have caused her to suffer a nervous breakdown. Nancy speeds away from Tony's bar when she catches Harry flirting with his mistress, Honey Parker (Vickers). On the way home, she encounters a satellite[4] and its 30-foot-tall radioactive occupant. The giant (Mike Ross, who also plays Tony the bartender) tries to steal her famous Star of India diamond; diamonds power his ship. Nancy escapes and

returns with the sheriff (George Douglas) and his deputy (Frank Chase), but the satellite is gone. When Harry and Honey hear about it, they see an opportunity to toss Nancy back into the asylum, putting Harry in the driver's seat. "You'd make a wild driver, Harry with fifty million bucks."

No one believes Nancy saw the satellite or the giant, so Nancy strikes a deal with handsome Harry. If he'll help her search for the satellite, she'll commit herself if they don't find it. But they do find it! Harry

Allison Hayes and William Hudson. Photo from the author's collection.

empties his gun into the giant as it makes a grab for Nancy, then drives off, leaving Nancy in the clutches of the giant. She mysteriously shows up on the pool house roof, unconscious, and soon becomes a giant herself. The sheriff and Nancy's butler Jess (Ken Terrell) follow some giant footprints near the pool house, which leads them to the satellite. They realize that Nancy had been right all along; there is a giant and he must have been the one to bring Nancy home. (They never ask themselves the big question: How did he know where she lived?) They find Harry's gun. "He emptied it before he ran," Jess tells the sheriff. "At what?" the sheriff wonders. *At what? What do you think? At the giant you two nitwits have just been talking about.*

Meanwhile, Nancy comes to, busts out of the house, and goes looking for Harry. She finds him at Tony's with Honey. She kills Honey and carries Harry off toward some high tension wires. The sheriff opens fire, hits the transformer, and causes a short that electrocutes Nancy and Harry. (In the script, Nancy squeezes Harry to death while he shoots her in the face.) Roy Gordon has the closing line, "She finally got Harry all to herself."

William Hudson, who was a little stiff in *The Colossal Man*, is really good here. He gets good support from his two leading ladies and Frank Chase is a lot of fun as the deputy sheriff.

Yvette Vickers said, "Frank Chase was great fun when we did our jitterbug. He was the one who suggested that. 'Let's camp,' he said, but the whole picture turned out to be camp. He was at one of the screenings that the L.A. Connection[5] had at the Nuart. He was with his wife and children. It was nice. I was glad to see him. I didn't get along with Bill Hudson too well. It wasn't a dislike, but I certainly wasn't attracted to him in any way. I think he felt sort of rejected. He asked to date me or something and I didn't want to. I guess he assumed something I didn't think he had any right to assume. So I let him know that I was just doing my part, so there was coldness between us; nothing drastic. The scenes went well. They went very well. In that sense, I liked him. He was very professional. Allison I adored. We had the same agent. I met her in the scenes where they were shooting up at the mansion in the Hollywood hills. I can't remember the exact location, but it was around that area of Franklin and Waddles Park. She was real nice to me. (There have been a few women in this town who have been really nice, really warm, not very many because I seem to have a problem there, but she was.) She was so glamorous. I thought she was beautiful. She was very sweet to me; encouraging."

Bernard Woolner, a theater owner with connections at Allied Artists, produced this picture. Jacques Marquette photographed it. He figured an eight-day shoot would cost $89,000. Woolner squawked, "We can't bring a budget like that to Allied Artists. They know you can't make a picture for that amount."

(Which isn't true; Allied Artists made a lot of films for less than that.) So Marquette bumped the figure to $99,000.

Jacques Marquette said, "When I told Jerry Juran he had eight days to make the movie, he told me it couldn't be done. I said fine and threatened to fire him. 'Okay, okay,' he said, 'but I'm going to have to take another pill.' 'Good,' I told him. 'Take two.'"

Marquette said that Juran wanted to keep shooting scenes until he got them right, regardless of how much it cost. We think Marquette is talking through his hat. Juran may not have been a particularly good director, but he knew the score. He directed a lot of low-budget, short-schedule movies. He took every assignment that came his way and he was always on time and on budget. Juran told us, "Anyone who says they turned down a script for artistic reasons... Well, I think that's a lot of horse shit!" The fact that he

Somehow, 50 feet looks more like 400 feet on this poster, which has been incorrectly attributed to Reynold Brown. Look at the figures of the little people. Brown's work was never so stiff. Photo from the author's collection.

worked for Marquette before and after this film, and brought the 50 *Foot Woman* in for the amount Marquette said it should cost, seems to suggest that Marquette might be a little reckless with the truth. Steve Broidy told Bernie Woolner he should use the $10,000 that was left over to improve the lousy special effects. "Why bother?" Woolner told him. "It won't make a nickel more."

The 30 Foot Bride of Candy Rock

A jaunt through Dinosaur Springs, a rock formation with mysterious powers, turns Dorothy Provine into *The 30 Foot Bride of Candy Rock* (1959). Unlike the 50 *Foot Woman*, this was supposed to be a comedy, but it wasn't nearly as funny. In fact, it isn't funny at all: it's depressing. It was Lou Costello's last movie, and the only one he made without his long-time partner Bud Abbott.

Dorothy Provine said, "It was exciting for me because it was one of my first starring roles. But I don't think Lou Costello was very happy about it. He seemed a little lost."

On a personal note, even more depressing than this movie was the sight of Bud Abbott on the afternoon news: evicted from his home, sitting on the curb out front, and asking children to send him nickels and dimes.

The Incredible Shrinking Man

Richard Matheson sold his novel *The Shrinking Man* to Universal, with the stipulation that he would write the screenplay. Matheson retained the structure of his novel, which opens with his protagonist, Robert Scott Carey, being soaked by a warm glittery spray while sunbathing on his brother's boat. The next chapter finds Carey trapped in his cellar, now only six-inches tall, and being chased by a black widow spider. The narrative jumps back and forth between Carey's cellar adventures and how he got there. Producer Albert Zugsmith wanted a linear narrative and gave Matheson's script to Richard Alan Simmons to rewrite. Not having read both scripts, this is only speculation on our part, but we suspect that Simmons may have been responsible for some of the dialogue that makes Carey such a likeable character. Warmth was never Matheson's strong suit; it's certainly nowhere to be found in his novel.

Grant Williams and Randy Stuart get some bad news from William Schallert. Photo from the author's collection.

The Incredible Shrinking Man (1957) is director Jack Arnold's best sci-fi movie by far, and the only one not produced by William Alland. "In those days," said Arnold, "the studios would give out assignments to contract producers and contract directors. Albert Zugsmith was just given the assignment and, really, had nothing to do with the picture... He never read the book; he never read the script. I told him to just stay out of my way." (Zugsmith must have read enough of the script to know he wanted it in a linear form.)

Grant Williams, a studio contract player, was given the role of Robert Scott Carey. He was not Zugsmith's first choice, but he was the best choice, and certainly better than any actor the studio had under contract at the time. Universal would never have cast any of their A-list actors in the part—such as Jeff Chandler, Rock Hudson, Tony Curtis, or George Nader—but those people would not have been right for it anyway. All of the things that kept Williams from being a star made him ideal for the role of the 20th century "everyman" who comes face-to-face with the atomic age.

Jack Arnold said, "...almost three-quarters of the film was silent and it required real acting from Grant. It wasn't just a case of reciting banal dialogue as happened in so many sf films. Grant had to act; and I thought he gave an outstanding performance, but it didn't help his career. Universal didn't put him into an 'A' picture as they should have done; they just put him into more 'B' pictures. That's happened to us all in this business at one time or another—directors, actors, or writers. Lady Luck sometimes sits on your shoulders, but other times, she's busy elsewhere."[6]

The score by Irving Gertz, Herman Stein, and Hans Salter is perfect, but the melody that sets the melancholy tone for the entire film was a composition called "The Girl in the Lonely Room," which was written by Fred Carling and Ed Lawrence, and is heard during the opening credits and woven throughout the score.

Jack Arnold and Grant Williams get ready to shoot a tense moment from The Incredible Shrinking Man *(1957). Photo from the author's collection.*

The story is pretty simple. While vacationing on his brother's boat, Scott Carey is enveloped by a radioactive cloud. Six months later, he begins to shrink. The first half of the film deals with the breakdown of Carey's relationships. His brother (Paul Langton) can't afford to support him and suggests he earn a living by exploiting himself. He becomes estranged from his wife (Randy Stuart) and has a brief affair with a midget (April Kent). As the world he knows slips away, he becomes morose, tyrannical, and finally suicidal. "Easy enough to speak of soul and size and essential worth," Carey notes in his narration, "but not when you're three feet tall." Soon he's only three inches tall, and living in a dollhouse. He's chased into the cellar by his pet cat and presumed dead. His basement odyssey is like a plunge into another world. He lives in a matchbox, gets his water from a leaky heater, and in the end has to fight a tarantula for a chunk of stale cake and the right to rule his new kingdom. The battle between Carey and the spider is a masterpiece of technical achievement and still packs a punch.

After his victory over the spider—the symbol of all of his fears and doubts—Carey is small enough to crawl through the screen that had previously kept him a prisoner in his cellar. "I had thought in terms of Man's own limited dimensions," Carey says in his closing narration. "That existence begins and ends is Man's conception, not nature's. And I felt my body dwindling, melting; becoming nothing. My fears melted away, and in their place came acceptance. All this vast majesty of creation, it had to mean something. And then I meant something, too. Yes, smaller than the smallest, I meant something, too. To God, there is no zero. I still exist!"

Arnold needed all the help he could get from U-I's special effects department and he got it. They used every trick in the book to make the film believable: oversized props, process shots, split screens, and rotoscope mattes. Just when you've spotted where the split screen is, one of the characters (with a little help from the rotoscope department) steps over it.

Arnold said, "Sometimes a writer can make things awfully difficult. The shrinking man is living in a matchbox under a water heater and at one point in the story, the heater starts to leak. The problem: how to make giant water drops. We tried turning a giant faucet on and off, but that didn't work. Then I remembered something I found in my father's drawer when I was a little boy. I didn't know what they were used for at the time, but what I did was filled them with water and threw them at people. So I asked around the set if anyone had one of these things. Sheepishly, someone finally admitted that he did. I said, 'Give it to me.' I filled it up with water, took it up to the rafters, and dropped it. It looked like a drop and splashed on impact. I said, 'That's it,' and promptly ordered several gross of prophylactics. And they worked great. A few days later, when the picture was finished, I was called up to the front office and asked what the hell the prophylactics were for. I told them it was a rough picture and we had a wild party afterwards!"

The critics were not kind to the film, and Bosley Crowther led the charge. In his review in *The New York Times*, he wrote: "...unless a viewer is addicted to freakish ironies, the unlikely spectacle of Mr. Williams losing an inch of height each week, while his wife, Randy Stuart, looks on helplessly, will become tiresome before Universal has emptied its lab of science-fiction clichés." It should be mentioned that

Randy Stuart and Grant Williams. Photo from the author's collection.

Mr. Crowther was predisposed to hating sci-fi films and was, as far as your authors are concerned, an old poop.

Audiences couldn't have cared less what the critics thought. "Scared the pants off the kids and raised a bumper crop of goose pimples on the elders," Montana exhibitor Frank Sabin wrote in *Boxoffice* magazine.Universal's $800,000 film turned a $4 million dollar profit.

Notes:

1. Parla, Paul. "Remembering Attack of the Giant Leeches," *Movie Collector's World*, No. 506, pg. 85.
2. Ibid. pg. 84.
3. Barnum, Michael. "Susan Gordon, Almost Like Playing!" *Classic Images*, Jan 2008, pg. 6.
4. Had this movie been made a year before or a year later, the satellite would have been a flying saucer. It was a satellite to cash in on the Sputnik launch. Hanna may or may not have known the difference.
5. The L.A. Connection was a comedy group that would turn off the sound and add their own dialogue to movies.
6. Brosnan, John. *The Horror People*, St. Martin's Press, New York, NY, pg. 98.

CHAPTER FIVE

The Abominable Snowman

*The persistence of the widespread belief in the
Abominable Snowman among the mountain people of
Tibet has caused the cold eye of science to focus on it.*

—Pageant, June 1955

A tribe of natives in the Himalayan Mountains, known as the Sherpa, believe there is a half-man, half-ape living near the snow line: the Yeti. It came to be known as the Abominable Snowman when writer Henry Newman coined the term in a letter he wrote to *The Times* in 1921. Over the years, various mountain climbers have claimed to have seen this creature (always at a great distance) and its footprints. In the opinion of Eduard Wyss-Dunant, the leader of a Swiss expedition to the Himalayas, the tracks were probably made by a bear.

In the fifties, a rash of sensational articles about the Yeti kept the subject alive. *Popular Science* began one of its articles by saying the whole idea was fantastic, "Yet pre-man lived in caves just like those found in the Himalayas." A tongue-in-cheek piece in *Time* reported that holiday skiers at a French Alpine resort were "buzzing" about the arrival of an uninvited guest: "...the Abominable Snowman, bristling bogeyman of the Himalayas." In 1954, the year that *Argossy* magazine ran a story titled "I Know Monsters Live on Everest," *The London Daily Mail* sponsored a fifteen-week expedition to search for the creature. With public interest in the Yeti at an all-time high, the time was ripe for someone to make a movie about him. W. Lee Wilder was that someone.

The Snow Creature

There are some good things to say about Wilder's *The Snow Creature* (1954). It cuts together in a professional manner, Floyd Crosby's photography is very good, and the director succeeds (with some good split screen work) in turning Bronson Canyon into the Himalayan Mountains. But the script by Myles Wilder, the director's son, is a hopeless collection of sequences that in anyone else's film would have taken place off camera during a dissolve or a fade to black—all of the stuff too boring to actually show.

Paul Langton, the colorless actor who narrates the film, plays a botanist looking for rare plants in the Himalayas. Teru Shimada is his Sherpa guide. Langton tells us that the first few days of the expedition were uneventful and tedious, but we have to see them anyway. Later, after a lot of trekking, he tells us that they haven't found anything interesting. We have to see that, too. Finally, the Yeti (Lock Martin in a modified suit left over from *Invaders from Mars*) shows up and kidnaps Teru's woman. Teru tells Langton he wants to search for her, but Langton doesn't believe the Yeti exists and callously dismisses him. The fact that the woman is missing should have been cause for concern whether he believed in the Yeti or not, which makes Langton look like a prick. Teru understandably hijacks the expedition to look for his woman and Langton is forced to go with them. They never do find her, but they do find a Yeti, and Langton takes it back to Los Angeles, where it's kept in a refrigeration unit while customs tries to figure out whether he's an animal or a human being. (It might make a difference in the import tax.) It breaks loose and kills a few people before the police gun it down in the LA sewer system.

The Yeti attacks a security guard in W. Lee Wilder's The Snow Creature. *Photo courtesy of Bob Villard.*

Man Beast

Man Beast (1956) was even worse than *The Snow Creature*, a rock-bottom effort by producer-director Jerry Warren. Using the pseudonym B. Arthur Cassidy, Warren wrote his script around some mountain climbing footage he'd purchased, and a cast was assembled based on how closely they resembled the people in the stock footage. Rock Madison starred in the film. His only other credit is *Creature of the Walking Dead* (1965), another Warren film. Actually, there is no such person. Warren made the name up.

Even a filmmaker as cynical as Warren knew he had to have a snowman, so he and his wife, Bri Murphy, rented a white gorilla suit from Western Costume. Murphy had no idea she'd be asked to wear it. Warren was hoping he could persuade one of the crew to play the role, but nobody wanted to. So Murphy, who stood 5'1", had to do it. Because she was so short, the costume buckled at the chest, making it appear that the snowman had huge boobs. Looking at the rushes, the editor called Warren at the Lone Pine location and told him to get Bri out of the suit. He was falling in love with the monster! Desperate, Warren finally offered to pay someone to wear the suit. The photographer, Vic Fisher, handed Murphy his light meter. She stepped behind the camera and he stepped into the suit.

The story, what little there is of it, had a handful of people searching for the Yeti, unaware that their guide, George Skaff, is himself a fifth generation Yeti. He wants to mate with Virginia Maynor (whose real name was Asa Maynor) to breed out the Yeti strain. He never explains why he wants to do this and, frankly, we don't care.

Jerry Warren said, "I remember I needed a Mongolian village because I had to establish where the characters were... We couldn't possibly build a village and naturally we couldn't go to Tibet. So I took my actors and we climbed over the fence [at Paramount] and shot our scene on their Mongolian set!"[1]

It took Warren seven days to shoot his $30,000 feature, and he thought he'd have better luck selling it if he had another film to package with it. He borrowed Albert Cohen's five-year-old movie *Prehistoric Women*, promising to split the profits with him—a promise he had no intention of keeping. He and Murphy went cross-country, from one state's right distributor to another, telling them his $30,000 movie had cost $100,000.

Bri Murphy said, "You'd find out that a territory (say Dallas) was worth 14 percent, so you should get $14,000 out of Dallas, predicated on your negative cost of $100,000. Now, you're in the screening room with these distributors and they're answering the phone and they're talking to each other and they're smoking and they get up and leave for a while and then come back. And then they ask, 'What do you want for this piece of shit?'... And Jerry would say, 'Give me my $14,000 and I'll *throw in* the other picture.'"[2]

The Abominable Snowman of the Himalayas

The last and best of these Yeti movies was Hammer's *The Abominable Snowman of the Himalayas* (1957), and it was nothing to write home about. As one would expect from its author, Nigel Kneale, the script was intelligent, but unfortunately, not very exciting.

Arnold Marle wonders how many props Peter Cushing is going to play with in this scene from The Abominable Snowman of the Himalayas *(1957). Photo courtesy of Bob Villard.*

Scientist Peter Cushing joins forces with opportunist Forrest Tucker to search for the Yeti. Tucker kills one of the snowmen, but he wants to bring one back alive to restore his sullied reputation. As the story progresses, Tucker and his group reveal themselves to be more abominable than the snowmen they're after. Through no fault of the Yeti, everyone but Cushing comes to a bad end. Cushing assumes that the snowmen will kill him to revenge their dead comrade, but instead he finds them wise, sympathetic, and compassionate. When he gets back home, he tells everyone that the creature they were looking for doesn't exist.

Peter Cushing was fond of using props. During a conversation with Andre Morrell and Francis De Wolff in *The Hound of the Baskervilles* (1959), Cushing straightens a picture on the wall, wipes some dust from a table with the tip of his finger, picks up a stack of papers from the mantle over the fireplace, sets them back down, secures them with a heavy object, and finally stands on a chair so that he can pluck books and papers off of the top of a bookcase. Val Guest, who directed *The Abominable Snowman*, said they called him "Props" Cushing.

Val Guest said, "He would work it all out and not tell you anything about it until the take and then all these things would start happening. In [*The Abominable Snowman*] when they show him the Yeti's tooth, none of us had any idea what was going to go on in that scene. But it sure went on! He took a tape measure out, he scraped the tooth with a nail file; he came up with a magnifying glass, all during the scene, talking the whole time. It was quite hysterical."[3]

Momoko Kochi and the ape man (Sagata Sanshiro) from Half Human *(1958). Photo courtesy of Bob Villard.*

Half Human: The Story of the Abominable Snowman

Despite its title, *Half Human: The Story of the Abominable Snowman* (1958) was not an abominable snowman movie. It was a 1955 Toho film—*Jujin Yuki Otoko* (*Half Beast-Half Man*)—about an ape man living in the Japanese Alps with his son. His son is captured by an animal broker (Yoshio Kosugi) to use as bait. The snowman is captured when he tries to rescue his son. Before the broker can haul him away, the members of a primitive tribe try to stop him. These people have lived in seclusion for so long, they've become deformed from inbreeding. To them, the snowman is a god. The broker shoots their leader (Kokuten Kodo). The snowman is hauled away in a truck and the broker follows after them. The snowman's son hops on the truck and sets his father free. The broker shoots the boy, but his gun jams before he can kill the father. You know what that means.

There's a lot more to this movie, but a detailed description of all of the characters and subplots would fill a chapter. The original Toho version, which we have not seen, ran ninety-eight minutes. The truncated American version, produced by Robert Homel and directed by Kenneth G. Crane, ran seventy minutes. It seemed like 170 minutes. Crane scrapped over half of the original movie and added new, boring sequences with John Carradine, Russell Thorson, Robert Karnes, and Morris Ankrum. To save the cost of dubbing the film, Carradine narrates the story. If the producer and the director had deliberately set out to ruin this movie, they couldn't have done a better job of it.

Notes:

1. Weaver, Tom. *Interviews with B Science Fiction and Horror Movie Makers*, McFarland, Jefferson, NC, pg. 371.
2. Weaver, Tom. *Monsters, Mutants and Heavenly Creatures*, Midnight Marquee Press, Baltimore, MD, pg. 154.
3. Weaver, Tom. *Attack of the Monster Movie Makers*, McFarland, Jefferson, NC, pg. 112.

CHAPTER SIX
BRIDEY MURPHY AND HER FRIENDS

*A great deal of publicity has been given lately to
hypnotized persons who supposedly recall an existence
prior to birth. In all cases we must ask ourselves: "Do
hypnotized people always tell the truth?"*
—The Curse of the Demon

In 1956, American International Pictures (AIP) released a movie called *The She-Creature*, the story of a carnival huckster (Chester Morris) who hypnotizes the woman he loves (Marla English) and takes her back to a time when she was an armor-plated prehistoric monster. Morris then materializes the monster so it can commit the murders that he predicts. "She came out of the ocean, just as I said she would," he tells everyone. "She'll come again. She comes from the beginning of time, huge and indestructible. And I'm the force that gives her life." So the idiot admits to being a co-conspirator in the murders. How stupid can you get?

AIP's advertising department made the following claim: "It can and did happen! Based on authentic facts you've been reading about!" What facts could they have possibly been talking about?

In Pueblo, Colorado, a young businessman named Morey Bernstein who was fascinated by hypnosis, wanted to try an experiment in regression. Bernstein believed the human mind could be taken back in time to a period before birth. He chose for his subject a young housewife named Virginia Tighe. He hypnotized her and took her on a journey back to the first year of her life. "I want you to keep going back," he told her, "back through time and space... now you are going to tell me what you see..." And she did. She described a child maliciously picking the color off a freshly painted metal bed in retaliation for the spanking she'd just received. "What is your name?" Bernstein asked. "Bridey Murphy," she replied in a rich brogue. She continued to chronicle her previous life as a spirited, saucy-tongued girl of 1798 Ireland who died at the age of sixty-six. Bernstein's book, *The Search for Bridey Murphy*, sold over 170,000 copies. Paramount made a movie out of it, but AIP beat them to the punch by three months with *The She-Creature*.

Bernstein's book turned reincarnation into a fad. It was the subject of songs and nightclub acts. There was even a Bridey Murphy dance, often performed

Paul Blaisdell as the She-Creature (1956). Photo from the author's collection.

at the many "Come as you were" parties where Reincarnation cocktails were often served. One Oklahoma boy committed suicide and left a note explaining that he wanted to investigate the Bridey Murphy theory in person. Naturally, moviemakers wanted to strike while the iron was hot.

The Influence of Bridey Murphy

In W. Lee Wilder's *Fright* (1957), Nancy Malone strongly resembles the Bridey Murphy character in Bernstein's book. She tells her psychiatrist, Eric Fleming, that she once lived in the year 1889. Under hypnosis, she speaks German and believes herself to be the Baroness Maria who is hopelessly in love with a married man named Rudy. Fleming discovers there was a woman named Maria Vetsera: the eighteen-year-old mistress of Crown Prince Rudolph of Austria. Unable to consummate their relationship, the lovers committed suicide. Delving into Miss Malone's past, Fleming learns that she was raised by an Austrian nurse, from whom she apparently learned to speak German and who gave her the knowledge of the scandalous suicide.

Peter Stevens (Jock Mahoney) is a pilot haunted by dreams about dying in a plane crash during World War I. He tells his fiancée (Leigh Snowden) he thinks he may have lived a previous life. "Reincarnation is impossible—I think—isn't it?" she replies. Stevens sees a picture of the pilot he believes himself to have been, which ultimately leads him to the home of the dead pilot's widow (Ann Harding). She thinks Stevens is out of his head until he describes the brooch that her husband gave her, a brooch that no one else had ever seen.

Written by Norman Jolly and William Talman (Hamilton Burger on TV's *Perry Mason*), *I've Lived Before* (1956) opens strong, but loses its momentum after about twenty minutes and becomes repetitious and dull. Director Richard Bartlett made two more movies after this one, both with Jock Mahoney, before finding his niche in television.

Reincarnation seemed like a ripe subject for comedy and it's surprising that *Hold That Hypnotist* (1957)—the forty-fourth entry in the long-running Bowery Boys series—was the only movie to take advantage of it. A greedy doctor (Robert Foulk) "hypnotizes" Huntz Hall and takes him back to a time when he was in possession of Bluebeard the Pirate's treasure map. The hypnotist wants to have Hall committed so that he can get his hands on the loot, which turns out to be jewelry from a recent robbery.

This was one of the movies made after Leo Gorcey left the series. It was produced by Ben Schwalb, written by Dan Pepper, and directed by Austin Jewel, who was, and continued to be after this film, an assistant director.

The Undead

The most imaginative and unique of these Bridey Murphy spin-offs was Roger Corman's *The Undead* (1957), a curious mix of black magic, horror, sci-fi, and the supernatural written by Chuck Griffith. Unfortunately, it runs out of steam about halfway through and seems to spin in circles. It opens with the Devil (Richard Devon) talking to the audience, dispelling any sense of reality and the need to provide rational explanations for the events that follow.

A prostitute named Diana Love (Pamela Duncan) is hypnotized by an unscrupulous psychotherapist, Quintus Ratcliff (Val Dufour), and taken back to her previous life during medieval times. As Helene, she is falsely accused of witchcraft and is to be executed at sunrise. She hears Diana's voice and wonders if she actually is a witch. With Diana's help, Helene escapes. Quintus isn't at all upset that his interference may have altered the course of his history as he just

Allison Hayes makes Richard Garland an offer that he's somehow able to refuse in Roger Corman's The Undead *(1957). The* Boxoffice *review called it "a witch's brew that smells more than it scares." Photo from the author's collection.*

wants to observe things firsthand. He uses a machine to connect his brainwaves with Diana's so that he can travel back in time. He's fascinated by the girl's dilemma. As Helene, she can escape the headman's axe and live the rest of her life with her lover, Pendragon (Richard Garland), but only at the sacrifice of her later lives. Die now, live later. Live now, die forever. She chooses death, rushing from Pendragon's arms and onto the chopping block. The axe severs her head and with it goes Quintus's connection to the future. He is hopelessly trapped in the past with the Devil laughing in his ear.

Chuck Griffith: "Roger said 'Give me a Bridey Murphy.' I told him that by the time we got the thing out, it would be a dead issue. Then the Paramount movie based on Bernstein's book bombed, so Roger changed the picture from *The Trance of Diana Love* to *The Undead*, which is a zombie title. The whole thing was originally written in iambic pentameter (all of the stuff in the past). The scenes were separated by synclines done by the Devil. It was the best piece of writing I'd done up until that time or maybe since, I don't know. Roger loved it when he first read it. Then he showed it around and nobody understood it, so he told me to translate it into English a couple of days before we had to shoot. And it was gone, you know. It was a mess then. It was fifty-five thousand dollars, fifteen trees with Spanish moss and a fog machine. That was a big deal for Roger then."

Actor Mel Welles, who played a bewitched grave digger with a penchant for singing grim little ditties, agreed with Griffith. "It would have been one of the classic films of all time if Roger had shot the script as it was originally written. It made that medieval regression part come off very ethereal, very Hansel and Gretelish, and would have been very charming. But Roger lost his nerve; didn't want to do it. I remember all of us were very disappointed, Bruno Ve Sota especially."

Griffith: "[Bruno] was supposed to back up against the wall and [Allison Hayes] was supposed to swing an axe that went through [his] neck, right into the wall. Then the body was supposed to slide down the wall, squirting blood, and the head was to stay on the axe blade. No attempt was made to do that. Bruno was really dying to do it."

Roger Corman: "It was a very strange film. There was a lot of interest in the Bridey Murphy phenomenon, so this was an attempt to do kind of a fantasy-horror along that line. I haven't seen it for a long, long time. I was maybe a little too ambitious for ten days and seventy or eighty thousand dollars. This is one of the things I learned: over the long run, we were better off making a small picture for a small amount of money than trying to make a big one and cheat it."

The Bride and the Beast

Ed Wood's script for *The Bride and the Beast* (1958) was written around some footage that producer-director Adrian Weiss had purchased from an old Sabu movie. Charlotte Austin played a woman who discovers, under hypnosis, that she was once a gorilla. The film ends with her husband, Lance Fuller, pondering the implications of Miss Austin's choice to run off with a pack of gorillas and leave him behind on their honeymoon. Adrian Weiss told your authors the film was a minor classic.

Charlotte Austin said, "Lance and I broke up laughing so badly one night that we couldn't shoot for an hour and a half. We were in a truck, supposedly traversing the African veldt. The stock shots of zebras and giraffes and rhinos and elephants would be added later. I happened to look out of the side of this fake truck we were in and there was a round barrel with twigs stapled to it. It was turning around and around and I saw at the bottom two little feet running on a treadmill turning this barrel. It was one of the Weiss family. They had a stuck in a cousin or an uncle or something to run this treadmill to make it look like we were moving. I turned to Lance and we just fell apart. We couldn't work. These feet were running, running, running—like a gerbil—to move this barrel with twigs nailed to it."[1]

After *The Search for Bridey Murphy* became a bestseller, reporters were sent to Ireland for a little fact checking and they found a number of holes in Virginia Tighe's account. There was no record of Bridey Murphy's birth or death or the house she supposedly lived in. After all was said and done, it turned out that Miss Tighe had simply been recounting stories told to her when she was a child by an Irish neighbor. Interest in reincarnation dwindled after that. "I kind of wish Bridey would have stayed in Ireland," wrote one beleaguered exhibitor, after running the Paramount movie. "The only thing that kept us from going into a trance was the high school seniors selling tickets to make more money for a trip."

Notes:
1. Baumann, Marty. *The Astounding B Monster*, Dinoship, NY, 2004, pg. 33.

CHAPTER SEVEN
TEENAGE TERRORS

*Remember how it felt to run over the hills in the
moonlight? To hide in a stream and wait in silence
until... Remember how wonderful it was when you
sprang suddenly and you dug in with your fangs—the
soft throat, the gush of warm blood? Yes, I want you to
remember. You must remember!*
     —I Was a Teenage Werewolf

Gather round, all you cats and kittens. Let us make the scene. Up ahead, there's a deserted road, stretching beyond the horizon into the future. There is no one in sight. Then we hear them, a faint buzz at first, and then we see them, coming blackly up the road like a dark cloud. It's the Black Rebels, dozens of them, on their motorcycles. The sullen, good-looking one is Marlon Brando, their leader. Ask him what he's rebelling against and he'll glibly reply: "What have you got?" Brando was thirty years old when he made *The Wild One* (1954), but he was expressing the feelings of a lot of young people at the time.

No longer children, but not yet adults, teenagers enjoyed none of the perks and all of the disadvantages of both. It was a real drag, man, like Downersville, you dig? Their parents told them that the teenage years were the best years of their lives, but how was that possible if their parents were calling all of the shots? Protests were generally met with indifference and everything that seemed important was trivialized. *You'll look back on this one day and wonder what all of the fuss was about.* Parents forgot what it was like to be young, and they forgot how real the pain could be, so the kids learned to keep the important stuff to themselves—like sex, for instance. Something happened to parents whenever that subject came up, something awful. They turned red and lost the power of cohesive thought.

In Hollywood movies, teenagers were healthy, wholesome subordinates. Adolescent girls like Deanna Durbin achieved mass popularity in the forties by radiating mindless good cheer wherever she went. Andy Hardy might have a few anxious moments, but Judge Hardy was always there to sort things out. Teenage sexual impulses were reduced to saccharine cases of puppy love. Displays of affection were restricted to a peck on the cheek. This was during the reign of the Hayes office when sexual displays of any kind were discouraged and often forbidden. Husbands and wives couldn't be shown in the same bed together. For some reason, sex was the only subject that you were better off knowing as little about as possible.

As far as the kids of the fifties were concerned, parents were a bunch of L7s, like real squares, like Nowheresville. They'd messed up everything. With the fear of nuclear devastation hanging over their heads, teenagers began to wonder if they had a future. As a result, they didn't want to act like, dress like, or be anything like their parents. They had money now. They bought their own threads and spent what was left on fast music and fast cars. (And fast women if a guy got lucky.) The purchasing power of the young changed the cultural and economic landscape. Adults fought back, creating what came to be known as "the Generation Gap."

Censorship always exercises its biggest control over the most popular media, so we can thank television for taking some of the heat away from the movies in the fifties. Filmmakers were finally able to talk about sex, but the Breen office still didn't want to see anyone engaged in it. And while once-forbidden subjects like drug addiction, infidelity, and teenage sex were suddenly fair game, the Breen Office discouraged any talk of divorce.

The Breen Office hated *Blackboard Jungle*. They didn't want to see the American school system trashed and they certainly didn't want to see a bunch of teenagers running amok with switchblade knives. But MGM was fighting for its life. Television had taken its toll, and the studio couldn't survive on family films anymore. They had to woo people back with something they couldn't get at home.

Glenn Ford played the teacher at war with his students in the movie based on Evan Hunter's sensational novel. Ford's son, Peter, suggested Bill Haley's "Rock Around the Clock" for the film's opening credits, forever linking rock and roll music to juvenile delinquency. The song became the teenage national anthem and disrupted the entire record industry, the first rock and roll record to occupy the Hit Parade for fifteen weeks.

In 1953, the FBI reported that half of all the burglaries and car thefts were committed by children under the age of eighteen. A Senate subcommittee looked into the matter, and after a lot of posturing, came to the conclusion that comic books may have contributed to the problem.

Many people found *The Wild One* and *Blackboard Jungle* disturbing, but when all was said and done, neither film touched them where they lived. Motorcycle gangs were on the outskirts of mainstream society. The film may have been based on a real incident, but it was an isolated one. And the shenanigans in *Blackboard Jungle* only happened in the inner-urban areas of the big cities with their slums and filth. But Nicholas Ray's *Rebel Without a Cause* (1955) laid the problem of juvenile delinquency right on their middle class doorsteps. It wasn't about some gang member on some distant tenement street. It was about the stranger in their own homes, the kid they didn't understand anymore, the one who was always getting into trouble. Ray's movie was a huge success and its star, James Dean, became the poster boy for the emerging youth culture. For the first time, a movie acknowledged the role that parents played in creating a delinquent and how difficult and painful it was for a kid to fit in, to be one of the crowd.

Everyone at Columbia, including Sam Katzman, was surprised when Katzman's low-budget, highly fictionalized biography of Bill Haley and the Comets, *Rock Around the Clock* (1956), took in $4 million, sending a clear message that there was money to be made in the newly created teenage market. Other producers were quick to take advantage of it, and no one did it better than American International Pictures. Owned and operated by a down-on-his-luck ex-theater owner named James Hartford Nicholson and a struggling attorney named Samuel Zachary Arkoff, these two men made a fortune from double-feature packages aimed at teenagers, which were designed for quick pay-offs at drive-ins and secondary hardtops.

"The first few pictures were not great pictures," said Leon Blender, AIP's sales manager. "The exhibitors wouldn't look at them because if they looked at them, they wouldn't buy them. They would look at Jim's ad campaigns and press sheets instead."

"Jim Nicholson and I would make up a title, decide how to approach the advertising, and then I'd go off and do the campaign," explained Albert Kallis, the company's resident illustrator. "We'd send the layouts to the theater owners and if they liked it we'd make it."

I Was a Teenage Werewolf

AIP specialized in teenage melodramas and sci-fi movies, but it wasn't until they combined the two that the company really struck gold. *I Was a Teenage Werewolf* opened in the summer of 1957, and in a few short months had made $2 million on an $80,000 investment.

"To take first things first," wrote the reviewer for the *L.A. Examiner*, "the title is a magnificent piece of composition. It has a haunting quality about it and I ought to caution you that if you let it pierce your consciousness it will echo in your brain in a constant refrain."

The title was a lift from a 1956 edition of *Dig* magazine. One of Nicholson's daughters told him about it. Nicholson thought it was the perfect title for the movie that producer Herman Cohen wanted to make. Cohen had just made a film with Barbara Stanwyck and Sterling Hayden that tanked. He took a tour of the country to find out why. He discovered that movie attendance by people over twenty-five had dramatically declined; 52.6 percent of the people who went to the movies once a week or more were between the ages of ten to nineteen. *Motion Picture Herald*, an exhibitor magazine, reported that the most frequent moviegoers were high school teenagers from well-off families. Cohen intended to aim his next picture at that audience. He wrote a script with Aben Kandel called *Blood of the Werewolf* and took it to Jim Nicholson. He and Cohen had both worked for Jack Broder. At one time, they'd discussed forming a partnership, but ultimately, Cohen left Broder's to make his own movies, leaving Nicholson behind to look for another partner.

Michael Landon as the Teenage Werewolf. *Photo from the author's collection.*

Initially, Cohen wanted Sherman Rose to direct the picture because their relationship on *Target Earth* had been a smooth one. But Rose had landed a steady gig cutting trailers for National Screen Service, so Cohen gave the job to Gene Fowler, Jr., a film editor. Fowler is the one who deserves the lion's share of the credit for making *Teenage Werewolf* as good as it is. Behind Cohen's back, he rewrote a lot of Cohen's silly script and Cohen was pretty sore about it. He never let it happen again.

Michael Landon is terrific as Tony Rivers, a troubled youth in desperate need of guidance. And Malcolm Atterbury is equally believable as his widowed father whose job keeps him away from home most of the time. Tony's short temper is always getting him into trouble. He flies off the handle at a Halloween party and beats one of his friends senseless. Looking at the frightened faces of his friends, Tony realizes he's out of control. He seeks help from psychiatrist Alfred Brandon (Whit Bissell), who unfortunately is a lunatic. "Mankind is on the verge of destroying itself," he tells his sniveling assistant (Joseph Mell). "The only hope for the human race is to hurl it back into its primitive dawn... to start all over again." Brandon is positive that

Tony's disturbed background makes him the ideal subject for his experiment in regression. Through drugs and hypnosis, Brandon takes the boy back to the time when he was a werewolf. (This is another nod to Bridey Murphy.) Once Tony realizes he is the one responsible for a series of brutal murders, he returns to the doctor and begs for help. Brandon takes him back one more time so that he can film the transformation. After Tony becomes the werewolf again, he kills Brandon and his assistant.

There's a very nice father-and-son moment early in the film where, in a matter-of-fact tone, Tony's father mentions that he got a call from the school principal about a fight that Tony was involved in. "Sometimes you have to do things the way people want them done," he tells Tony. "That makes 'em happy and they leave you alone. I used to have a foreman like that. Every time I assembled a motor my way he beefed, but when I assembled it his way..." Tony cuts his father off. He tells his father he doesn't like to be pushed around, but his father gently insists that sometimes you have to do what you're told. He apologizes for not having dinner with him, but he's on night shift again. "There are a couple of lamb chops in the icebox. I seasoned them the way you like. Just put 'em in the pan." Tony chuckles and says, "Dad, I can cook a chop." As he starts out the door, his father says, "Tony, think over what I said, would you? I mean about not being so stubborn. It might make things easier all the way around." A few seconds after he's gone, Tony throws a bottle of milk at the wall.

Variety said, "Michael Landon delivers a first-class characterization as the high school boy constantly in trouble and has okay support right down the line. Yvonne Lime is pretty as his girlfriend who asks him to go to the psychiatrist and Whit Bissell handles the doctor part capably, although some of his lines are pretty thick."

The film went slightly over budget when Herman Cohen insisted that the werewolf should not be seen when it kills Michael Rougas as he walks alone through the woods at night. Fowler shot the scene with Landon in the werewolf makeup. Cohen wanted the whole thing played with the werewolf off camera. It was probably the right decision.

I Was a Teenage Frankenstein

Herb Strock, a more pliable director, was hired to helm Cohen's next three pictures: *I Was a Teenage Frankenstein*, *Blood of Dracula* (both 1957), and *How to Make a Monster* (1958). *Teenage Frankenstein* shifted the focus from the teenage victim to the adult despot who is obsessed with obedience. This served as the blueprint for almost every Herman Cohen film that followed.

There are no healthy relationships in Cohen's misogynistic, sadistic films, which sheds more light on his psyche than he probably realized. The women in his films are always depicted as deceitful, emasculating shrews. When asked why he killed the innocent young ingénue at the end of *Konga* (1961), Cohen replied, "I wanted to use my carnivorous plants. She was a very pretty girl and very sexy and I thought the audience would get a big kick out of seeing her killed..." Obviously *he* did.

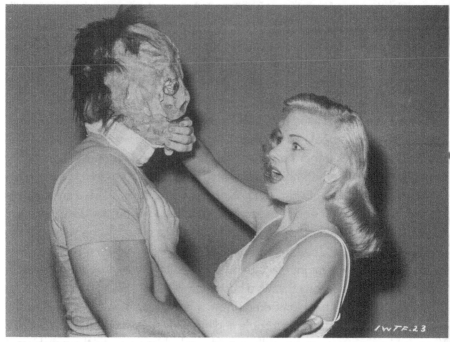

Angela Blake wrestles with Gary Conway in I Was a Teenage Frankenstein *(1957) Photo from the author's collection.*

Whit Bissell played a modern day descendant of the Frankenstein family in *Teenage Frankenstein*, obsessed with creating a teenage boy. "I shall use only the ingredients of youth, not the worn-out body inhabited by an over-taxed brain," he tells his reluctant assistant, Robert Burton. (The assistants in these films were always reluctant, spineless wimps.) No sooner is this statement out of his mouth than a teenage hot-rodder (Gary Conway) is killed in a car accident right outside his door. If the film had any wit, the body would have been hurled through his living room window. In no time flat, the doc's stitched-together teenager, dressed in a pair of Ivy League slacks and a form-fitting T-shirt, is happily lifting weights in his secret laboratory, waiting for Frankenstein to replace his hideous face.

Herbert Strock said, "We did a scene where Whit Bissell cuts a leg off with an electric saw. You didn't actually see it. You heard the sound of the blade cutting through the bone and then he picks up this phony leg and holds it in front of the camera with blood all over it. The censors said, 'You can't show him cutting off a leg on camera. You'll have to cut the scene.' I argued that it took place off camera but they insisted they saw him cut into the leg. I had to run the film for them again."

The critic for *The New York Times* said, "It forces one to acknowledge the impression that such films may aggravate the mass social sickness euphemistically termed juvenile delinquency." If he meant the kids might be provoked into tearing the theater apart because the film was so lousy, there might be something to what he said.

The picture was already in production, scheduled for a January release, when a conversation with Bob O'Donnell—the owner of a chain of theaters in Texas—threw everything into fourth gear. O'Donnell was outspoken in his support for little companies like AIP and Allied Artists, and over lunch one afternoon, he told Nicholson and Arkoff that he was tired of being gouged by the major studios. "I hate to give those bastards Thanksgiving week," he grumbled; Thanksgiving week was always a profitable one for exhibitors. Remembering that O'Donnell had done good business with *Teenage Werewolf*, Nicholson mentioned they had *Teenage Frankenstein* in the works. O'Donnell promised to open the picture at his 2400-seat flagship theater, The Majestic, if he could have another movie to go with it. This was a big deal for Nicholson and Arkoff as their pictures rarely played flagship theaters. When the situation was explained to Herman Cohen, he and Aben Kandel quickly wrote *Blood of Dracula* and the two pictures were shot back to back.

Half sheet poster from Blood of Dracula *(1957). "Our films concerned teenagers who had doubts about their parents, their teacher or what-have-you. That these doubts influence a teenager to go bad. I felt this would appeal to a teenage audience, which it did."— Herman Cohen. Photo from author's collection.*

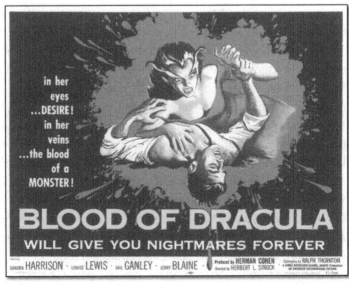

in her eyes
...DESIRE!
in her veins
...the blood of a
MONSTER!

BLOOD OF DRACULA
WILL GIVE YOU NIGHTMARES FOREVER

SANDRA HARRISON · LOUISE LEWIS · GAIL GANLEY · JERRY BLAINE · Produced by HERMAN COHEN · Screenplay by RALPH THORNTON · Directed by HERBERT L. STROCK

Blood of Dracula

Sandra Harrison gave a very good performance in *Blood of Dracula* as the troubled youth who was placed in the Sherwood's School for Girls by her father (Tom Brown Henry) and his new wife (Jean Dean). Her quick temper attracts the attention of her frigid (possibly lesbian) science teacher (Louise Lewis), who thinks that if the governments of the world realize people can be turned into vampires, they'll stop making bombs. She's not only frigid, she's crazy. Through hypnosis and the power of an ancient Carpathian amulet, Sandy becomes her guinea pig. Sandy kills the old bag once she gets wise to her, but dies during the struggle in what has to be one of the worst directed moments in screen history.

As you can tell from reading the synopsis, *Blood of Dracula* was simply the *Teenage Werewolf* again. Why Cohen didn't call it *I Was a Teenage Dracula* is a mystery.

One thing you can always count on in a Herman Cohen film is a lot of boring, time-eating police station sequences, during which the audience is subjected to a summation of facts and events that they already know. Someone inevitably says, "The newspapers will have a field day." Since the police play no part in bringing Cohen's despots to justice, all of these sequences could be excised without damaging the narrative in any way. It's nothing more than lazy writing and a way of giving the director a bunch of junk that he can shoot in a single day.

Teenage Monster

Independent producer Jacques Marquette couldn't help but notice that AIP was on to a good thing with their teenage melodramas. He quickly changed his deceptively titled *Meteor Monster*—originally titled *The Monster on the Hill*—to the deceptively titled *Teenage Monster* (1957), although *Charlie, the Hairy Halfwit* would have been closer to the truth. Marquette's western melodrama about a disfigured, brain-damaged teenager is ill conceived at best, and a blatant rip-off at worst. The original title suggests that it was aimed at the sci-fi market, but other than the meteor that burns Charlie's face and fries his brain, there are no sci-fi elements in the story. Forget for a moment that it's poorly made. More importantly, it is not what it purports to be. I saw this movie when I was ten years old and I distinctly remember feeling cheated. I would have felt a lot better if I'd seen a movie just as crummy with a stupid-looking monster. It would have been just as cheap and easy to make, so why didn't they? And why did they hire a 50-year-old stuntman (Gil Perkins) to play their teenage killer? A shoe made with the indifference and disregard that went into this picture would fall apart before the salesman could get it out of the box.

"You've been a bad boy again, haven't you, Charlie?" his mother (Anne Gwynne) says sadly as the body count rises. She knows her son is a murdering psychopath, but doesn't do anything to stop him. Whatever Charlie says to his mother in response is impossible to understand; he sounds a lot like Blacktooth on the old Soupy Sales TV show. But the characters in the film don't have any trouble making sense out of his grunts and groans. Marquette said they were supposed to "intuitively understand" what he was saying. Gil Perkins said he spent the better part of a day dubbing unintelligible noises to replace his dialogue because writer Ray Buffum thought he sounded too intelligent.

In the end, Charlie is shot by the sheriff (Stuart Wade). To our way of thinking, he should have shot the mother too, and he might want to think about the writer and the producer. Anyone taken in by this fraud may find some consolation in the knowledge that Marquette and Buffum never saw a dime of their profit participation in this picture.

Invasion of the Saucer-Men

A new character emerged during the bumper crop of post-*Rebel* youth films: the teenage hero. This relatively clean-cut guy could enjoy hotrods, girls, rock and roll, and even an occasional thumb-of-the-nose to authority, but he knew where to draw the line. Young ladies could trust him and only narrow-minded, hypocritical adults could possibly object to his behavior. He made his first appearance in AIP's *Invasion of the Saucer-Men* (1957), the companion feature to *Teenage Werewolf*. Steve Terrell was the star of the film, and the first sci-fi hero who wasn't a doctor, policeman, military man, scientist, or some other authority figure. All of the authority figures in *Saucer-Men* are blundering nitwits. It's up to Terrell and his friends to deal with the little green men from Mars. Once they discover that the Martians are vulnerable to bright light, Terrell and his buddies circle the invaders and fry them with their hotrod headlights. If you're looking for a laugh from this sci-fi comedy, you'd have better luck finding a teenage actor in the cast.

Paul Blaisdell's little green men from Mars. Photo from the author's collection.

Giant Gila Monster

The teenage hero of the *Giant Gila Monster* (1958) was an auto mechanic (Don Sullivan) who finds the time to build his own hotrod and write rock and roll songs between lube jobs. Sullivan wrote the three incomprehensible numbers he sings in this film, and one of them, "The Mushroom Song," will stick with you like a bad meal. In a sequence designed to tug at the heartstrings, he sings it to his little crippled sister (Janice Stone), then has the nerve to sing it again at the local record hop. Even the Gila monster won't stand for it a second time. It pokes its head through the side of the building, interrupting Sullivan in mid-verse. Once it's sure the song has been put to rest, it leaves. Sullivan gets even. He loads his hotrod with nitroglycerin and sends it crashing into the lizard, blowing it and his hotrod to smithereens.

The producer, Gordon McLendon, owned six radio stations and ten theaters in Texas. He told *Variety*, "If we can sell pictures, we can make pictures." *Gila Monster* was shot back-to-back with *The Killer Shrews* and sent out as a package with modest success in Dallas and Fort Worth. The two pictures, made for a total cost of $138,000, were eventually sold to AIP.

The Return of Dracula

If you take Uncle Charlie from Alfred Hitchcock's *Shadow of a Doubt* (1943) and replace him with Count Dracula, you have *The Return of Dracula* (1958) from producers Jules Levy and Arthur Gardner. Norma Eberhardt has the Teresa Wright role and Francis Lederer is Dracula—although Dracula is posing as a cousin that Norma and her family have never met, called Bellac Gordal. Like Uncle Charlie, Dracula is on the run, chased out of Europe by vampire hunter John Wengraf, who eventually catches up to him. But, as with Hitchcock's film, it's leading lady Eberhardt who brings Dracula to justice.

Written by Pat Fielder and directed by Paul Landres, this film was overshadowed by Hammer's *Horror of Dracula*. It isn't as good or as graphic as the Hammer film, but there was one scene that proved to be quite a surprise: a close-up of a stake being driven into the heart of a vampire. The film switched to color as the blood came gushing out. (There's an identical moment in Hammer's *Dracula* which was entirely in color.) Giving good support to the film's creepy quality is Gerald Fried's score, which borrows heavily from "Dreams of a Witches Sabbath" from *Symphonie Fantastique* by Hector Berloiz.

Frankenstein's Daughter

The critic for the *New York Times* called *Frankenstein's Daughter* (1958) a cheap, dull piece of claptrap. Most fans think it's the worst Frankenstein movie ever made. We hated it when we were kids, but as immature, brain-damaged adults, we now think it's a lot of fun, which is not to say that it isn't a cheap, dull

Donald Murphy and Wolfe Barzell don't understand why Harry Wilson was hired to play Frankenstein's daughter. Photo courtesy of Bob Villard.

piece of claptrap. It features the most hapless cast of characters since *Godzilla.*

First, there's Johnny Bruder (John Ashley), and he's worried about his girl-friend, Trudy Morton (Sandra Knight). She's been having nightmares in which she sees herself as a monster, prowling the city at night. Poor Trudy spends a lot of time in her bedroom to keep from being accosted by her uncle's assistant, Oliver Frank (Donald Murphy), whose name is really Frankenstein. He can't keep his hands off Trudy. Her uncle, Carter Morton (Felix Locher), is a feckless old fool who can't seem to get his house in order. Having lost his job, he's forced to work out of his home on a formula he believes will wipe out all of the destructive forces that plague mankind: a concoction that's turning his niece into a monster. Carter and Oliver bicker like a pair of old hens and Carter doesn't get along with his gardener (Wolfe Barzell) either. The cops haul him away for stealing drugs from the place he used to work. This gives Oliver the run of the place. He's the one who's been spiking Trudy's fruit punch with Carter's miracle drug. In a secret two-story room behind a bookcase in the lab—that somehow Carter knows nothing about—Oliver has been doing what all of the Frankensteins do: he's making a monster and the gardener is helping him. Oliver's judgment is often impaired by his lust for the ladies, though he can't get laid to save his life. Neither can Johnny's best friend, Don Harold (Harold Lloyd, Jr.). His girlfriend, Suzie Lawler (*Playboy* playmate Sally Todd), is nothing but a tease. In the very first scene of the movie, we see that Don can't even get a goodnight kiss. But Suzie has problems of her own; she can't convince anyone that she saw the monster that Trudy keeps talking about. She's also angry at Trudy for taking Johnny away from her. To get even, Suzie makes a play for Oliver, thinking that Trudy wants him too, although nothing could be further from the truth. Not re-alizing who she's dealing with, Trudy treats Oliver the same way she treated Don. Oliver becomes enraged, smacks her with his car, and grafts her head onto his creation. Still, nobody has it any worse than the two cops (John

Zaremba and Robert Dix). These poor guys are on duty around the clock. And let us not forget the monster (Harry Wilson). It's so stupid, it sets itself on fire.

What is this, Dan, some kind of a joke? Please tell me you didn't hire Harry Wilson to play Frankenstein's daughter. What could you have been..? No, Dan, if we were making Frankenstein's Uncle, *he'd be perfect. I can't believe you did this. What? Yes, you're right, Dan, I don't know what Sally Todd would look like if she were run over by a car, but I can tell you this: she wouldn't look like Harry Wilson. Jesus H. Christ! We can't get away with this. The audience will... Now what are you doing? What are you...? You put lipstick on him. That's... That's great, Dan. Yeah, that makes all the difference.*

John Ashley said. "I knew when we were making the film that it didn't seem very frightening. There I was with this table between me and this monster and I'm rocking it back and forth and I couldn't believe that what we were doing was going to somehow be terrifying because it was on a big screen. It could only be worse. I say this to you now, in retrospect, but these are not thoughts I would have shared at the time. You don't want to hurt anyone's feelings. The fellow that directed that film was doing his best. But when you don't have any time and you don't have any money, there's only so much you can do no matter how talented you are."

The Blob. *Photo from the author's collection.*

The Blob

The Blob (1958) was the brainchild of two men: a film distributor named Jack H. Harris and the head of visual aids for the Boy Scouts of America, Irvine H. Millgate, The story they cooked up is so simple it seems like anyone could have thought of it. An indestructible blob from outer space eats people and gets bigger. That's it. Theodore Simonson fleshed out their story and Kate Phillips gave it a polish. The authority figures in their scenario aren't anything like the ones in *Invasion of the Saucer-Men*. They work with the teenagers to tackle the menace.

The picture was directed by Irvin S. Yeahworth in three weeks at a cost of $128,000. Yeahworth, a maker of 16 mm religious shorts, put up a third of the budget, Harris put up a third, and the other third came from Mike Friedman, the owner of a company that made film reels, cans, and cases. Harris sold the picture to Paramount for $300,000, and it grossed $4 million.

The Blob could never be mistaken for a Hollywood movie. It's too rough around the edges for that, which is part of its charm. The absence of polish gives the picture a fresh, homespun quality that works to its advantage. The viewer doesn't expect as much out of it, but it delivers just the same. Steve McQueen is the star of the film, and his performance, like most of the performances, is good but uneven. The special effects usually work, and Ralph Carmichael's understated score is quite effective. Paramount jettisoned his main title theme and substituted a pop song written by Burt Bacharach and Mack David. All in all, it's a pretty good little picture. It's a shame that director Yeahworth could never get it out of low gear.

How to Make a Monster

Herman Cohen was at it again with *How to Make a Monster* (1958). A new regime takes over American International and they don't want to make any more monster movies; they want to make musicals. Makeup man Robert H. Harris is told that his services won't be needed, and he doesn't take this lying down. "I'll use the very monsters they mock to bring them to an end," he tells his sniveling assistant (Paul Brinegar). Harris has invented a foundation cream that paralyzes the will. He uses it on two young men (Gary Clarke and Gary Conway), makes them look like monsters, and orders them to kill the studio executives. After they've taken care of business, Harris invites them to his home to show them his Chamber of Horrors. He tells the boys he wants to cut off their heads to add to his wall. They don't take kindly to the idea, even for posterity, and beat a hasty retreat. Police Captain Morris Ankrum shows up in time to arrest them for murder.

The highlight of the movie is its one musical number, "You Gotta Have Ee-Ooo," written by Skip Redwine and Paul Dunlap. John Ashley sings their song surrounded by a bevy of dancing beauties. These poor ladies probably had no more than one rehearsal if that, as it takes about ten seconds before they're hopelessly out of sync. It's absolutely wonderful.

Earth vs. the Spider

In Bert Gordon's *Earth vs. the Spider* (1958), June Kenney and her boyfriend Gene Persson find her missing father's truck in a ditch. Thinking he may have been injured and crawled into a nearby cave for shelter, they enter the cave and find his shriveled corpse and a giant tarantula. They call in the authorities, who spray the spider with poison and drag the thing back to town for study. It is housed in the school gymnasium where it is brought back to life by the throbbing rhythm of a rock and roll band.

Three years after he made *The Spider*, Bert Gordon took Jim Nicholson and Sam Arkoff to court. Arkoff blamed Bert's wife for this just as he blamed Alex Gordon's wife for the trouble they'd had with Alex. Both men claimed that Nicholson and Arkoff were diverting the profits from their pictures to their other production companies.

Sam Arkoff said, "We would determine what production company we would use by the state of the profit and loss division. In other words, whenever a picture would get into a certain kind of profit, or it would begin to pay off profits, then you had to pay taxes above the minimum level of taxes. Then we'd dump another picture to be made in that corporation. So we'd get a new write-off coming very quickly because we made the picture so fast and got 'em out so fast. This is how the thing would work, in essence, like revolving companies."

So Bert and Alex were right; Jim and Sam were playing the old shell game. Wow, like, I mean Disappointmentville. Who would have thought there were crooks working in the motion picture business?

Arkoff said that he begged Alex Gordon not to leave, but Ronnie Ashcroft was standing outside Jim Nicholson's office one afternoon when he heard Nicholson and Arkoff trying to figure out a way to get rid of Alex. As it turned out, they got rid of just about everybody. The company had reached the point where they had to make better pictures to survive and there was no place for people who complained about being cheated.

Sometime in the 1980s, a Los Angeles TV station aired a week-long tribute to AIP, and actress Shelley Winters was on hand the night they screened *Bloody Mama* (1970). She took the opportunity to publicly remind Arkoff that she was still waiting for her share of the profits on the picture. She's probably still waiting. Jack Rabin always wondered how a picture made as cheaply as *Viking Women and the Sea Serpent* (1958) could never turn a profit. Edward Bernds said he never saw a dime from the two pictures he made until they were sold to television; Jim and Sam needed his signature to close the deal.

Edward Bernds said, "I had to sign away my residual rights or I wouldn't get my money. I could have taken them to court, but it would have been tied up in litigation for years. Sometimes you just had to take what you could get."

Sid Pink's lawyer believed that a picture could play in every theater in the world and never show a profit, judging by the way Jim and Sam kept their books. Roger Corman, who always maintained that AIP was an honest company, finally admitted in a recent interview that there were two sets of books.

The Headless Ghost and Ghost of Dragstrip Hollow

By 1959, the teenage monster movie had worn out its welcome. AIP brought it to a close with two laugh-free comedies, *The Headless Ghost* and *Ghost of Dragstrip Hollow*. The first picture was hastily put together by Herman Cohen to package with a bigger picture he was making at the time. The less said about it the better. Even Cohen didn't like it.

The second picture, written by Lou Rusoff, was a mixed bag of drag racing, ghosts, gags, and songs. It was a sort of trial run for the later Frankie and Annette beach party movies, the sort of musicals the studio moguls in *How to Make a Monster* had been talking about. The movie ends with one of the silliest denouements ever committed to film. Playing himself, Paul Blaisdell admits that he is the one responsible for the mysterious things the kids had seen because AIP wouldn't let him be in *Horrors of the Black Museum*.

Half sheet poster for The Headless Ghost.*(1959). Photo from the author's collection.*

Blaisdell was another casualty in Nicholson's and Arkoff's housecleaning. Only Roger Corman remained, and he would be instrumental in helping AIP upgrade its image. The company couldn't stay alive with the cheap combinations any more. They needed to make films that were good enough to play as single attractions. Corman was going to make Edgar Allan Poe's *House of Usher*

(1960) in color and CinemaScope to see if they could get away with it. Daniel Haller, Corman's art director, didn't agree with Nicholson and Arkoff's decision to use the sets from *Dragstrip Hollow* for what was supposed to be their first picture with class.

Dan Haller recalled, "...Jim and Sam went to Europe on a buying spree. At the same time, they still owed Roger some dough and Roger was kind of pissed off at them. So Roger said to me, 'Let's really spend some money and make this a good film.' Then I told Roger about what Jim and Sam wanted me to do, which was to re-use the old sets, which I thought would look really shitty. Roger said, 'All right, let's pull out all the stops. Spend $5,000!' So I went over to Universal and for $2,000 we were able to rent three horse trucks full of scenery and eventually piece it all together and make it into something that looked fairly good."[1]

Teenagers from Outer Space

Teenagers from Outer Space (1959) wanted to use our planet as a breeding ground for something that looks suspiciously like a giant lobster. They're a miserable bunch, these invaders. They talk like robots and give the impression they have never known or ever will know a moment of joy, which is pretty much the way you'll feel if you watch more than five minutes of this movie. It will fail to meet your lowest expectation and the blame falls on the shoulders of Tom Graeff, who wrote, produced, and directed it.

The Shaggy Dog

The time couldn't have been better for a parody of these teenage monster movies when Walt Disney made *The Shaggy Dog* (1959), but Disney—the most conservative studio in Hollywood—was still making family films. *The Shaggy Dog* was pretty much what you would expect: a very broad fantasy-comedy with Fred MacMurray as an ex-mailman who hates dogs. Tommy Kirk was his son, turned into a Bratislavian sheepdog by a spell that can only be broken by an act of heroism. Written by Bill Walsh and Lillie Hayward, and directed by comedy veteran Charles Barton, it was a pretty sorry affair, but a smash hit nevertheless, grossing well over $9 million.

Teenage Zombies

There's an old adage in Hollywood: No one ever set out to make a bad movie. It should be added that there were plenty of people who never set out to make a good one, either, and Jerry Warren was one of those people. Using the name Jacques Lecotier, Warren wrote *Teenage Zombies* (1959) in a week and took even less time to shoot it.

Katherine Victor plays Dr. Myra, working feverishly in her island laboratory to create a nerve gas that will turn people into zombie-like slaves. With a little help from her pet gorilla and her goon, she captures four teenagers (Don Sullivan, Mitzi Alpertson, Paul Pepper, and Bri Murphy), tosses them into cages, and plans to use them as guinea pigs.

Bri Murphy said, "I'm telling you, Ed Wood had nothing on Jerry Warren! I saw *Ed Wood* and I said, 'What's the fuss about? We did crazier stuff than this!' Jerry makes Ed Wood look like Mother Teresa, doesn't he?"[2]

As the decade came to an end, youth-rebellion films were ultimately replaced by the wholesomeness of the *Beach Party* series and Elvis Presley's post-army musicals. The phony baloney payola scandal put an end to rock and roll music for a while, and the new singing idols were clean-cut, all-American kids. And look what happened to Elvis; the Army turned him into Dan Dailey.

And what happened to American International Pictures? Roger Corman's *House of Usher* was a huge success, both critically and commercially. The company continued to grow and the Nicholsons and the Arkoffs were flying high. They spent the holidays together. They went on vacations together. They did lots of things together. That all changed when Nicholson fell in love with a young actress named Susan Hart.

There was a tearful picture of Nicholson's wife, Sylvia, taken outside the courtroom on the day she filed for divorce. She got half of Nicholson's AIP stock in the settlement, which put Arkoff in the driver's seat. He used his new power to get even with Nicholson for breaking up the family. Important meetings were held without Jim's knowledge. Major decisions were made without his input. Disgusted and fed up, Nicholson cut his work days short. "If Sam wants to run the company by himself, let him," he told Susan. Still not satisfied, Arkoff wouldn't let Susan Hart appear in any AIP movies. "No nepotism at AIP," he told the press, ignoring the six years that his brother-in-law wrote and produced movies for the company. For Nicholson, it was the last straw. He left the company, signed a six-picture deal with 20th Century-Fox, produced one movie, and died from a brain tumor before it was released.

AIP continued to flourish. In 1976, it merged with Filmways—a merger that pushed Arkoff out of the driver's seat. Five months later, Arkoff resigned, and he spent the rest of his life rewriting AIP's history with some success. Arkoff's name now precedes Nicholson's name in articles written by people who don't know any better. Arkoff's self-serving remarks are never questioned.

Arkoff was never a filmmaker. He was a dealmaker. The only time he was on a set was when there was trouble. Nicholson was the creative member of the team. He was the one who cooked up the titles and initiated the projects, and he was the one most often quoted by the press. Arkoff would get his two cents in every now and then, but for the most part, he was content to play the cigar-chomping mogul who didn't give a damn what anybody thought of their films, expressing contempt for what he called arty-farty types. Once he had his money, however, Arkoff changed his tune. He wanted respect and, furthermore, he wanted to be thought of as a filmmaker. People wrote books about Roger Corman, but they weren't writing books about Sam Arkoff. So, he wrote his own book and took credit for everything. Quotes that had previously been attributed to Jim Nicholson were suddenly coming out of Arkoff's mouth.

Jim? Jim who? Oh, Nicholson, sure, great guy and a great title man—best in the business. Once in a while, he was a big help around here.

Roger Corman said, "Some people tell you they're not interested in commercial success and that all they want to do is good work and I think for the most part, those people are not being honest. Then there are people who tell you they're only after commercial success and that they don't care about the quality of their films and I don't think those people are telling the truth, either. I think they care very much. They just don't want to admit it."

Notes:
1. French, Lawrence. "*California Gothic, The Corman/Haller Collaboration,*" Video Watchdog No. 138, pg. 19.
2. Weaver, Tom. *Monsters, Mutants and Heavenly Creatures*, Midnight Marquee Press, Baltimore, MD, pg. 158.

CHAPTER EIGHT
The Hand is At Your Throat!

*The Tingler will break loose in the theatre while
you are in the audience. As you enter the theatre you
will receive instructions... how to guard yourself against
attack by THE TINGLER!*
—Columbia Publicity

The first old-fashioned horror film to come out of Hollywood since 1946 was written by Curt Siodmak, whose credits include *The Wolf Man* (1941), *I Walked with a Zombie* (1943), and *The Beast with Five Fingers* (1946). Siodmak wrote a psychological horror piece called *A Face in the Water* in which a surly plantation foreman murders his boss for his wife and his money. A witness to the crime puts a hex on him. "Cursed shall be the murderer these eyes have seen. Cursed shall be the mind of the wrongdoer. He shall be like an animal that haunts the jungle... the jungle shall haunt him to his death." Sure enough, the killer loses

Barbara Payton wonders what's happening to Raymond Burr. Photo courtesy of Bob Villard.

interest in the woman he murdered for and spends most of his time cavorting with the jungle wildlife. On one of his nightly prowls, he is horrified by his reflection in a pool of water. The audience was not supposed to see his reflection, leaving them to wonder if he was actually becoming an animal or simply suffering from a delusion created by a guilty conscience.

Curt Siodmak wrote the script so he could direct it. He wanted to show his brother Robert—a successful director of stylish film noirs—that he could do it too. Jack Broder liked Siodmak's script, but he wanted him to make one itty-bitty compromise. Instead of all of this silly ambiguity, he wanted the plantation foreman to turn into a gorilla.

Bride of the Gorilla

Barbara Payton was the principal asset of *Bride of the Gorilla* (1951), although she was an actress better known for her sexual escapades and hard drinking than she was her acting. She was under contract to Jack Warner, who didn't like all of the adverse publicity she was generating. To teach her a lesson, and hopefully bring her back into line, he loaned her to Broder.

Raymond Burr was desperate when he auditioned for the part of Payton's lover. He promised to slim down, but Broder didn't think he could do it. Payton threatened to walk off the picture unless Broder gave him a chance: an act of kindness for which Burr was forever grateful. Their performances are the best thing about this silly, highly compromised horror melodrama. As for Curt Siodmak's direction, let us be charitable and simply say he posed no threat to his brother.

Bela Lugosi Meets a Brooklyn Gorilla

Duke Mitchell and Sammy Petrillo were a couple of low-rent comedians who did an impersonation of the decade's most popular comedy team, Dean Martin and Jerry Lewis. Jack Broder thought they were hysterical and starred them in *Bela Lugosi Meets a Brooklyn Gorilla* (1952), a movie written to showcase their talents. Jerry Lewis got wind of what Broder was up to and stormed into his office and the two got into a screaming match. Hal Wallis had Martin and Lewis under contract. He offered to buy the negative from Broder so he could burn it. Broder was willing to sell it to him, but, unfortunately, the two men couldn't agree on a price.

Mitchell and Petrillo play themselves in the film, on their way back from entertaining the troops in Guam. They fall out of their plane and find themselves on a South Sea Island, where Bela has developed a formula that can turn men into apes, and Mitchell becomes his first victim. It all turns out to be a dream, a very unfunny dream.

The director of this $100,000, seven-day jungle epic was William "one shot" Beaudine. No stranger to bottom-of-the-bucket productions, Beaudine began his career in silent films—a career that was derailed by the 1929 stock market crash. He migrated to England, and when he returned to Hollywood, the only work he could find was on poverty row quickies. At one time, he wanted to be the world's best director. With that avenue closed to him, he decided to be the world's fastest director. An executive from the front office once came to the set of one of his five-day sagebrush sagas and told the director to hurry up. Confused, Beaudine looked at the man and said, "You mean somebody is actually waiting for this crap?"

Boris Karloff

Scared Stiff (1953), starring the real Dean Martin and Jerry Lewis, was a limp remake of a Bob Hope comedy called *The Ghost Breakers* (1940). Both films were directed by the underrated George Marshall, who should have let sleeping dogs lie. Audiences were better served by a pair of Victorian costume melodramas from Universal, both featuring Boris Karloff in supporting roles.

Karloff was Charles Laughton's servant in *The Strange Door* (1951), based on Robert Louis Stevenson's "The Sire de Maletroit's Door." Laughton is a seething ball of hate who doesn't take rejection well. For twenty years, his brother (Paul Cavanagh) has been a prisoner in his dungeon—his punishment for marrying the woman that Laughton loved. Laughton forces his niece (Sally Forrest) to marry a scoundrel (Richard Stapley) who he hopes will ruin her life. Apparently, producer Ted Richmond and director Joseph Pevney were either unable or didn't care to stop Laughton from climbing the walls. His performance is outrageous and wonderful.

Pevney was supposed to direct *The Black Castle* (1952). This time, Karloff was a doctor in the service of another revenge-seeking swine, this time played by Stephen McNally. Pevney was assigned to another picture at the last minute and was replaced by Academy Award winning art director Nathan Juran. Jerry Sackheim wrote both pictures, and this one is slightly better than *The Strange Door*. Right off the bat, the audience sees Richard Greene and Paula Corday in their coffins, minutes away from being buried alive. We know they're alive because we hear Greene's thoughts, and in a flashback we learn how he came to be in such a precarious position.

Nathan Juran said, "The big problem I had on that picture was when the producer wanted a shot of Richard Greene with the leopard. He didn't want to use a double or any camera tricks. I didn't think it was such a good idea, but I told the trainer to convince Greene that it was. The trainer told him that the animal played with little children in the park in Thousand Oaks and that it was harmless. Greene agreed to do the shot and when it was over, the trainer shook his hand. 'I really admire you for doing that,' he told him. Greene said, 'What did I do? It was no big thing. You told me yourself that the animal is tame as a kitten.' 'Yeah,' the trainer replied, 'but you never know with an animal like that.'"

As seven million television sets found their way into homes each year, studio moguls began to panic. Between 1950 and 1953, over three thousand hardtops closed their doors. One writer glibly suggested that the exhibitors should run movies in the streets to drive people back into the theaters. Vested interests accused television of rotting people's minds, as if all of the junk movies that the studios cranked out were somehow elevated to an educational status by virtue of being shown on a larger screen. Characters in movies took potshots at the new medium. In *All That Heaven Allows* (1955), the television became the last refuge of lonely women and looked very much like the Grim Reaper as it was rolled into Jane Wyman's home. In Arch Obler's *The Twonky* (1953), a TV sprouts legs and follows Hans Conried everywhere he goes, making his life miserable. Why Obler, a man who'd made his reputation as a radio writer, would feel so hostile to the new medium is puzzling. Radio shows like *Dragnet, Our Miss Brooks, Gunsmoke*, and dozens of others became staples of early television. Old radio scripts were recycled for the new medium, which, in those days, was little more than a radio with pictures. Obler was responsible for starting the short cycle of 3-D movies that effectively kicked off a new wave of horror films.

Julian and Milton Gunzburg developed "Natural Vision 3-Dimension," but they couldn't get any of the studios interested in it until Obler used it to shoot *Bwana Devil*, a low rent jungle adventure, independently financed and distributed. It opened in two Los Angeles theaters, and business was so good that United Artists quickly stepped in and took over the distribution. After it grossed $15 million, Universal, Columbia, and Warner Brothers tripped over each other in a race to produce the first "major studio" 3-D film.

House of Wax

Warner's *House of Wax* (1953) was a remake of the studio's *Mystery of the Wax Museum* (1933). It starred Vincent Price as a brilliant sculptor, horribly disfigured by a fire set by his greedy business partner. Price's wax figures are destroyed along with his ability to recreate them, so he murders people who look like his old statues and covers them with wax. Phyllis Kirk is to be his Marie Antoinette, rescued from her wax bath at the last possible second by Frank Lovejoy and an army of policemen.

The critics were not happy with the film. *The New York Times's* Bosley Crowther called it "a bundle of horrifying claptrap." In *Commonweal*, John P. Sisk grumbled: "When audience and actors intermingle, the essential tension breaks down; the result may be orgy, nightmare, or ecstasy, but it is not drama." Writing in the *New Republic*, Parker Tyler felt that 3-D challenged the frontiers

Phyllis Kirk is lost in the House of Wax.*(1953). Photo courtesy of Bob Villard.*

of esthetic experience and put into question "the disputed margin between pornography and artistic representation."

But critics have little effect on a film like this. In the first week of its release, *House of Wax* broke house records in Detroit and Chicago, and was the number one box office attraction for four straight weeks nationwide. Made for $685,000, the movie earned over $2 million in the first month, which was an incredible sum when one considers there were only 2,000 theaters that could show 3-D movies at the time.

A Bucket of Blood

Six years later, Roger Corman made a black comedy version of *House of Wax* called *A Bucket of Blood* (1959), and it was the most incisive study of the beat generation to come out of Hollywood either before or since.

Disillusioned by war and the industrial revolution, the beat generation rejected materialism, mainstream religion, and politics. They'd abandoned the American Dream and went looking for one of their own. They smoked dope, wore sandals, listened to jazz, and spouted free-form poetry. For the most part, these bohemians were ignored

Dick Miller and "Murdered Man" from A Bucket of Blood *(1959). Photo from the author's collection.*

by the media except as comic foils. They were often called Beatniks: a play on the Soviet satellite Sputnik.

Corman shot his film in five days for $50,000 on sets left over from *Diary of a High School Bride* (1959). It was written by Charles Griffith, who was a bit of a bohemian himself. The characters in his script sit around a bleak little coffee house called The Yellow Door, eating wheat germ bagels while they listen to the resident bitter poet and prophet, Maxwell Brock (Julian Burton). Amidst the marijuana smoke moves Walter Paisley (Dick Miller), the Yellow Door's not-so-bright busboy. Walter wants to be an artist so that he can make a lot of money and marry Carla (Barboura Morris). One night, as he hopelessly attempts to sculpt a bust of his lady love, he hears the cries of his landlady's cat trapped in the wall. Using a knife to rip the wall apart, he accidentally stabs the cat. As he grieves over the animal's death, he recalls one of Brock's poems, "Let them die, and by their miserable deaths become the clay with his hands that he might form an ashtray or an ark." Walter covers the cat with clay, knife and all, and takes "Dead Cat" to the Yellow Door. "Why'd you stick a knife in it?" Leonard de Santis (Anthony Carbone) asks. Leonard is his boss. Walter innocently replies, "I didn't mean to." The cat is put on display at The Yellow Door and Walter becomes a minor celebrity. One of his fans (Jhean Burton) slips him a pack of heroin to show her appreciation. Walter has no idea what heroin is. An undercover cop (Burt Convey) sees the exchange and follows Walter home to arrest him. Confused and frightened, Walter splits the cop's skull with a frying pan and covers his body with clay. He shows "Murdered Man" to Carla and Leonard. Carla is impressed, but Leonard is appalled. Quite by accident, he discovered there was a cat beneath the clay, something that Walter assumed everyone knew all along. Leonard is ready to phone the police when an art collector (Bruno Ve Sota) offers him $500 for the cat. Greed overrides Leonard's morality; he gives Walter $50, pockets the rest, and remains silent as the body count continues to rise.

The Maze

Allied Artists entered the 3-D race with *The Maze* (1953), written by Dan Ulman and directed by William Cameron Menzies. Richard Carlson starred as Gerald MacTeam, who was urgently summoned to Craven, the family castle in Scotland, shortly before his marriage to Kitty Murray (Veronica Hurst). In a letter, he cancels their engagement without an explanation. She goes to the castle and finds him curiously aged and very cranky. He wants her to leave, but she insists on staying. She's locked in her bedroom at night and hears strange noises outside of her door. Through her window, she sees a maze of shrubbery surrounding a pond. Someone or something is moving through the maze, but she can't tell what it is. One night, she sneaks out of the house, gets lost in the maze, and encounters a giant frog. The frog makes a beeline for the castle and leaps out of the highest window to its death. MacTeam explains that the frog was actually Sir Roger Phillip MacTeam, born April 5th, 1750. "The human embryo goes through all stages of evolution," he tells Kitty. "At one point the embryo is an amphibian. Sir Roger never developed beyond that stage physically... but he continued to grow and develop mentally." What Gerald does not explain is why he didn't tell Kitty the truth in the first place. Why all of the secrecy? And what kind of a moron would sacrifice his life for the sake of an overgrown, selfish frog. The more you think about this picture, the more ridiculous it is. And it's boring.

The Mad Magician

Bryan Foy and Crane Wilbur, the producer and the writer of *House of Wax*, concocted another 3-D vehicle for Vincent Price called *The Mad Magician* (1954). Again, Price is a victim-turned-killer, only this time, all of the characters he murders have it coming. His boss, Donald Randolph, has tied Price to a contract that prevents him from performing his own stunts, even the ones created on his own time. He's victim number one. Randolph ran off with Price's wife, Eva Gabor, who is delighted to learn that Price killed her husband. The only reason she married him was for his money. She's victim number two. John Emery suspects that Price murdered his business partner, but is willing to keep quiet about it so long as he can keep Price under his thumb. He's victim number three. It isn't as good as *House of Wax*, but it's a lot of fun nevertheless, and Price gives the kind of over-the-top performance that ultimately made him the decade's number one horror star—a title he held throughout the sixties.

Phantom of the Rue Morgue and Gorilla at Large

Phantom of the Rue Morgue, based on Edgar Allan Poe's *Murders in the Rue Morgue*, and *Gorilla at Large* (both 1954) proved that you can never have enough gorilla movies. In the first film, Karl Malden chews up the scenery, as only he can do, as the madman who uses a gorilla to murder the women who reject him.

"It was a silly picture," Malden recalled. "It was one of those 3-D pictures that were so popular at the time. Merv Griffin had a part in it. We all went on to better things."

Gorilla at Large was filmed at the Nu Pike amusement park in Long Beach, California—a location used for the climax of *The Beast from 20,000 Fathoms*. In its heyday during the forties, The Pike was quite a place, with rides, attractions, a ballroom, and a plunge. But in the fifties, it became dirty and seedy, and was hardly competition for the newer, cleaner amusement parks like Disneyland and Knotts Berry Farm. By the mid-sixties, it became a sleazy hangout for sailors

Delores Dorn is about to wrestle with the Phantom of the Rue Morgue*(1954). Photo courtesy of Bob Villard.*

and unsavory characters—hardly a place you'd want to take your family unless you were broke. Walking along the boardwalk, a sign above one of the hamburger joints boasted that it was "always a safe place to eat," while one of the tattoo parlors had a sign in the window that read, "We tattooed your dad." As you climbed that first big hill on the roller-coaster, the sight of several dead cars hidden beneath the tracks was nothing short of alarming. Every time you took one of the hairpin corners, you wondered if your car might leave the tracks and go sailing into the ocean. The bumper cars were a lot safer and were a lot of fun if you didn't mind getting a little grease on your clothes. They were the old-fashioned ones without all of the padding; the kind where you really got a jolt when someone smacked you.

By the late sixties, the Pike was all but forgotten until a TV crew filming an episode of *The Six Million Dollar Man* discovered the mummified body of bank robber Elmer McCurdy covered in wax hanging in the Laff in the Dark ride. It wasn't the sort of publicity that would lure middle class families back to the park.

By 1955, the 3-D cycle had run its course. Some historians blamed the headaches caused by the Polaroid glasses, but the real culprit was the cost of exhibiting 3-D movies. Already feeling the pinch of a dwindling audience, exhibitors were asked to shell out a small fortune for new high-reflection screens, special lenses, and dual-projector systems. Toss in the expense of wiring theaters for stereo sound and the tab was astronomical. And while Warner Brothers was pushing 3-D, 20th Century-Fox was promoting CinemaScope—the studio's new widescreen format, often called the poor man's Cinerama. Nobody knew which process was going to win the battle and the poor exhibitors were caught in the middle.

In a self-serving remark, Fox's Darryl Zanuck said that any process that needed glasses was bound to fail. As Fox stood to make a lot of money by leasing their CinemaScope lenses to other studios at $25,000 a pop, his opinion was more than a little suspect. Zanuck insisted that movies needed width, not depth, a remark open to interpretation.

Bud Abbott and Lou Costello meet the mummy. "Some kids got scared and screamed their lungs out," said exhibitor Harry Hawkson, "but then there was the sound of laughter." Photo from the author's collection.

Abbott and Costello Meet the Mummy

Following the success of *Abbott and Costello Meet Frankenstein* (1948), Bud and Lou met everyone from Captain Kidd to the Keystone Cops and just about every monster in Universal's archive. By the time they met the mummy, the comedians had worn out their welcome. *Abbott and Costello Meet the Mummy* (1955) was their last movie for Universal. Bud and Lou had exhausted all of their old vaudeville routines, which had always been the highlight of their films. Aside from answering the burning question of how a shovel can be a pick, there isn't much to say about their mummy movie. It's full of recycled gags that give it a sort of window-worn look. In most markets, it played as a second feature.

Cult of the Cobra

U-I's *Cult of the Cobra* (1954), also released as a second feature, proved to be one of the studio's more satisfying horror entries, and was much better than the movie it supported. On leave in Asia, six soldiers infiltrate a secret religious ceremony of a cult that believes people can transform into snakes. They're discovered when one of them (James Dobson) takes a flash picture of the cere-

Faith Domergue. Photo courtesy of Bob Villard.

mony. "The Cobra Goddess will avenge herself! One by one you will die!" warns the high priest (Ed Platt). Dobson is bitten by a cobra and rushed to the hospital. He's on his way to recovery when a second bite kills him. "Only a snake with a brain could have got into that ward last night and singled out that same kid," the doctor concludes. Dobson isn't the last of the soldiers to die and in some respects, the disrespectful louts have it coming. They were warned what would happen if they were caught. "What will they try to do, kill us?" David Janssen asked the Hindu they bribed to sneak them into the temple. "The word *try* is unnecessary. They *will* kill you," he assured them. During their escape from the temple, they kill one of the guards and set fire to the place. And Dobson stole the basket that held the snake that bit him.

Faith Domergue is the Cobra Goddess who follows the boys back to the States to punish them. She takes up residence in the apartment across the way from Marshall Thompson, who has just been told that his girlfriend, Kathleen Hughes, plans to marry his best friend, Richard Long. He needs a relationship so desperately that he forces himself on Domergue, becoming possessive and demanding and, like her, a stalker. Long senses that there's something peculiar about Domergue, but he's hardly in a position to suggest that Thompson use a little restraint. Thompson is so blinded by his need for a female prop, he wouldn't have listened anyway.

Miss Domergue was studio hopping when she made this picture: finishing a western at Republic during the day while working on this picture at night. It's one of her best performances.

The Cat Girl

The transformation of an alluring female into a murdering creature is also the subject of *The Cat Girl* (1957), a low-key British remake of Val Lewton's *The Cat People* (1942), and a joint effort between Anglo-Amalgamated in England and American International in America. AIP gave Anglo a script by Lou Rusoff and his services as an executive producer. His primary job was to make sure the picture wasn't too British. The audience would have been better served if he'd made sure it wasn't too boring.

The Black Sleep

The Black Sleep (1956) was a throwback to the horror films of the forties, and was set in 1870s England, sporting the biggest horror cast anyone had seen since *Abbott and Costello Meet Frankenstein*. Basil Rathbone played a surgeon who was obsessed with curing his comatose wife of her brain tumor. His experiments result in a cellar full of brain-damaged maniacs, including Lon Chaney, Bela Lugosi, Tor Johnson, and John Carradine. "Down with the infidels!" Carradine roars as he leads a revolt against Rathbone, looking as if

Above: Patricia Blair is menaced by Lon Chaney, John Carradine, Tor Johnson, George Sawaya, and Sally Yarnell in The Black Sleep *(1956). Below: Kurt Katch and Alvaro Guillot from* Pharaoh's Curse *(1957).. Photos courtesy of Bob Villard.*

he just stepped off the set of *The Ten Commandments*. It's a climax that doesn't come any too soon.

Bela Lugosi and Tor Johnson went on a promotional tour for the picture, and to save money, they stayed in the same hotel rooms. Lugosi had recently gone through the cure for his drug addiction and it had taken its toll, leaving him as hardy as an empty paper sack. Night after night, he complained about his non-speaking role in the picture and life in general. He told Johnson he wanted to kill himself. One night, fed up with Lugosi's whining, the 400-pound ex-wrestler picked up Lugosi and dangled him out of their eighth-floor window. "You want to die?" Johnson asked. "Just say the word and I'll let you go!"

Pharaoh's Curse

Pharaoh's Curse (1957) was a pseudo-mummy movie directed by Lee "Roll 'em" Sholem. Sholem spent one location-day chasing the sun from one end of Death Valley to the other, and shooting what amounted to the first fifteen minutes of the picture. Mark Dana is the hero of the piece, ordered to rescue some archeologists from the Valley of the Kings. He arrives shortly after the infidels have opened the tomb of a high priest, whose spirit enters the body of Alvaro Guillot and (like my interview with Arthur Franz) it ages him terribly. As Guillot's body rots, he goes on a murder spree. Ambling away from one of his victims, he is about to make his escape through a secret tunnel in the catacombs when Dana grabs his arm. It snaps off in his hand like a dry twig. It's the most memorable moment in the picture, but one can't help but wonder how someone so brittle could possibly kill anyone. Sorry. We forgot. You don't question art.

Mark Dana has all of the warmth and charm of a gas cap. If he were any stiffer, he wouldn't be able to walk. He was much better as Mr. Clean and the Man from Labatts on some early sixties TV commercials. As Simira, the Cat Goddess, Ziva Shapir is appropriately aloof, while the rest of the cast is simply okay. Les Baxter's atmospheric score helps.

Voodoo Island

A developer sends Boris Karloff to *Voodoo Island* (1957) to see if it's a safe place to build a hotel. It isn't. Some of the people who accompany Karloff on this expedition are eaten by the hungry plants that pepper the place. Voodoo chief Frederich Ledebur sends Karloff, and what's left of his entourage, back to the States with a message for the developer: We don't want your stinking hotel. The only thing this exercise in tedium has going for it is location filming in Kauai. Naturally, when you go to a lush and colorful location like that, you make your movie in black and white.

The Naked Jungle

Carl Stephenson's short story and radio play, "Leiningen Versus the Ants," was the basis of George Pal's exciting *The Naked Jungle* (1954)—one of the producer's best and least talked about films. Charlton Heston played Leiningen, a fearless man who tries to save his plantation from a swarm of army ants known as Marabunta. "You're up against a monster twenty miles long and two miles wide! Forty square miles of agonizing death! You can't stop it!" district commissioner William Conrad tells him. Conrad played Leiningen in 1948 when the story was adapted for the radio.

A mail-order bride was added to Stephenson's story by screenwriters Ben Maddow and Ranald MacDougall. (Maddow was on the blacklist at the time, so writer Philip Yordan was happy to take some of the money and all of the credit for his work.) Eleanor Parker played the bride and she's every bit as tough as Charlton Heston's self-made, self-righteous Leiningen.

The New York Times said, "It is a tight dramatic conflict between Mr. Heston as the plantation master and Eleanor Parker as the wife he has imported, sight unseen—a real psychological situation between an egoist and his mail-order bride. And with him getting steamed because the lady turns out to have been married before and her showing baffled indignation in a two-person war of nerves, this becomes a quite interesting conflict, based on the husband's vanity."

The Naked Jungle was quite a surprise for this 11-year-old kid, who had no idea what the film was about. Halfway through the story, Charlton Heston pulls the hat off John Dierke's corpse, which has been eaten by the army ants. I knew I was in good hands. There are even a couple of shots of stop-motion ants!

Curucu, Beast of the Amazon

Curt Siodmak went to Brazil to make *Curucu, Beast of the Amazon* (1956) in color, starring Beverly Garland and John Bromfield. Siodmak claims he never physically recovered from making the picture and it serves him right. I was nine years old when I saw it and it taught me a valuable lesson, one that every kid who grew up in the fifties had to learn in order to survive: keep your expectations low.

Usually, you had to wait thirty or forty minutes before you got to see the monster, but Curucu showed up in the first three minutes, and what a disappointment he was. He looked as if he'd just stepped out of a Mardi Gras parade. Oh well, you say to yourself, there's nothing to do but accept it. But later, *much* later, when Curucu is cornered and staring down the barrel of John Bromfield's rifle, he removes his head and we see that it's Tom Payne, one of the characters in the film.

"BOOOOOOOOO!"

Snack bar items were hurled at the screen in mass. Never in my life had I seen an audience so angry. Nobody heard why Payne was masquerading as a monster. Nobody cared. We'd been had. Universal had taken our money under false pretenses and there was nothing we could do about it. It was, in essence, a cinematic mugging. Adding insult to injury, the lousy movie wasn't over. There

John Bromfield, Beverly Garland, and Curucu, one of the all-time stinkers. Photo from the author's collection.

Beverly Garland from Curucu, Beast of the Amazon (1956). Photo courtesy of Gary Smith.

was still another thirty minutes to go because Miss Garland had yet to learn the secret of tissue shrinking from the headhunters. Whether she did or didn't was of no concern to me. I preferred to spend those thirty minutes watching the traffic outside of the theater, waiting for my ride home.

Beverly Garland said, "There was a scene I had to do with a boa constrictor where it was supposed to be squeezing me to death. I was told to hold the head with one hand and its tail with the other while it was wrapped around me so it couldn't constrict. Curt Siodmak yelled for 'Action!' So I began rolling, kicking, and screaming and suddenly Curt jumped up and told the cameraman to stop shooting. I asked: 'Why did you stop the camera?' And he said he thought the snake was killing me. And I said, 'Jesus Christ! Isn't that what you wanted? Aren't I supposed to act? Let's do it and get this thing off of me!' Then there was the scene where John [Bromfield] and I are captured by a bunch of natives and we escape when the village catches fire. When they shot the flamethrowers at the huts, they went up like whoosh! I turn around and John is gone. I mean he just took off. And I thought to myself, *This is it, Bev. You're going to die.* I broke into a run and went right through the fire. I singed my hair and my eyebrows. I hope to Christ they got it on film."

Voodoo Woman

There is nothing quite as exciting as a jungle movie shot entirely indoors on a sound stage the size of a two-car garage. *Voodoo Woman* (1957), starring Marla English, Mike Connors, and Tom Conway, is such a movie. It was written by Russ Bender, produced by Alex Gordon, and directed by that master of inertia, Edward L. Cahn. Conway, looking comatose and ridiculous in a fuzzy headpiece, is collaborating with a witch doctor to create an indestructible, obedient female. Once he's successful, he intends to march her down the hallowed halls of the universities that had mocked him to show the fools who called him mad that he's even madder than they thought. But first, he has to find the right woman to work his magic on: a woman who will kill for him. Ruthless sociopath English comes to the village looking for diamonds, and she's just what Conway has been looking for. He promises to show her where the diamonds are if only she'll be his guinea pig. He waits until after he has turned her into an indestructible monster before telling her that there are no diamonds, which proves to be a bad career move on his part.

Al Kallis art for Voodoo Woman *(1957). The critic for* Boxoffice *wrote: "Comparing this for merit with its running mate [*The Undead*] is like asking a man whether he prefers to be shot to death or hanged." Photo from the author's collection.*

Alex Gordon took his fiancée to a sneak preview of the picture, hoping to impress her. Considering how truly miserable this movie is on every possible level, it's hard to believe that he could have thought she'd be anything but depressed. But low-budget filmmakers don't think or talk about their movies the way everybody else does. They talk about the record number of set-ups they got on such and such a day or how they were able to borrow a prop from some other movie or how much money the picture made. They talk about everything but the quality of the picture. Anyone who has ever worked on a low-budget movie is probably familiar with the following statement: For the time and money and for what it was, it wasn't a bad little picture. *For what it was.* That's the escape clause. Unless we know what it was, it's a remark without meaning. If Alex Gordon could have seen *Voodoo Woman* through the eyes of his fiancée, he would have well understood why she gave him back his engagement ring.

Alex Gordon was an enthusiastic film fan who was happy to be working in the industry. He was proud that he was able to make a movie in six days for $65,000, even a movie as crummy as *Voodoo Woman.* He was a sweet guy. He was 80 years old when he died in a nursing home in 2003. Mike Connors told the *Los Angeles Times*, "Alex was a cheerful, happy-go-lucky guy, always laughing and smiling. He was one of the nicest people I've known in the business in 50 years. He was one of those guys that just ate, slept, and loved to talk movies. If you sat down and started asking questions about old movies, he was in seventh heaven."

Zombies of Mora Tau

This campaign did not appear in the pressbook for either of these movies. Photo from the author's collection.

A ship carrying a cargo of diamonds sinks along the African coast and all hands are lost at sea. They return from the dead as the *Zombies of Mora Tau* (1957). "They're still guarding those cursed diamonds," Marjorie Eaton tells Gregg Palmer. Eaton is the wife of the Captain of the sunken ship. She believes that if the diamonds are scattered to the winds, it will lift the curse and her husband will, at last, rest in peace. She hopes that Palmer will turn the diamonds over to her, but after risking his neck to get them, he wants to sell them. Eaton warns him that the zombies will find him wherever he goes. "They'll be sold in every capital in the world!" he tells her. "What will they do—picket the jewelry stores on Fifth Avenue?" Not only is his argument a good one, it could well be the plot of a sequel. In the end, the old woman's tears touch Palmer's better nature and he gives her the diamonds, which she happily scatters.

The script was written by blacklisted writer Bernard Gordon using the name Raymond T. Marcus, and is scary and exciting. But in the hands of director Edward L. Cahn, it became just another flat potboiler. In Ted Newsome's interview with Gordon, the writer recalled a scene where the zombies awkwardly rise from their coffins. Gordon thought they could shoot the scene again with the coffins in an upright position. "Look, I got six days to make a 90-minute movie," Cahn snapped. "You think I got time for retakes?" Gordon didn't realize who he was dealing with. If the zombies had taken ten minutes to climb out of those coffins, it wouldn't have made any difference to Cahn. What did he care? He manages to successfully suck the energy out of every sequence. The film plays out as if it were directed by a zombie. "It all happened so fast," one of the sailors remarks over the death of his boss. In a film where nothing happens fast, it's a line that's always good for a laugh.

From Hell It Came

Gregg Palmer was back in *From Hell It Came* (1957) as a native prince put to death for the murder of his father by the people who actually committed the crime. The conspirators want Palmer dead because he's consorting with an American atomic research team. Palmer vows that he will return from the grave and kill the people who framed him; which he does as a walking tree known to the island people as the Tabonga, a creature of revenge.

Tod Andrews, Tina Carver (who has the worst scream in the world), and the rest of the actors in this film know they've hit bottom. They're so detached from the material that they might as well have the script in their hands while they say their lines. One standout sequence has two South Sea native women (Suzanne Ridgway and Tani

The Tabonga (Chester Hayes) watches Suzanne Ridgeway sink to her death in a pit of quicksand in one of the all-time classics, From Hell It Came (1957).]

Marsh) locked in mortal combat. You've never seen a more listless struggle in your life. These two ladies are ever so careful not to injure themselves and expend so little energy that they probably could have gone at it for days if the Tabonga hadn't shown up and tossed one of them into quicksand. The survivor halfheartedly runs back to the village to report to the witch doctor (Robert Swan) that she just saw the Tabonga. The witch doctor, obviously not used to thinking on his feet, asks, "How do you know it was Tabonga?"

We confess that we don't know if it's Tabonga or Tobanga or Tabanga. The guy who narrated the trailer called it the Baranga.

> You say Tabonga and I say Tobanga,
> You say Tabanga and I say Baranga,
> Baranga, Tabanga, Tabonga, Tobanga,
> Let's call the whole thing off.

The Disembodied

The companion feature to *From Hell It Came* was *The Disembodied* (1957) with Allison Hayes as a double-dealing, cold-blooded murderer with a lot of sex appeal. "You bad, bad woman," Dean Fredericks tells her. "You think I'm bad?" she asks. He kisses her, long and hard. She slaps his face just to show him who's boss. Allison wants to kill her husband (John Wengraf), but we don't know why. We also don't know why she can't seem to do it; she has voodoo powers. We see her in action. She is, in fact, a voodoo priestess. She's in love with Paul Burke, yet she becomes excited when it looks like he might be killed by one of her zombies. She is an enigma.

The high point of the movie is the exotic dance that Miss Hayes performs with suitable abandon, choreographed by A.E. Okonu. "It never came off the way it should have," she remarked. "It came off as more of a bump and grind number instead of a voodoo dance." Before she went into her gyrations, director Walter Grauman cleared the set. Miss Hayes noticed a very serious-looking man with his arms crossed, standing in the corner. "You! Out!" she demanded. The man meekly complied. Later, she learned it was Walter Mirisch, the head of the studio.

In 1934, Alex Raymond and Don Moore created a comic strip based on the adventures of real-life hunter Jim Bradley, nicknamed Jungle Jim. Sam Katzman bought the rights to use the character in a series of low-budget programs starring Johnny Weissmuller. Weissmuller was well-known for playing Tarzan in twelve features for MGM and RKO, and though the Olympic swimming champ had gotten a little too beefy to play Tarzan, he still looked okay with his clothes on. When Katzman lost the right to use the character's name in 1954, he made three more jungle dramas with Weissmuller playing Jungle Johnny. Nobody noticed the difference. Weissmuller continued to play Jungle Jim in twenty-six episodes of a television series. One episode had Jim trapped in a cave by a giant lizard. "We'll never get out of this alive!" some guy whines. With a huge rock held above his head, ready to pitch at the lizard, Jim says to the guy, "Relax. We've been in tighter spots than this."

The Four Skulls of Jonathan Drake

The Four Skulls of Jonathan Drake (1959) was a voodoo "thriller" written by Orville H. Hampton (strike one), produced by Robert E. Kent (strike two), and directed by Edward L. Cahn (strike three. You're out!). The title implies that Jonathan Drake (Eduard Franz) is a collector of skulls, but this is not the case. He is slated to be the fourth victim of the Drake family curse. It seems that in 1759, his great-grandfather, Sir Wilfred Drake, slaughtered a tribe of Jivaro Indians. Since then, all of the Drakes have had their heads lopped off on their sixtieth birthday. Their skulls are then returned to the family vault by Zuta (Paul Wexler), the Jivaro servant of Dr. Emil Zurich (Henry Daniell), whose job it is to carry out the curse.

Other than Henry Daniell's rather fruity performance and an unsavory sequence in which he demonstrates the proper procedure for shrinking heads, the film has little to offer unless you want to hear the score from *Teenage Frankenstein* again and derive some pleasure from watching a parade of automobiles pull in and out of the Drake driveway.

Curse of the Faceless Man

"The skies have been dark since yesterday, when father returned from the Senate in Rome," Tina Enright (Elaine Edwards) says under hypnosis in *Curse of the Faceless Man* (1959). Tina is the reincarnation of the senator's daughter, Lucilla. "I feel that something is going to happen. There has been no rain, no clouds, just the gray light over Pompeii that depresses me as I look from my window and see Vesuvius. And I remember the curse placed upon my family by the slave Quintillus Aurelius."

Quintillus Aurelius was in love with Lucilla. Denied that love, his curse brings about the volcanic eruption of Vesuvius, which makes him, despite his lowly status, a pretty powerful guy—though not a very bright one. It isn't until after he's set things in motion that he realizes his precious Lucilla will probably be roasted alive unless he can take her to the ocean, where she will be safe. Before he can save her, he's covered in lava. Kept alive by the radioactivity in the ground and later revitalized by x-rays, Quintillus insists on completing his rescue mission, though he's a dollar short and 2000 years too late.

Richard Anderson delivers the worst performance of his career as the hero. He gives the impression that he thinks the film is beneath him, but if that were true, he wouldn't be in it. Edward Small was behind this picture, but he wanted no credit for the films he made at this level. His producer was Robert Kent, and Edward L. Cahn directed it. General Ankrum narrated it, but like the film's producer, he chose to remain anonymous as well.

The Curse of Frankenstein

In June of 1957, Warner Brothers released *The Curse of Frankenstein*, a so-so color version of the Mary Shelley classic by Hammer Films in England. Hammer was a small-time, family-run operation headed by Enrique Carreras and William Hinds. Enrique's son, James, was in charge of production. His son, Michael, served as an executive producer. Hind's son, Tony, was persuaded to put his writing aspirations aside and come aboard as a producer. Carreras and Hinds took a lease on a derelict house on the banks of the Thames, which became their base of operations until 1966. Known as Bray Studios, this was where director Terence Fisher, writer Jimmy Sangster, production designer Bernard Robinson, photographer Jack Asher, and composer James Bernard worked their magic. These people were the backbone of Hammer's success story. And let us not forget actor Peter Cushing, who deserved a lifetime achievement award for his ability to deliver the most outlandish gibberish with a sense of dignity and absolute conviction. At the very least, he should have been knighted for being the most beloved horror personality since Boris Karloff.

In the early part of the decade, Carreras and Hinds had a deal with American theatre owner and film distributor Robert Lippert, giving them a limited access to the U.S. market. Eliot Hyman was the one who really opened the market for them and his

Newspaper ad for The Curse of Frankenstein *(1957). Photo from the author's collection.*

continued affiliation with Hammer was instrumental in their success story. Hyman was the president of Associate Artists Productions: a successful syndicator of Hollywood films to American television. He was also co-owner of Seven Arts Productions. Hyman put up half of the money and a script by Milton Subotsky for Hammer to make a color Frankenstein movie. But Subotsky's script borrowed too heavily from Universal's Frankenstein movies and Hammer was worried about a potential lawsuit. Jimmy Sangster was asked to write a new script. Peter Cushing, who had just won a BAFTA TV award, was signed to play Baron Frankenstein. Christopher Lee, who stood six-foot-five-inches, landed the role of the monster. "I don't have any lines!" he complained to Cushing. "You're lucky," Cushing remarked. "I've seen the script."

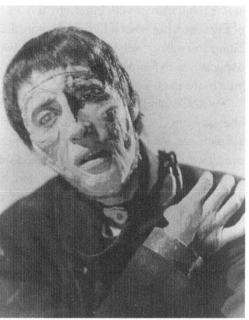

In a frame story, Victor Frankenstein has an hour before he's to meet his death on the guillotine. He hopes to convince a priest that it was his creation, not he, who committed the murders for which he is about to be executed. Yet as the story unfolds in a flashback, Frankenstein admits to killing an old man (Paul Hardtmuth) and playing a part in the murder of his servant Justine (Valerie Gaunt). It

Christopher Lee as Frankenstein's monster. *Photo courtesy of Gary Smith.*

takes Frankenstein over an hour to tell his story, which leaves the priest no time to save him even if he wanted to.

One of the film's most effective moments is the first appearance of the monster, wrapped like a mummy from head to toe. The camera moves in quickly as he dramatically rips the gauze from his hideous face. But, in retrospect, the events that lead to this frightening moment make the whole thing funny.

Frankenstein needs help to operate the machinery that will bring his creation to life, but his assistant, Paul Krempe (Robert Urquhart), has washed his hands of the blasphemous experiment. While Frankenstein attempts to cajole him back to the lab, a bolt of lightning hits a switch and starts the machinery rolling. By the time Frankenstein returns, his creation is alive and hostile. So it seems that Frankenstein didn't need Krempe's help after all and his own participation proved to be unnecessary as well.

Once Krempe opts out of Frankenstein's experiment, the scenes between the two men become repetitious and silly. Paul's continued presence in Frankenstein's home is supposedly motivated by his concern for Elizabeth (Hazel Court), Frankenstein's wife. He begs her to leave, but he won't tell her why and he won't go to the police. Why Frankenstein continues to give this spineless wimp free access to his home is a mystery. The film would have been more interesting if it had spent less time with Krempe and devoted a little more time to Frankenstein's relationships with Elizabeth and Justine. We know that Justine is jealous of Elizabeth, but what if Elizabeth shared similar feelings about Justine? A few biting and telling exchanges from these two women might have been amusing, especially with Frankenstein caught in the middle. As it stands, the women are little more than window dressing.

Peter Cushing's suave, sociopathic, and virile Frankenstein was a welcome change from Colin Clive's weak-kneed portrayal of the Baron in the old Universal pictures. While Clive preferred the company of his idiot assistant to his pretty wife, Cushing is sexually active, dividing his amorous activities between his wife and his servant. It must be said, however, that he still spends far too much time in the lab. If he really wanted to create life, he should have spent more time in the bedroom; it would have been less messy and a lot more fun.

The film opened in London a month before it played in the U.S. The critics were appalled that the film seemed to delight in showing the anatomical details as Frankenstein assembled his creation. "I put it among the half-dozen most repulsive films I have ever encountered," wrote C.A. Lejeune in the *Observer*. It broke box-office records in England, and in America it took in more than $4 million. Theaters in San Diego, Boston, Buffalo, and Hartford did a full week's business in two days! It established Hammer Films as the big Kahuna in the horror market.[1] By the time they'd completed the sequel, three studios were bidding for the distribution rights.

The Revenge of Frankenstein

The Revenge of Frankenstein (1958), distributed by Columbia, began where the previous picture left off, with Frankenstein (Cushing) headed for the guillotine. Off camera, we hear a struggle and the whack of the blade. Later, we learn that it was the priest who lost his head, shoved under the blade by a misshapen prison guard named Karl (Oscar Quitak) in exchange for the new body that Frankenstein promised him. This additional piece of information makes the frame story in the first film even more ridiculous.

Using the name Dr. Stein, Frankenstein opens a hospital for the poor in the village of Carlsbruck. Whenever he needs a part for his new creation, he simply takes it from one of the riffraff in his clinic. He is recognized by Hans Kleve (Francis

Matthews), an eager young doctor who wants to assist the Baron in any way he can. Together, they transfer Karl's brain to a new body (Michael Gwynn). When Karl learns that Frankenstein intends to put him on display for the medical world to gawk at, he takes off. His first order of business is to burn his old body. But he's caught in the act by a sadistic janitor (Richard Wordsworth), who beats him, causing damage to his brain. Karl takes on the appearance of his old, twisted self. He pushes his way into a posh dinner party and begs Frankenstein for help, calling him by name. News of Frankenstein's true identity provokes his patients to attack him, but the clever doctor has

Michael Gwynn from The Revenge of Frankenstein *(1958). Variety called it "a high grade horror film, gory enough to give adults a squeamish second thought and a thoroughly unpleasant one." Photo courtesy of Gary Smith.*

made preparations for just such an emergency. Hans transfers the Baron's brain into an artificially created look-alike body, and Dr. Frank opens a new practice in London. It's the one and only time Frankenstein's experiment doesn't end in disaster. Frankenstein becomes the living proof of what he set out to do. Apparently, he's no more interested in being a medical freak than Karl was. In lieu of presenting himself to the medical world, he continued his efforts to create an artificial man well into the next decade.

Night of the Demon/Curse of the Demon

Columbia didn't think much of *Night of the Demon* (1957). It sat on the shelf for a year before they changed the title to *Curse of the Demon*, cut thirteen minutes out of it, shuffled scenes around, and used it to support *The Revenge of Frankenstein*. Charles Bennett wrote the screenplay based on Montague James's *Casting the Runes*. Bennett sold his script to Hal Chester, who gave it to Cy Endfield for a rewrite. Endfield was on the Hollywood blacklist at the time, so Chester happily took his credit. Director Jacques Tourneur made his own changes in the script during pre-production.

Pass the parchment quick or you'll have a date with this guy.
Photo from the author's collection.

Charles Bennett said, "I think the job Jacques Tourneur did with what Hal Chester gave him was awfully good. Hal Chester, as far as I'm concerned, if he walked up my driveway right now, I'd shoot him dead."[2]

John Holden (Dana Andrews) is investigating Julian Karswell (Niall MacGinnis) and his cult of Devil worshipers. Holden doesn't know that Karswell has translated an ancient volume that has given him supernatural powers—powers he uses to force his followers to finance his extravagant lifestyle. Karswell doesn't want anyone poking into his business and has already killed Holden's colleague, Professor Henry Harrington (Maurice Denham). Harrington's niece Joanna (Peggy Cummins), knows Karswell is responsible for her uncle's supposed "accidental" death and uses her skills as a psychologist and a schoolteacher to persuade Holden that Karswell is a force to be reckoned with. And she has her work cut out for her. Holden is proud of the fact that he's "not a superstitious idiot like ninety percent of humanity." When he refuses to stop his investigation, Karswell secretly passes a parchment to him. Holden has three days to pass the parchment back to Karswell, without his knowing it, before the demon from Hell comes for him.

Tourneur believed that horror was best left to the viewer's imagination and completed the movie without ever showing the demon. Against Tourneur's wishes, Chester added the monster scenes that were probably directed by Cy Endfield. Chester's decision was probably a wise one. Tourneur may have been aiming his picture at adults, but it was the kids who paid to see it. The appearance of the monster at the beginning and end of the picture satisfied that audience and, though it wasn't Chester's intention, added a level of suspense to the rest of the picture that wouldn't have been there otherwise. The audience knows that Holden is in danger; they've seen the demon. Unless Holden can overcome his pride, he will be hoisted by his own petard. It's a terrific movie, and one that seems to get better with every viewing.

Back from the Dead

Back from the Dead (1957) was another tale of witchcraft, written by Catherine Turney from her novel *The Other One*. Peggie Castle is possessed by the spirit of her husband's previous wife, Felicia. Peggy tells her sister, Marsha Hunt, that she feels like she's "losing herself," but Hunt attributes it to her pregnancy. Apparently, Felicia wasn't a very nice person. "I loved my daughter in spite of the evil in her," her father (James Bell) tells Hunt. "But she's been dead for six years. I don't want her back."

There's one unintentionally funny moment where Arthur Franz, as Peggy's husband, forces her to listen to one of Felicia's favorite records: a reprise of the film's disturbing main title. Franz looks almost psychotic in his enjoyment of the piece, unaware that Peggy can't stand it. This is the only moment that your authors can recall with any clarity, which more than suggests that the movie is pretty low on thrills.

Arthur Franz said, "We made that picture in one or two weeks. The director was a guy named Charles Marquis Warren. He did quite well for himself as the producer and writer of *Gunsmoke*."

Bell, Book and Candle

James Stewart and Kim Novak—the stars of Alfred Hitchcock's Vertigo—were reunited for Columbia's *Bell, Book and Candle* (1958), based on the successful Broadway play by John Van Druten. Stewart was the publisher bewitched by Novak on the eve of his wedding to Janice Rule—one of Novak's enemies in college. But her sweet-revenge game backfires. She falls in love with Stewart and loses her magic powers.

The easy charm of Van Druten's play somehow got lost in the translation from stage to screen. Columbia was never very good at making comedies, especially during this period, and this one is no exception. Daniel Taradash's script is tired, and Richard Quine's direction is flat. This was Stewart's last movie as a romantic lead.

The runaway success of *The Curse of Frankenstein*, coupled with the release of Universal's classic (and not so classic) horror films to television a few months later, made the old monsters viable properties once again. The result: *Blood of Dracula, Return of Dracula, I Was a Teenage Werewolf, I Was a Teenage Frankenstein, Frankenstein's Daughter,* and Allied Artists CinemaScope production of *Frankenstein 1970* (1958).

Frankenstein 1970

As the credits come to an end on *Frankenstein 1970*, we see the names Aubrey Schenck and Howard Koch—the same guys who made *Voodoo Island*. Expectations hit rock bottom. But wait, here's Jana Lund and she's running for

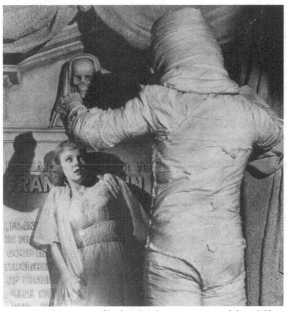

Jana Lund gets a good look at Frankenstein 1970 and doesn't like what she sees. Neither will you. Photo courtesy of Gary Smith.

her life. She looks terrified as she pauses to catch her breath and look over her shoulder at the monster coming after her. We can't see its face, but its gnarly claws are visible and its arms are riddled with stitches. At the rate it's going, dragging one leg behind it, it doesn't seem possible that it can ever overtake Jana, but never mind that. Things are looking up. Things are definitely looking up. The monster chases her into a lake. She backs away from it, screaming and sobbing as she begs for her life. Closer it comes until it has her by the throat and plunges her into the water. What a way to open a picture. This is going to be great!

"Cut!"

Who said that? What is this? It looks like a movie crew. Oh no! They're making a movie. We've been duped again! Is that Don Barry in the director's chair? He might as well turn to the camera and flip us off.

BOOOOOOOOO!

Writers Richard Landau and George Worthing Yates probably thought that this was a clever way to open a picture. It might have been if there was something as exciting later on, but there wasn't. The filmmakers move into Frankenstein's castle and the movie turns into a gab-fest. The exciting opening ultimately works against the picture. It reveals that its makers know what the audience wants to see, but for some reason they have no intention of giving it to them.

Baron von Frankenstein (Boris Karloff) has allowed the movie crew to invade his privacy in exchange for a chunk of money that will allow him to purchase the atomic reactor he needs to make his monster. Karloff's over-the-top performance, which leaves no piece of scenery unchewed, is the only thing that makes the film bearable—though it's hardly a reason to watch it. It has the distinction of being the only movie I ever saw where the beginning and the end ignited hostility from the audience.

Howard Koch said, "I was *afraid* to say to him it was too much! That's not right, but again I tell you we weren't great talents, we were just trying to make movies. All I was really concerned about was the schedule—which is not a good thing to admit, but I had the pressure of the fact that we couldn't go over the $105,000. I just was glad to get the scenes done."[3]

The Haunted Strangler

Karloff is a little more restrained in *The Haunted Strangler* (1958). The role was written for him by Jan Read, and Karloff plays James Rankin. He's convinced that a man named Edward Styles (Michael Atkinson)—known as The Haymarket Strangler—was innocent of the murders for which he was hanged two decades ago. As Rankin delves into the facts, it begins to look as if a young doctor named Tenant may be the real killer. Tenant performed the autopsies on the strangler's five victims. He collapsed when Styles was buried and suffered a mental breakdown, but no one knows what happened to him after a nurse whisked him away from the mental hospital where he was confined. Rankin's wife (Elizabeth Allen) wants him to drop his investigation, but Rankin is determined to find the truth. He digs up Styles's coffin and finds the scalpel that Tenant used to slash his victims. Staring at the blade, Rankin undergoes a mental and physical change and becomes the strangler once again. Rankin is Tenant: something even he didn't realize.

The Haunted Strangler is handsomely mounted and well-acted. Robert Day's direction is sober, and the psychological implications of a man hell-bent on bringing about his own downfall makes for an interesting ride, but not for the younger audiences for which it was intended.

In this excerpt from producer John Croydon's unpublished autobiography that appeared in a 1984 issue of *Fangoria* magazine, Croydon recalled making the picture:

"A major concern was how to achieve [Karloff's physical] transformation without complicated and expensive processes. We called Karloff, Robert Day, and the makeup man to Walton Studios to discuss the metamorphosis. We talked about monsters, ghouls, and ghosts and were not getting very far when I noticed a twinkle in Karloff's eye. "Mind if I try my own?" he asked. "Go ahead," I replied. He turned his back and seemed to be remolding his features. We he swung back again, we were stunned. He had removed his false left upper and lower molars, and drawn his mouth awkwardly sideways, sucked in his lower lip so that the upper teeth overlapped, his cheek drawn inwards. The left eyebrow and lid were lowered, his left arm drawn up and useless, as though he had suffered a major stroke. In a thickened tone, unlike his own softly modulated voice, he asked, "Will this do?" What was there to say? Our psychopathic monster had materialized before our very eyes and that was how Karloff played the role. It was perfect."

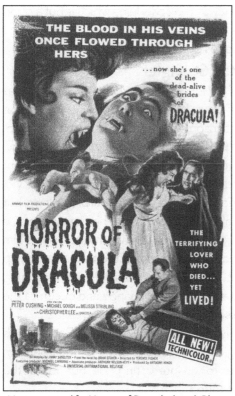

Newspaper ad for Horror of Dracula *(1958). Photo from the author's collection.*

Christopher Lee takes a bite out of Melissa Stribling in Horror of Dracula *(1958) Photo from the author's collection.*

Horror of Dracula

Hammer's *Dracula* (1958)—called *Horror of Dracula* in America—proved to be an even greater success than their Frankenstein films. For over two decades, Bela Lugosi had been the quintessential Dracula, but Christopher Lee's portrayal of the vampire count aggressively challenged Lugosi's title. Tall, dark, and handsome, Lee was the personification of forbidden sex.

Michael Carreras said, "The greatest difference between our Dracula and anybody else's was the sexual connotations. There was no real horror in it; the women were eager to be nipped by Dracula and I think that gave it a fresh look."[4]

As Dracula's nemesis Dr. Van Helsing, Peter Cushing was excellent as always. He was the one who thought of making a cross out of two candlesticks that holds Dracula at bay long enough for the sunlight to kill him at the film's exciting climax. Lee's disintegration is a far cry from Lugosi's off-camera staking in the 1931 version and proved to be so shocking that some of it had to be trimmed. These scenes, thought to be lost, have recently turned up in a Japanese print, and there is talk of restoring it for a DVD release.

Jimmy Sangster's streamlined version of Bram Stoker's novel is solid, and Terence Fisher's directing is good, but as always, deliberately paced. When he fails to provide the energy needed for the action scenes, James Bernard's terrific score picks up the slack.

As expected, the critics hated it. "I came away revolted and outraged," wrote Nina Hibbins in the *Daily Worker*. C.A. Lejeune was equally distressed, and she expressed her regret that a film in such sickening, bad taste was being shown in America. The bigwigs at Universal couldn't have cared less what the critics thought. The box office returns told them all that they needed to know. They cut a deal with Hammer to remake all of their classic horror movies. From that point on, Universal slashed the budgets on their own horror films. *The Thing that Couldn't Die* (1958), *Monster on the Campus* (1958), and *Curse of the Undead* (1959) were cheaply produced for the express purpose of supporting Hammer's color imports.

The Thing that Couldn't Die

The setting for *The Thing that Couldn't Die* is a modern rural ranch. Carolyn Kearney is dowsing for water when she discovers, buried deep in the ground, an old chest containing the living head of Gideon Drew (Robin Hughes)—a warlock beheaded by Sir Francis Drake. Using hypnosis, Drew recruits the ranchers to search for his body, corrupting them in the process. The innocent Carolyn Kearney becomes a tramp, Jeffrey Stone turns into a brooding alcoholic, his fiancée (Andra Martin) becomes a lascivious tease, and a mentally deficient handyman is compelled to commit murder. The audience has every reason to believe that the movie will really kick into gear when head and body finally meet, but alas, they're in for a bit of a disappointment. There's just enough time left for Drew to in-

The Thing That Couldn't Die *(1958). Photo courtesy of Gary Smith.*

sult everyone in the room before William Reynolds backs him into his coffin with a crucifix. Reynolds tosses the crucifix into the coffin, shuts the lid, and that's that. Only Drew's skeleton remains.

Half sheet poster for Curse of the Undead *(1958). Photo from the author's collection.*

Curse of the Undead

Michael Pate plays a vampire gunslinger in Edward Dein's *Curse of the Undead*, hired by Kathleen Crowley to deal with nasty rival Bruce Gordon. Pate isn't the fastest gun in the west, but since he's already dead, he always wins. Eric Fleming is the preacher who kills Pate in broad daylight with a cross-engraved bullet.

If only this movie was half as exciting as the Reynold Brown poster, it would have been quite a show, but it's so boring that the characters are constantly screaming at one another to keep the audience awake.

Blood of the Vampire

Just before production began on *Horror of Dracula*, producers Robert S. Baker and Monty Berman hired Jimmy Sangster to write a Hammer-like horror movie called *Blood of the Vampire* (1958). It was in color and handsomely mounted, but that's about the best that can be said for it.

Donald Wolfit, made up to look like Bela Lugosi, is in charge of a prison for the criminally insane. He uses the blood of the inmates to keep himself alive while he works on a cure for his rare blood disease. So he really isn't a vampire at all, even though a stake is driven through his heart in a pre-credit sequence.

The Mummy

Hammer's *The Mummy* (1959) was not a remake of the Boris Karloff classic, which had been a mix of horror and romance aimed at adults. Instead, it was a remake of *The Mummy's Tomb* (1942), which was a monster movie made for children. The plot is pretty simple: He who robs the graves of Egypt dies! Peter Cushing is one of the despoilers of Princess Anaka's tomb and Christopher Lee is the mummy sent to kill him. Lee's spirited portrayal is a marked improvement over the crippled character played by Lon Chaney.

This poster art for The Mummy *(1959) was painted by Reynold Brown. Unfortunately, Universal opted to go with the original British poster art, which was pretty stiff. Photo courtesy of Gary Smith.*

Christopher Lee said, "I had to carry these women... as dead weights through the studio swamp, which was full of underground machinery crashing against my legs. I paced the walk out and it came to eighty-three yards and there were three takes. I pulled all the muscles in my neck and shoulders on that film."[5]

The Man Who Could Cheat Death

Anton Diffring was *The Man Who Could Cheat Death* (1959), Hammer's remake of Paramount's *The Man in Half Moon Street* (1945). A year earlier, Diffring had played Dr. Frankenstein in an unsold Hammer television pilot. For some reason, Terence Fisher has the actor deliver a lot of his dialogue with his back to the people he's supposed to be talking to, staring off into space as if he's in a trance. He does it so often that it becomes laughable. But it's not a bad picture. Predictably, it ends with Diffring crumbling to dust, the way all films end that have characters that have lived too long. The continental version had a topless shot of Hazel Court.

Hazel Court said, "Appearing topless in a film at that time was very unusual, and I was one of the first in Britain to do so. It was very beautifully shot. The studio was cleared except for only the most necessary personnel for that shot. Only a few people have ever seen the version of the film that has that shot in it."[6]

It is important to note that it wasn't just color, gore, and sex that Hammer brought to the table: it was respectability. Working with modest $400,000 budgets, their movies simply looked better than their American counterparts. Equally important, Hammer never played down to the audience. They got a lot of flak for taking a Grand Guignole approach to the material, but that's neither here nor there. Hammer did for the horror movie what Sergio Leone did for the western in the sixties. But like the horror filmmakers before them, they too returned to the same watering hole one too many times. The approach that had once been fresh grew stale from repetition. Sir James Carreras once said, "At Hammer Films, we make the movies where the monsters bite the women's titties." With few exceptions, the buxom young starlets in their flimsy nightgowns were the only points of interest—no pun intended.

Horrors of the Black Museum *half sheet poster. Photo from the author's collection.*

Horrors of the Black Museum

One of the most notorious films of the decade was Herman Cohen's *Horrors of the Black Museum* (1959), which was inspired by a tour through Scotland Yard's Black Museum. Among the 100-year-old collection of murder weapons, Cohen spotted a pair of binoculars. The slightest pressure on the focus released two spikes from the eyepieces. It had been a gift to an unsuspecting woman from the lunatic stable boy she had jilted.

Cohen wanted Vincent Price to play Edmond Bancroft, the bestselling author who commits the murders he writes about. But the actor was out of his price range. Cohen found the perfect actor to play his sadistic, woman-hating despot in the fey histrionics of Michael Gough. "No woman can hold her tongue!" Gough tells his lackey (Graham Curnow). "They're a suspicious, unreliable breed!"

This was an unusually sadistic film for its time, and as such, it caused quite a stir. "Producers have relied on sensationalism without subtlety or characterization, situation or dialog," wrote the London reviewer for *Variety*. "In virtually every category of craftsmanship, this picture bears evidence of only an ounce of thought for every pound of CinemaScope footage," said *New York Times* critic Richard Nason. "The plot might deserve detailed consideration as a serious treatment on violence," wrote David Pirie in *A Heritage of Horror*, "if it were not executed quite so titillatingly."

Story-wise, the most outrageous thing about the movie is when Michael Gough announces that he possesses the Jekyll and Hyde formula. Not that this film is ever grounded. Like most of Cohen's films, it has a comic book mentality, but the introduction of something so fantastic during the last quarter of the film is sloppy writing to say the least.

Black Museum was American International's biggest film to date, in color, scope, and HypnoVista! "It actually puts YOU in the picture," the ads claimed. This modern miracle was a thirteen-minute lecture on hypnotism tacked at the front of the picture, delivered by Dr. Emile Franchel, a hypnotherapist. "The doc gets the jump on his audiences—at least the young ones—right off by telling them that only idiots and fools can't be hypnotized," wrote Jack Moffit in the *Hollywood Reporter*. "Thereafter at the previews, the kids hastened to prove their mental health by yawning when the doc told them to, forcing their hands apart at his bidding, shivering when he suggested a blue light was cold, and mopping their brows when he said a red light was blistering." This prologue was Jim Nicholson's idea and was only seen in America.

My World Dies Screaming

PsychoRama was the gimmick used to promote *My World Dies Screaming* (1958), a mystery promoted like a horror film and given a more horrific title— *Terror in the Haunted House*—when it was sold to television a few years after its theatrical release.

Suppressing the memory of the axe murder she witnessed as a child, Cathy O'Donnell has nightmares about the house in which the murder took place. After her marriage to Gerald Mohr, she's more than a little upset when she learns that their intended honeymoon house, which belongs to Mohr, is the house from her nightmares. Throughout the picture, subliminal words and images flash on the screen to increase the suspense.

A demonstration of PsychoRama was held for the press at the Beverly Canon theatre in Hollywood. Hazel Flynn, a reporter from the *Hollywood Citizen News*, was one of the people in attendance. In her column, she questioned the right of the filmmakers to mess with the public's subconscious. One Iowa theatre owner used it to stimulate interest in his snack bar and had his best month ever. The National Association of Broadcasters and the Federal Communications Commission eventually outlawed subliminal advertising.

Rhino's DVD release of this picture did not include Gerald Mohr's eight-minute explanation of PsychoRama and Rhino took it upon themselves to insert some new, not-so-subliminal images into the picture.

Gimmicks like PsychoRama and HypnoVista began with William Castle, a journeyman director whose lack of talent as a filmmaker was overshadowed by his P.T. Barnum approach to ballyhoo. Early in his career, Castle learned the value of a good gimmick. Sometime in the forties, he was directing an unsuccessful play called *Not for Children* starring Ellen Schwanneke. Castle broke the windows, painted swastikas on the walls, and told the newspapers that the vandalism resulted from Miss Schwanneke's cablegram to Hitler refusing his request that she return to Germany. Actually, Hitler had only asked if Miss Schwanneke would be interested in being his guest at an art festival. She wasn't, and Castle offered to send a cablegram to Hitler on her behalf. He took it upon himself to tell Hitler that Miss Schwanneke wanted no part of him or his government and hand-carried a copy of that cablegram to the New York papers, along with the pictures of the damaged playhouse. Castle said they played to packed houses for weeks.

Castle had directed dozens of programs for Columbia and Universal when he turned to television to become a producer. He was working on the *Men of Annapolis* TV series when he saw Henri-Georges Clouzot's *Diabolique* (1955)—the movie that changed his life. He wanted to make a thriller movie with plot twists like Clouzot's, but he knew he didn't have Clouzot's directorial skills, so he cooked up a gimmick to sell his picture.

Robb White, one of the writers on Castle's TV series, became his partner. It was White's understanding that they would be splitting the cost of Castle's suspense thriller, but Castle was never quite able to come up with his half, so White had to shoulder the full amount: $86,000. It wasn't until they started to make the picture that White understood why Castle called himself the Earl of Deferral. According to White, Castle never paid for anything.

For a percentage of the picture, Howard Koch and Aubrey Schenk helped Castle navigate his way through the ins and outs of production. When they were invited to a screening of the picture, Koch told White it was the worst movie he'd ever seen in his life and he'd never get his money back. When Castle couldn't sell the picture, White started to worry as they owed a lot of money in deferrals. He and Castle were looking at jail time if they couldn't make good on their debts. Steve Broidy came to the rescue and bought the picture.

Macabre

Ever since the days of *Frankenstein* and *Dracula*, customers were warned to see horror movies at their own risk. The more ambitious exhibitors often had nurses on hand in the lobby with smelling salts at the ready—it was the oldest gag in the book. Bill Castle upped the ante and persuaded Lloyds of London to insure everyone who saw *Macabre* (1958) for $1000 against death-by-fright. The gimmick is what sold Broidy on the picture, and it grossed over $3 million.

The Screaming Skull and I Bury the Living

Both American International's *The Screaming Skull* (1958) and UA's *I Bury the Living* (1959) offered free burial plots to anyone who died of fright, but there was no insurance company backing them up. You can bet *your* life that hell would have frozen over before they would have made good on their promise.

The Screaming Skull was independently made by producers T. Frank Woods, John Coots, and John Kneubuhl. Kneubuhl also wrote the script, which is pretty flimsy. Alex Nicol directed it and played Mickey the gardener. There are only four other characters in the film: Eric and Jenni Whitlock (John Hudson and Peggy Webber), a couple of newlyweds who have come to live in Eric's secluded palatial home; and their neighbors, the Reverend Edward Snow and his wife (Russ Conway and Tony Johnson). These four people are obsessed with Mickey. They're always talking about him and when they're not talking about him, they're looking for him. If every member of the audience was given a dollar for every time one of the characters mentioned his name, they'd have more than enough to bury themselves. With all of the attention that's showered on Mickey, one would assume that he must be a pretty interesting guy. Not so. He's slovenly, unfriendly, and retarded. And he's obsessed with Marion, the first Mrs. Whitlock, who supposedly died from a nasty spill. The audience is led to believe that Mickey is trying to drive Jenni out of the house by making her believe that Marion is haunting the place. To no one's surprise, Eric turns out to be the culprit. He killed Marion for her money and now he wants Jenni's. Knowing he can't get away with the same gag twice, he sets the stage to make Jenni's death appear to be a suicide. Marion's ghost comes to the rescue and kills Eric. This surprising turn of events is the only interesting thing about the picture.

I Bury the Living had exactly the opposite problem. The climax sabotages what had otherwise been an innovative and thoroughly off-the-wall exercise in claustrophobic terror. Richard Boone is Robert Kraft—the owner of a small town department store—who must take charge of the local cemetery for a year as part of his civic duty. All he has to do is keep the books, and Andy McKee (Theodore Bikel), the elderly caretaker, does everything else.

On the wall in McKee's cramped little office is a large push-pin map of the cemetery. White pins indicate plots that have been purchased. Black pins mark the plots that have been filled. Boone accidentally pushes black pins into the plots of a couple of newlyweds, who die that same day in an auto accident. Boone can't shake the feeling that he somehow caused their deaths. To prove to himself that it was nothing more than coincidence, he arbitrarily sticks another black into the map and that person dies of a heart attack. His three business associates try to convince Boone that it's nothing more than coincidence and, to prove their point, insist that he put black pins in their plots. They die, too. Driven to the brink of madness, Boone replaces the black pins of the people he thinks he's killed with white ones. Then, fearing that they might actually crawl out of their graves, he barricades his office.

"That's the way we wanted the picture to end," said the film's producer-director, Albert Band. "You would hear them outside, pounding and scratching to get at him. But the distributors wouldn't have it. They thought it was too unpleasant."

And so writer Louis Garfinkle concocted a new ending in which McKee confesses to the murders as an act of revenge for being forced into retirement. How McKee managed to make it appear as if his victims died of natural causes is never explained. Still, Band's intense direction, Boone's sincere performance, Edward Vorkapic's innovative and frightening art direction, all supported by Gerald Fried's haunting score, make *I Bury the Living* one of the most effective horror films of the decade. It would have been even better as a half-hour *Twilight Zone* episode, with Band's original ending, of course.

House on Haunted Hill

Bill Castle already had a new gimmick in mind to sell his next, and most popular, film: *House on Haunted Hill* (1959). Castle told White of another tale of deception and murder that ended with a skeleton rising out of a vat of acid. White's script has more holes than a block of Swiss cheese, but audiences didn't seem to care.

Vincent Price invites five people—Richard Long, Carolyn Craig, Alan Marshal, Julie Mitchum, and Elisha Cook—to spend the night in a haunted house, for which they will each be paid $10,000 if they survive. Before they have a chance to say yes or no to his proposition, the caretakers lock them in and there's no way out.

Elisha Cook is convinced the house is haunted and it looks like he's right. A falling chandelier almost kills Carolyn Craig the minute she sets foot in the place. Richard Long is knocked unconscious in an empty room. At first blush, it appears that Price's wife, Carol Ohmart, has committed suicide by hanging herself. She appears outside of Craig's second story room, mysteriously floating in the air. The rope that had been around her neck crawls through the window like a snake and wraps around Craig's ankles. But Ohmart isn't dead. She and her lover, Alan Marshall, are hoping to scare Miss Craig into such a state of hysteria that she will kill Price with the gun she has been given as a party favor. And it works, or so they think. Miss Craig races to the cellar, Price shows up on cue, she shoots him and runs off to tell the others what she's done. Before they return, Marshall tries to toss Price's body into a vat of acid. At this point, the screen goes black. We hear a struggle and a splash. Ohmart comes to the cellar to celebrate their victory. A skeleton rises out of the acid. "Come with me," Price's ghostly

Half sheet poster for House on Haunted Hill *(1959). Photo from the author's collection.*

Vincent Price. Photo courtesy of Bob Villard.

voice tells her. Ohmart screams and the skeleton pushes her into the vat. Now we see that the skeleton is on wires, manipulated like a puppet by Price, who was wise to their little scheme all along; he loaded Craig's gun with blanks.

From start to finish, *House on Haunted Hill* doesn't make a lick of sense. The whole thing depends on the assumption that frightened people always run to cellars.

Castle's gimmick for this film was Emergo. "The thrills fly right into the audience!" claimed the newspaper ads. Hidden by a curtain, in a box above the screen a plastic, luminous skeleton was sent flying across the audience as the skeleton in the movie rises out of the acid bath. As Price reels the onscreen skeleton in the luminous skeleton returns to the box. Castle was on hand for the premier engagement of his stunt. That night, the skeleton was apparently suffering from stage fright. It missed its cue, came staggering out of the box a couple of feet dangled for a few seconds, and beat a hasty retreat. The audience laughed. Gathering its courage, the skeleton came out of the box again. The wire snapped and it fell into a crowd of delighted children. At subsequent screenings, the children came armed with weapons to shoot it down. Castle didn't care so long as they came, and the picture was a huge success. The enterprising manager of a New Orleans theater modified Castle's carny-style stunt for a screening of *The Bat* (1959) and enjoyed the best box office he'd had in months.

The Tingler

With his credibility as a moneymaker established, Castle returned to Columbia to make *The Tingler* (1959) in Percepto. After introducing himself in a prologue, Castle warned the audience that "some of the sensations, some of the physical reactions which actors on the screen will feel will be experienced, for the first time in motion-picture history, by certain members of the audience." Castle went on to explain that these "unfortunate" people will experience a strange, tingling sensation from time to time, but he assured them that they could protect themselves simply by screaming. "Remember," he concluded, "a scream at the right time may save your life!"

What they actually experienced was the vibration of the little war surplus motors attached to the bottom of every tenth seat in specially selected theaters. Milt Rice supervised the installation, which took about four hours. According to an article in *Variety*, Percepto cost $250,000, which when added to the campaign and negative costs, set Columbia back $1 million. This is pretty hard to believe. More likely, $250,000 was the total cost of the picture and the installation, but even that seems excessive.

After Castle's prologue, the audience is introduced to Vincent Price, a pathologist who discovers a grotesque, caterpillar-like parasite that grows from the base of the spine during moments of extreme fear. It can only be neutralized by screaming. A deaf mute (Judith Evelyn), frightened to death by her husband (Philip Coolidge), gives Price the opportunity to liberate one of these creatures for study. Before he can return it to Evelyn's corpse, the Tingler escapes and causes havoc in the silent movie theater she owned. It works its way from the auditorium to the projection booth and attacks the projectionist. The reel comes to an end and the Tingler's shadow is projected on the screen. This is the point where the onscreen audience and the theater audience merge, and Castle's gimmick goes into action. The screen goes black. Vincent Price warns everyone that the Tingler is loose in the theater: the cue for the projectionist to flip the switch on the motors. An actress planted in the audience screams and faints, and screams from the audience join the screams on the soundtrack.

"It failed to arouse the customer seated in front of this viewer yesterday, a fearless lad who was sound asleep, snoring," wrote Howard Thompson in *The New York Times*. The critic urged Castle to forget about gimmicks and concentrate on keeping people awake.

Robb White said, "We didn't want to buy thousands of vibrators without knowing whether or not they would really work out, so we scouted around until we found a theater in the Valley that was running *The Nun's Story* [which] was going to close on a Sunday night and *The Tingler* was going to open on Monday. We got in a huge crew of people to spend the day attaching the vibrators to the seats. But that night, just at the most tragic moment of *The Nun's Story*, somebody touched the master switch and the seats began vibrating in wave after wave. There was absolute pandemonium!"[7]

"We can no longer expect the distributor to create the excitement needed to sell tickets," Castle told *Variety*. "We must do it ourselves."[8]

The Tingler is the oddest of the five Castle/White collaborations, creating a universe unto itself where there's nothing unusual about a man allowed to witness the execution of his brother-in-law and then strike up a conversation with the doctor performing the autopsy. Price thinks nothing of living with a woman who might poison him; In *House on Haunted Hill*, Price humorously says to Carol Ohmart, "Remember the fun we had when you tried to poison me?" Price's wife, Pamela Lincoln, reacts with casual indifference when she sees the Tingler for the first time and is only interested in it as a means to kill Price. By the time Judith Evelyn is terrified by a series of what appears to be supernatural events, it all seems a matter of course.

In addition to the Percepto gimmick, the film contains two standout moments. The first is Vincent Price's LSD trip. It's supposed to be frightening, but in Castle's hands, it's just silly and more than a little embarrassing. Castle may have been a master showman, but a good director he wasn't.

The second sequence is something straight out of *House on Haunted Hill* where Judith Evelyn is haunted in her own apartment. She runs to the bathroom, where she finds a bathtub full of blood from which a bloody hand reaches out for her. The set was in black and white. The actress wore a gray robe and her face and hands were covered in white makeup. Only the blood was in color, an effect that was quite startling at the time.

Castle and White made two more films then severed their partnership, which was, from the beginning, as shaky as the Tingler seats. They never saw each other socially and all of their script conferences were conducted over the phone. There is no mention of White in the recent documentary *Spine Tingler! The William Castle Story*.

So far, we have resisted naming the theaters where we saw these films because we know that nobody cares. But, since this chapter is as much about ballyhoo and theater exhibition as it is making horror films, we have to indulge ourselves for a moment to talk about The Cozy: possibly the worst theater in the world. The walls had no ornamentation whatsoever, the floor was cement, and the 350 seats, many of them broken, had no cushions. Some of these seats were behind large pillars that completely blocked the view of anyone stupid enough to sit in them, and the restrooms were located on either side of the small screen. We never went inside the bathroom just as we never dared to buy anything from the snack bar.

One afternoon, after we'd been there for at least forty minutes, we saw a woman march into the men's restroom. After what seemed like an awfully long time, no less than seven angry guys stormed out. We wondered what they'd been doing in there all that time. The woman never did come out.

Built in 1927, The Cozy was located at 320 S. Broadway in downtown Los Angeles. "Make it a Cozy habit" read the sign above the entrance, and much to our shame and to the detriment of our mental and physical health, we did. Every weekend, The Cozy showed four horror pictures. We never knew which ones. "Always four big hits" was all the newspapers told us and calling the theater was an exercise in frustration. The woman who answered the phone was Hispanic, not fluent in English, and she spoke with a thick accent. After thinking about it for a moment or two, we realized *The Cough* had to be *The Couch* (1962), just as we knew that *King Kong vs. Gonzalez* had to be *King Kong vs. Godzilla* (1962). But when she reported that The Beast and The Monster were on the program, we were left with a myriad of possibilities. *Brown Child in the Attic* turned out to be *Paranoiac* (1962).

As often as not, the marquee was equally confusing. It wasn't big enough to hold four titles, so each title had to be distilled, which often created some interesting interpretations. Not that it mattered, as the Cozy regulars didn't care what was on the screen. They paid their fifty cents to have somewhere to sleep, on the seats or on the floor—it didn't seem to matter. And we're talking about a floor that wasn't just sticky: it was mushy with who knows how many decades of crap. We were convinced the health department refused to go near the place.

As you might have already guessed, the place stank of bad breath and B.O. and if there was a ventilation system of some kind, it was never working. The only fresh air came from the large crack in the ceiling above the screen. One hot summer day, I was horrified to see the manager, dressed in a wife-beater shirt, wipe the sweat from under his armpit and absently run his hand through the popcorn. And yet this same guy meticulously displayed posters and dozens of photographs for each and every movie he showed—items that came from his own collection, we later found out. Now that's showmanship!

Notes:

1. Technically, Frankenstein stories are science fiction, but your authors have always viewed them as horror movies and so did *TV Guide* magazine. **Movie—Horror** was their heading for the Frankenstein films when they appeared on Shock Theatre and who are we to argue with *TV Guide*?

2. Earnshaw, Tony. *Beating the Devil, The Making of Night of the Demon*, National Museum of Photography, Film & Television Pictureville and Tomahawk Press, England, 2005, pg. 26.

3. Weaver, Tom. *Interviews with B Science Fiction and Horror Movie Makers*, McFarland & Co., Jefferson, NC, pg. 217.

4. Brosnan, John. *The Horror People*, Plume Books, New York, NY, 1976, pg. 106.

5. Frank, Alan. *Horror Films*, Hamlyn Publishing Group Ltd., London.

6. Court, Hazel. *Hazel Court Horror Queen*, Tomahawk Press, Sheffield, England, pgs. 82-83.

7. Weaver, Tom. *Science Fiction Stars and Horror Heroes*, McFarland, Jefferson, NC, 1991, pg. 428.

8. *Variety*, review, June 10, 1959, pg. 3.

CHAPTER NINE
CREATURES, THINGS AND TREACHEROUS TREKS

*Kent, there's no question about it now. Whatever they
are, humans, animals or monsters, they're here, and
they've come up from the center of the earth!*
—Superman and the Mole Men

The surprise hit of 1958 was Ray Harryhausen's *The 7th Voyage of Sinbad*. *Time* magazine, never a champion of horror films, called it "one of the best monster pictures ever made for children. In fact, it is so horrifyingly good that some parents may want to scout it before letting their children see it." *Parents Magazine* gave it their Special Merit Award. *Newsweek* called it an "Arabian Nightmare" in a new process called Dynamation, "which in place of the customary jerk of monster animation presents them for the most part with high realism."

The New York Times said it was a "briskly-paced fantasy adventure" and *Variety* agreed: "A bright, noisy package for youngsters and adults alike." Audiences lined up around the block to see it.

The Magic Carpet
Before *The 7th Voyage of Sinbad*, the only Arabian Nights fantasy to mix magic with monsters was Alexander Korda's

The Cyclops. Photo courtesy of Bob Villard.

The Thief of Bagdad (1940). The films that followed were little more than (to quote Harryhausen) "cops and robbers stories in baggy pants." Dancing girls and derring-do were favored over monsters and mayhem, and by the 1950s, the genre had fallen into Sam Katzman's hands. Katzman's costume movies were so lackluster that his boss, Harry Cohn, thought he could use one of them to break his contract with Lucille Ball. She owed the studio one more picture and Cohn didn't want to pay her. He was certain she'd refuse to do *The Magic Carpet* (1951), and if she did, she would violate the terms of her contract. But Lucy fooled him, "I'd love to do the movie."

"I nearly got killed on that one," said Miss Ball's co-star, John Agar. "They had constructed this carpet with a motor on it, powerful enough to lift it into the air with a dummy riding it. But the trouble was it *looked* like a dummy. So the director [Lew Landers] said, 'Put the other dummy on it.' That was me. But the motor wasn't strong enough to lift a man into the air, so at a certain point in the suspension, I had to help push the carpet forward. Well, you could see the snag, so we took the scene several times until I finally said, 'This is going to be a take,' and really pushed hard. I sent myself off balance, the carpet went falling and I had to grab hold of the piano wires to save myself from falling thirty feet.'"

Sinbad

Howard Hughes's miserable *Son of Sinbad* (1955) was deservedly playing to empty houses while Harryhausen was trying to promote *his* Sinbad picture. Going from door to door with his high-powered illustrations in hand, he was met with indifference until he approached Charles H. Schneer with the idea. It sounded good to Schneer, but he insisted on making the film in color, which posed a problem for Harryhausen. His stop-motion figures were often photographed in front of process screens. "And the minute you duped it by projection, your colors deteriorated and [the image] got grainy," he recalled. "In those days I had to flash the film with light in a laboratory to reduce contrast on

Kerwin Mathews and Kathryn Grant. Photo from the author's collection.

the raw stock before plate photography. Then I had to come up with a rear projection system in which the grain of the screen was reduced with a vibrating source. Sometimes the problems are unavoidable."[1]

The budget for *Sinbad* was set at $650,000. It should have been two or three million, but Columbia wasn't willing to gamble a small fortune on such a risky project. To cut costs, Schneer decided to shoot the movie in Spain. The Alhambra in Granada saved them the cost of building the Caliph's palace, and the replica of Columbus's ship, the *Santa Maria*, moored in Barcelona harbor, served as Sinbad's ship. Photographer Wilkie Cooper, who took six months to shoot *The Thief of Bagdad*, was taken aback when he was told he'd have to get everything in the can in three short weeks. To that end, he often worked around the clock, stealing the extra lights he needed from the stage where Stanley Kramer was shooting *The Pride and the Passion* (1957).

Columbia contract player Kerwin Mathews was cast as Sinbad, a serendipitous choice. Besides being a handsome, likeable guy, his ability to give the impression that he was actually looking at Harryhausen's monsters was a godsend, especially during the show-stopping duel between Sinbad and a sword-swinging skeleton. Kathryn Grant, another contract player, was appropriately sweet and wholesome as Princess Parisa, though it would have been better if she'd been more like the character she played in *The Big Circus* (1959): spunky and sexy. She serves as both the love interest and catalyst of the story. Torin Thatcher is the evil magician Sokurah, a role he plays to the hilt.

Above: The dragon that guards Sokurah's lab. Below: The show-stopping swordfight with the skeleton. Photo from the author's collection.

Bernard Herrmann's magical score under the main titles kicked the movie into fourth gear. Five minutes later, having stopped on the island of Colossa for water, Sinbad and his men encounter the Cyclops chasing after Sokurah and the magic lamp. As Sinbad and his men battle the Cyclops, Sokurah summons the genie of the lamp (Richard Eyer) to protect them. But on the way back to the ship, the boat is capsized, the lamp falls from Sokurah's grip, and the Cyclops retrieves it. Sokurah offers Sinbad a fortune in jewels to take him back to the island, but Sinbad has bigger fish to fry; he must return to Bagdad with the Princess. Their marriage means an end to the war between Bagdad and Chandra, and once they reach Bagdad, Sokurah continues to plead his case, but to no avail. While Parisa sleeps, Sokurah shrinks her to the size of a doll. Sinbad, unaware that Sokurah was responsible for her condition, asks the magician if he can restore her. There is such a potion, he tells Sinbad, but one of the ingredients is the shell of an egg from the Roc: a two-headed bird that can only be found on Colossa. This remarkable coincidence is lost on Sinbad. He doesn't even suspect that Sokurah may have something to do with Parisa's mysterious malady, which makes him more than a little thick. Back on Colossa, Sokurah tricks Sinbad again by splitting the men into two groups and sending Sinbad's group through the Valley of the Cyclops where they are captured and caged by the monster. Sokurah passes by their cage with a smile, making no effort to save them. Later, after Sinbad and his men have escaped, Sinbad tells Parisa, "I do not trust the magician." It's a comic highpoint.

As Sokurah mixes the potion that will restore the Princess, Sinbad gives him the eggshell. If writer Kenneth Kolb had his wits about him, Sokurah would have chuckled and tossed the eggshell aside, letting Sinbad and the audience know the whole thing had all been a ruse. But, there is very little wit in Kolb's screenplay and Nathan Juran falls short as a director. Neither of them played much of a part in the film's success; it was Harryhausen's monsters—the Cyclops, the serpent woman, the Roc, the skeleton, and the dragon that won the audience over. Because of him, Columbia's modest investment paid off handsomely, and the picture grossed $6 million.

Ulysses

The highlight of the Dino De Laurentiis/Carlo Ponti co-production of *Ulysses* (1954) was a sequence where Ulysses (Kirk Douglas) and his men are captured by the Cyclops Polyphemus. No less than seven writers tackled the screenplay based on Homer's *The Odyssey*, Ben Hecht and Irwin Shaw among them, and yet they were no match for Ken Kolb's humble effort. Though the movie was lavishly produced, it was mediocre at best and didn't perform well at the box office.

Hercules

The Italian import that really took the country by storm was *Hercules* (1958), starring Steve Reeves, who was the former "Mr. America" and "Mr. Universe." His co-star was the beautiful Sylvia Koscina as Princess Iole. Director Pietro Francisci told the story of Jason and the Golden Fleece from Hercules's point of view. Joseph E. Levine bought the U.S. distribution rights for $120,000 and spent over $1 million to promote it. He thought it was one of the worst movies he'd ever seen, but he figured he could make a couple of bucks on it. The critic for *The New York Times* felt that Levine's "deafening barrage of publicity" gave the film a prominence that it didn't warrant, making the business of reviewing it unnecessary. It grossed over $7 million and kicked off a wave of Italian mus-clemen movies that continued well into the next decade. Steve Reeves's salary jumped from $12,000 to $150,000 and he became the king of peplum movies.

The Sword and the Dragon

The Sword and the Dragon (1959) was a 1956 Russian fantasy based on the *byliny* tales of the bogatyr Ilya Muromets. It was written by Mikhail Kochnev, directed by Aleksandr Ptushko, and starred Boris Andreyev, Shukur Burkhanvov, and Andrei Abrikosov. It featured (according to the advertisements) over 100,000 people and 11,000 horses and was four years in the making. That may be hype, but we wouldn't want to bet on it. It's an epic! One sequence has what looks like a million soldiers piling one on top of the other to create a mountain, and some guy rides his horse to the top to observe the enemy forces. One of the film's highlights is a pudgy demon whose cheeks balloon like the cheeks of a glass blower to create a mighty wind. And, of course, there was a three-headed dragon. Being a large prop it didn't do much, and unfortunately for all of the director's efforts, neither did the film.

Rumor has it that Roger Corman re-edited and re-dubbed this movie in the early 1960s, but it's never mentioned in any of the books written about him and is nowhere to be found in his filmography. Corman did, however, have much to do with the anti-epic *The Saga of the Viking Women and Their Voyage to the Waters of the Great Sea Serpent* (1958).

Viking Women and the Sea Serpent

Kirk Douglas was getting a lot of press while he was making *The Vikings* (1958), so Jack Rabin and Irving Block thought they should take advantage of it. They had Lawrence Louis Goldman whip up a script while Block did some dynamic sketches of Viking warriors in mortal combat with a sea serpent. They took the script and their drawings to Roger Corman, assuring him that for a mere $20,000 and a small piece of the profits, they could bring those drawings to life. Corman took their drawings to Jim Nicholson and Sam Arkoff at American International and they agreed to

Sultry Abby Dalton was the star of Viking Women and the Sea Serpent *(1958). Photo courtesy of Bob Villard.*

give him the $100,000 he needed to make his ten-day picture. Corman said he was "suckered" by Rabin and Block, and if he learned anything from the experience it was "never to be sold on a film by a mere presentation." Considering how reckless with the truth AIP was in *their* salesmanship, this is a pretty funny remark.

Abby Dalton, Susan Cabot, June Kenney, Betsy Jones-Moreland, Lynn Bernay, and Sally Todd are among the brave Viking women in Corman's film. They set sail to search for their men, who have failed to return from a hunting excursion.

On location at Cabrillo Beach, Corman waited impatiently for Kipp Hamilton, the film's star. After a few frantic phone calls, Corman learned that she'd gotten a better job. Corman gave her part to Abby Dalton and Abby's sister was hustled out of bed to take the part that Abby was supposed to have played. After what seemed like a lifetime to Corman, he called for action and the women pushed their boat into the water. It hadn't gone ten feet when the flimsy rudder fell off. The women and the boat were carried out to sea.

Betsy Jones-Moreland said, "We were all of a sudden on our way to Hawaii! We had no engine; we had *nothing*! We had no one to come get us! Roger is walking up and down on the beach and he is slamming his hat on the ground, then picking it up and walking a few more steps and slamming it down again. Finally, he had to call the Coast Guard as we were floating away."[2]

Already behind schedule and making every effort to keep a couple of steps ahead of the union, Corman couldn't be bothered with shooting the scene again. He added a couple of lines to the script to cover the loss of the rudder. "We can't handle this boat with just an oar!" one of the women says to Abby Dalton. "We've got to," she replies.

Things went from bad to worse when, at Iverson's Ranch, they suffered another mishap. Corman called for action on a scene where the Viking women were supposed to ride bareback toward a pile of rocks at full gallop and bring their horses to a stop. Abby's sister was thrown from her horse, hit her head on a rock, and had to be taken to the hospital. She was still groggy when Corman showed up with a release for her to sign, absolving him of all responsibility. Her role was given to June Kenney.

The Viking women eventually find their men, held captive in Bronson Caves by some ruthless thugs called the Grimaults. Their leader is a sadistic brute named Stark, played by Richard Devon. After much trial and tribulation, the Viking women and their men make their escape in one of the Grimault boats with Stark close behind. As the water was a little dangerous, Devon had some concerns about straying too far from the shore. As they paddled out to sea, he got the feeling that Corman wanted to eat up as much film as possible and wasn't going to cut the shot anytime soon. He yelled an obscenity at Corman and bailed out of the boat. Sloshing clumsily back to the shore, Devon was hit by a wave that slammed him into the water. The sheepskin he was wearing took on ballast, making it almost impossible for him to get on his feet again. "If I ever get my hands on you," he screamed, "I'll strangle you."[3] By the time he reached the shore, Corman was nowhere to be found.

As for those marvelous special effects that Rabin and Block promised, they were not so special after all. Scenes of the ocean, photographed for rear projection, were stupidly filmed from cliff tops, giving the impression that the Viking boat was floating in the air like Winkin', Blinkin', and Nod. One of Block's matte paintings effectively cut the heads off the actors as they enter the Grimault castle, and the sea serpent was nothing more than a little hand puppet worn by Irving Block.

Standing in a pool of water they'd built using tarps and with the puppet on his hand, Block couldn't understand why the cameraman was taking so long to get the shot. "Turn that damn camera on or we're gonna lose the thing!" he snapped. Finally, his impatience got the better of him and he flipped the switch himself and felt a surge of electricity race through his body. "That was the biggest scare I had in my life," he said. "Maybe it's good for someone doing science fiction—it turns your brains inside-out."

Port Sinister

In Jack Pollexfen and Aubrey Wisberg's *Port Sinister* (1953), a giant crab ever so briefly menaces the people who come to Port Royal in search of pirate treasure. James Warren is the scientist who is certain that the island will rise from the ocean floor on such-and-such a date, and he's right. Before he can get his act together, however, Paul Cavanagh and his gang of thugs hijack his boat and take Lynne Roberts with them. Warren hires a drunken pilot (House Peters, Jr.) to fly him to the island, but they run out of gas. Miracle of miracles, they float to the very spot they were searching for. Will they be able to rescue Miss Roberts before the island sinks again? Who cares?

A few years later, *Port Sinister* was re-released as *The Beast of Paradise Island* on a double bill with tepid jungle melodrama *Creatures of the Jungle*, aka *The White Orchid* (1954). What an exciting afternoon that was.

The Mole People

John Agar was depressed as he waited for his next scene in *The Mole People* (1956). He didn't like the direction his career seemed

John Agar and Cynthia Patrick. Photo courtesy of Gary Smith.

to be heading. He'd made four pictures for Universal: two of them second string programmers, and two science fiction pictures. The programmers were bad enough, but sci-fi movies were the kiss of death to an actor's career and now he was making another one with a first-time director, Virgil Vogel—it was the worst one yet. Never mind the story, the dialogue was insufferable. "Nobody talks like this," he'd told producer William Alland, who was incensed by this remark. He told Agar that he'd paid a man $1,000 a week to write that dialogue! Agar told him he'd been cheated. For months, he'd begged the front office to give him better pictures and look where it got him: *The Mole People*. You wouldn't catch Jeff Chandler or Tony Curtis in a picture like this. It was enough to drive a guy to drink.

All of a sudden, Universal's biggest star, Rock Hudson, was standing beside him. He'd wandered over from one of the other stages where he was starring in the kind of a picture Agar would have given his right arm to make. After looking things over, Hudson innocently asked, "How'd you get mixed up in a thing like this?" Agar held his tongue. He made one more film for Universal, *Joe Butterfly* (1957), where he received fifth billing. After that, he left the studio to do better pictures. His very first role was in *Daughter of Dr. Jekyll* (1957), which was even worse than *The Mole People*.

Agar is Dr. Roger Bentley in *The Mole People*—an archeologist who, according to Bentley, is nothing but an underpaid publicist for ancient royalty. Artifacts lead Bentley, Dr. Jud Bellamin (Hugh Beaumont), and Etienne Lafarge (Nestor Paiva) to the top of a mountain in Asia where they find the remains of an ancient temple. The ground gives way and swallows one of their companions. The publicists go after him.

Virgil Vogel said, "Universal gave me three 18-foot rocks on rollers and a lot of black velvet—that was my set. All I had to do [one day] was shoot this one climb-down scene. But we worked so fast and so well that I actually finished everything I wanted by noon, so we spent the rest of the day shooting inserts—hands climbing, feet slipping, all that kind of stuff."[4]

The studio executives liked the climb-down bit so much that they told Vogel to add a little more when the film came in short. Anytime something was too terrible to make the final cut, they made up the difference with more climb-downs and stock footage. Even then, it came in too short, so a prologue was added with Dr. Frank Baxter explaining the various theories people had about the center of the Earth.

Vogel said, "Now we're at the preview and the climb-down scene is running. The suspense is terrific—you could just feel the tension in the audience, it really was good. The climbers went down deeper and deeper, into the very bowels of the Earth—it seemed like about five miles. They get down to the bottom, they turn the body over—and someone says, 'He's dead.' Dead? He should have been a grease spot! There were about 1,500 people in this theater and they all burst into incredible laughter!"[5]

Before they can climb back up, a cave-in seals the exit. Searching for another way out, the publicists follow a tunnel that leads to a tribe of Sumerian albinos. These jokers have lived their subterranean existence for so long that they've come to believe there is no other world but their own. The publicists pose a threat to their status quo. Bentley falls in love with Adal (Cynthia Patrick), one of the "marked ones," born with normal pigmentation. The film originally ended with her and Bentley living happily ever after, but Universal executives didn't like the idea of Bentley fathering Sumerian children, so they had Vogel shoot a new ending where she is killed by an earthquake.

One of the slaves of The Mole People *(1956). Photo from the author's collection.*

The big-eyed, wart-headed, humpbacked creatures that dominate the advertising for this film are not the mole people. They're the slaves of the Sumerians who whip, beat, and starve them. Bentley saves one of them from a beating, an act of kindness that pays off at the film's climax. As Bentley and Bellamin are marched into the chamber that houses the fires of Ishtar, the creatures revolt and kill the Sumerians. A cost-cutting decision by Alland ruined the first take. When the producer was told what it would cost to make the rubber humps, he told the makeup department to stuff the mole men's backs with newspapers instead. The newspapers were all over the floor by the end of the battle.

Superman and the Mole Men

Clark Kent (George Reeves) and Lois Lane (Phyllis Coates) head west to the little town of Silsby to do a story on the world's deepest oil well. But the foreman, Bill Corrigan (Walter Reade), has suspended operations and orders valuable equipment to be buried, but he won't say why. Later that night, Kent presses Corrigan for an explanation. Corrigan is convinced they've drilled to the center of the Earth. Samples of the soil taken at one-hundred-foot intervals glow in the dark, each successive sample more intense. He's afraid they're radioactive, but they aren't— just phosphorescent. It isn't long before strange little creatures are seen by the frightened citizens of Silsby. Hot-head Luke Benson (Jeff Corey) organizes a mob to kill them. They track the little creatures to a dam, and one of the mole men is shot. Superman catches him as he falls, but the other mole man escapes and returns to the well for help. Superman takes the wounded one to the hospital where, against the orders of his superior (Frank Reicher), Dr. Reed (John Baer) pulls the bullet out of his chest. Benson and the mob storm the hospital, but Superman blocks the entrance. "That little creature in there has a much right to live as you do," he tells them. "Don't forget, you invaded his world. You sunk a pipe six miles into the ground. When he climbed up, you set dogs on him; shot him." More mole men crawl out of the tunnel to rescue their pal, this time armed with a weapon. They almost kill Benson with it, but Superman inserts himself between the deadly ray and Benson. "You saved my life," Benson says. "It's more than you deserve," Superman tells him. The mole men return to the hole with their injured buddy and set fire to the well. As she watches the flames, Lois remarks, "It's almost as if they were saying you live your lives and we'll live ours."

Superman and the Mole Men (1951) was a low-budget Lippert movie bereft of special effects, yet it's superior to *The Mole People* in every way. The screenplay by Richard Fielding (a pseudonym for producer Robert Maxwell) is a welcome plea for tolerance in an intolerant era. Whitney Ellsworth, who would later produce the second season of the *Superman* television series, provided Maxwell with the outline of the story. Director Lee Sholem shot the movie in two weeks on the RKO lot.

George Reeves and Phyllis Coates played the same characters in the first season of *The Adventures of Superman* television series, which Robert Maxwell co-produced with Bernard Luber. The series sat dormant for over a year before Kellogg's, "the greatest name in cereals," agreed to sponsor it.

Bernard Luber said, "They weren't very happy with the show. They thought it was too violent for a kids' show, but we weren't making it for kids. We made it for adults and we got very good ratings. They cut some of the violence out of our shows after they went into reruns."

The last two episodes of the first season were an edited version of *Superman and the Mole Men* called "The Unknown People." Darrell Caulker's score was replaced by library music. Whitney Ellsworth took over the series after that and, with Kellogg's blessing, took the bite out of it.

The Brain Eaters

The Brain Eaters (1958) were another subterranean life form. These fuzzy little parasites don't eat brains: they control them. Leonard Nimoy tells us they've come to "free men from strife and turmoil," but we know he's full of wild blueberry muffins. Before long, they've taken over the sleepy little town of Riverdale and it's up to Ed Nelson to stop them before they take over the world.

Actor Bruno Ve Sota came up with the idea for this picture which he called "The Keepers." Gordon Urquhart turned it into a script, which Ve Sota took to Roger Corman. Corman liked the script and gave Ve Sota $26,000 to make it. Corman asked Ed Nelson, one of his stock company players, to produce it. It was a real seat-of-the-pants production. Nelson donated to several charities in Pomona (the town where he lived), and in return he was given access to police cars, uniforms, guns, and facilities. One of Nelson's neighbors, a carpenter by trade, built the thirty-foot cone that brings the parasites to the Earth's surface for a modest $250. The interior of the cone was shot in Nelson's garage. Most of the cast were friends of his, including Leonard Nimoy. "I showed him a trick or two to play the old man," Ve Sota

Insert poster for The Brain Eaters *(1959). Photo from the author's collection.]*

recalled, "which he used very little of and did much better." Nimoy was supposed to get $45 for his part, but he's still waiting.

Nelson made the parasites out of little wind-up toy ladybugs that he covered with fur from an old coat. He used pipe cleaners for the antennae.

Thanks to Ve Sota's flair for the bizarre, the film has an unsettling, nightmarish quality about it. It's loaded with dark shadows and Dutch-angles and, whether intentional or not, reflects the McCarthy-era paranoia. Unfortunately, while individual shots convey the mood Ve Sota was striving for, nothing cuts together, and it doesn't look like a real movie.

Corman sold Ve Sota's relentlessly grim little bootleg picture to American International, probably for three or four times what it cost him. Shortly after it went into release, Robert Heinlein leveled a $150,000 lawsuit against AIP, Corinthian Productions (the company that produced the film), Roger Corman, and screenwriter Gordon Urquhart for copying, imitating, and appropriating his serial, "The Puppet Masters," which had appeared some years earlier in *Galaxy* magazine.

Roger Corman: "They stole it. No question whatsoever. Bruno brought that script to me and I said I'd back it. It was a pretty nice little script. Then I got this letter from Heinlein's lawyer. I called Bruno and asked what it was all about. He said it was absolute nonsense. So I told my secretary to get me a copy of *The Puppet Masters*... They changed a few things so it wasn't exactly the same, but it was really obvious that they took it... We settled for a $5,000 amount because it was such a low budget picture."

X... the Unknown

Before *The H-Man* or *The Blob* there was *X... the Unknown* (1956), a radioactive, living mass of mud from the bowels of the Earth that "kills but cannot be killed." It melts flesh and feeds on radiation, growing larger with each meal.

This was supposed to be a sequel to *The Creeping Unknown* (aka *Quatermass 1*), but Nigel Kneale wouldn't let Hammer Films use his Quatermass character. Kneale wasn't asked to participate in the project, so who can blame him? But in every way, it's a Quatermass-like movie—intelligent, sober, and methodical.

On a gravel pit in Scotland during a military training exercise, a huge fissure opens and several of the soldiers suffer radiation burns. Yet Dr. Adam Royston (Dean Jagger), the head scientist at an atomic research installation, finds no trace of radiation present. Soon after, a container of radioactive material is stolen from his lab. He recovers the empty container, but there's no radioactive residual. "But that's impossible, isn't it?" asks one of his colleagues, Peter Elliott (William Lucas). "Yesterday I would have said yes, but this fact is inescapable," Royston replies. "The energy trapped in that trinium has been sucked right out of it, and, furthermore, that window was barred and these doors were locked all night. So whoever it was that came in here must be most... unusual." The "unusual" intruder steals more radioactive material from a local hospital. Royston believes they're dealing with a radioactive creature from the Earth's core, an intelligent life form that developed millions of years ago. Quakes and pressures have forced the thing to the surface to seek the radioactive energy it thrives on. "It's a particle of mud, but by virtue of its atomic structure, it emits radiation," Royston tells Inspector McGill (Leo McKern). "That's all it is, just mud. How do you kill mud?"

All of the performances are exceptionally good, but Dean Jagger and Leo McKern are flawless. This was Jimmy Sangster's first screenplay and it may well be the best thing he ever wrote. The censors found it "disgusting rather than frightening," a mix of "scientific hokum and sadism," and urged Hammer to abandon the project. Truth be known, Hammer deliberately put more objectionable material into their scripts than they intended to shoot so they'd have something to cut to appease the censors while leaving intact the scenes they wanted in the first place. *X... the Unknown* has some delightfully disgusting moments that serve the picture well.

Joseph Losey, who'd come to England to avoid testifying before the House on Un-American Activities Committee, was going to direct the picture under his pseudonym Joseph Walton. He was replaced by Leslie Norman. Some say it was for reasons of health, others claim Dean Jagger refused to work with a Commie sympathizer. By all accounts, Norman proved to be a major pain in the ass and never worked for Hammer again. Yet, in spite of his lack of enthusiasm for the project, his direction is crisp and sharp. *X... the Unknown* is one of Hammer's best films.

RKO had money in the picture and planned to package it with Bert Gordon's *The Cyclops*, but the studio collapsed and the picture sat on the shelf for over a year while RKO and Warner Brothers settled a dispute over the distribution rights. Warner used it to support *The Curse of Frankenstein*.

Unknown World

With the threat of nuclear holocaust hanging over their heads, a bunch of scientists drill to the center of the Earth in their Cyclotram, hoping to find a safe haven. They don't encounter the fuzzy little parasites, the mole men, or radioactive mud in the *Unknown World* (1951), but they do find poison gas and sterility. More important, our explorers begin their journey in Bronson Canyon, drill to the center of the Earth, and burst free in... Bronson Canyon. Which proves that in fifties sci-fi, no matter where or how far you go, all roads lead to Bronson Canyon.

This Jack Rabin/Irving Block film, released by Lippert, has a timely message to impart; take care of your planet, it's the only one you've got. But messages are better received when delivered in entertaining packages, and this movie is anything but that. The acting is so-so, Ernest Gold's score is boring, and Terry Morse's direction is pedestrian, though in all fairness, even Sidney Lumet would have had trouble pumping life into Millard Kaufman's dull script.[6] However, as fatiguing as this movie is, compared to The Incredible Petrified World (1959), it's an action-packed thriller.

The Incredible Petrified World

Petrified World was produced and directed by the master of malaise, Jerry Warren. It starred veteran actor John Carradine, who, in 1969, appeared before the students at Augusta College to discuss his career. "Coffee with Carradine" was the name of this intimate question-and-answer session. One young fellow asked Carradine how he felt about being typecast as a horror actor. Carradine bristled. "I'm not typecast as a horror actor! I've only been in nine horror films and I never played a monster!" Wasn't Dracula a monster? "Dracula was a man not a monster," Carradine assured everyone, a distinction that was obviously important to him, but lost on his audience. "I turned down the role of the Frankenstein monster and I never regretted it. Karloff took it and he never stopped regretting it."

At that time, off the top of my head, I could think of at least twenty horror films that Carradine had been in and he probably made twice that many in the years that followed, and none worse than The Incredible Petrified World.

Robert Clark, Phyllis Coates, Allen Windsor, and Sheila Noonan (Carol) take a dip in the ocean in Carradine's new diving bell. The cable snaps and they end up on the ocean floor, where they discover the petrified world (Arizona's Colossal Cave). The tension rises to a fever pitch as they encounter a lizard, a human skeleton, and an old man (Maurice Bernard) who's been living in the petrified world for eighteen years. The skeleton belonged to his friend, who we later find out he murdered, though we never learn why. The old man has designs on Coates, but before he can rape or murder her, an exploding volcano triggers an avalanche that kills him. We're treated to a few clips from One Million B.C. before the four are rescued by another diving bell.

The picture cost $15,000 to make, and Carradine was paid $2000 under the table for two days' work. With his consent, the actor was locked in Ronnie Ashcroft's stage overnight; Warren was afraid that if Carradine went home he wouldn't come back. Phyllis Coates, a childhood friend of Warren's, did the film as a favor and received no salary. After she read the script, she was afraid she'd never work again.

Robert Clarke said, "I worked for a deferred salary on that one. Jerry did pay me. It wasn't much, but he did pay me. He put us up in some sleazy motel and fed us hamburgers for lunch and dinner."

Phyllis Coates and Sheila Carol have a funny exchange in *Petrified World*. After reading a rejection letter from her boyfriend for the second time, Coates wads it up and tosses it away. Not knowing what the note said, Carol jokingly tells her that she should have kept it because it might be a while before she has anything else to read.

Coates: "When I need your advice, I'll ask for it."

Carol: "I'm sorry. I didn't realize..."

Coates: "You don't realize a lot of things and probably never will."

Carol: "I didn't mean to intrude. It was just a friendly joke."

Coates: "Friendly. (Laughs) Well you just listen to me, Miss Innocent. There's nothing friendly between two females. There never was and there never will be."

Carol: "Sorry you feel that way. I was hoping we could help one another."

Coates: "You don't need any help and neither do I, not as long as we have two men around us."

Believe us, this will be the longest fifty-nine minutes you will ever spend watching a movie.

The Night the World Exploded

There were two movies about dangerous rocks in the fifties, both released in 1957. The first was Sam Katzman's *The Night the World Exploded*, which was directed by Fred F. Sears who also served as the film's narrator. In the script by Luci Ward and Jack Natteford, pressure forces rocks to the surface where industry has weakened the crust. So long as these rocks—called Element 112—are immersed in water, they're dormant, but once they're dry, they suck nitrogen from the air, double in size, reach a temperature hot enough to melt steel, and explode. "It's almost as if the Earth was striking back at us for the way we've robbed it of its natural resources," Kathryn Grant muses. She's in love with her seismologist boss, William Leslie, but he's too wrapped up in his work to notice. Leslie has just invented a new machine that can predict earthquakes, which erupt at an alarming rate. Newsreel footage of natural disasters coupled with a few effects shots cribbed from a couple of Republic pictures provided what little spectacle this minimal-effort film has to offer. Once Leslie discovers the cause of the quakes, he gathers the world's leading scientists together for a demonstration of Element 112's destructive power. He drops one of the rocks into a plastic globe that he's hung from a tree branch and it explodes before the startled eyes of the scientists. It's a deliciously sublime moment and the closest the film gets to its title.

After worldwide cloud-seeding and dam-busting has buried Element 112 in water, Kathy tells her boss how good it feels to be safe again. Leslie finally gets wise and gives her the kiss that she's been hoping for. "Maybe I spoke too soon," she tells him. "The earth just started trembling again."

This ho-hum movie isn't bad enough to be amusing or good enough to be entertaining. It's a lot like an episode of *Science Fiction Theatre* and would have played better in that half-hour format. As it stands, it really doesn't have much to offer.

Reynold Brown art for The Monolith Monsters *(1957). Photo courtesy of Gary Smith.*

The Monolith Monsters

The Monolith Monsters was much better. Written by Norman Jolly and Robert M. Fresco from a story by Fresco and Jack Arnold, the film is structured a lot like *Tarantula*. Instead of a giant spider working its way to town, living skyscrapers of stone are on a collision course with the desert community of San Angelo. Unlike Element 112, water makes these rocks grow, and as they grow, they suck silicon from anything or anyone near them—effectively turning people into stone.

Before the credits roll, a meteor crashes in the desert, scattering crystal fragments everywhere. Geologist Phil Harvey takes a piece back to his lab. The next morning, his partner Grant Williams finds his petrified body, and the lab is covered with the crystals. How one little crystal could have grown tall enough to break into hundreds of pieces without crashing through the roof is a mystery. Why people continue to turn to stone when they're no longer in contact with the rocks is another mystery. Grant Williams is around the rocks during their growth-cycle all of the time and never even gets a headache.

This was supposed to be Jack Arnold's picture, but the studio assigned him to one of their more prestigious films—*The Tattered Dress* (1957). No doubt he was grateful that the job was given to John Sherwood. It's a decent piece of entertainment even though it doesn't follow its own rules.

Giant from the Unknown

Arthur Jacobs and Richard Cunha had gone into debt to buy a studio from an old friend who retired from the film business. It had a two-thousand-square-foot stage, dubbing facilities, and editing rooms. Jacobs and Cunha were happy doing commercials, but they had a friend who kept needling them to make movies. They kicked around a few ideas and decided to make a monster movie. They didn't have a lot of money, so it had to be something simple—something that didn't require special effects: something cheap. *Giant from the Unknown* (1958) was certainly that.

General Ankrum, this time in the role of an archeologist, comes to Pine Ridge with his daughter Sally Fraser. He is searching for proof that a bunch of Spanish soldiers led by a ruthless giant of a man named Vargas (Buddy Baer)—also known as the Diablo Giant—had come to the area over 500 years ago. They meet a friendly scientist, Ed Kemmer, who takes them to a spot known as Devil's Crag, where they find a number of Spanish artifacts, including the shield, helmet, sword, and armor plating worn by Vargas. A bolt of lightning resurrects Vargas, who has been in a state of suspended animation, preserved by something in the soil. He grabs his gear and goes on a killing spree.

Buddy Baer and Sally Fraser. Photo courtesy of Bob Villard.

The picture opens in the little town of Fawnskin, which is across the lake from the much larger town of Big Bear. A small group of concerned citizens have gathered in the street to listen to Oliver Blake. "I'm telling you, there's something mighty strange going on around here," he says. "First the cattle and the horses ripped apart, then old man Banks is found dead under mighty peculiar circumstances. Just ain't natural." We never do find out whom or what is responsible for this mischief. It can't be the Diablo Giant because he hasn't been resurrected yet.

These opening scenes were the first ones that were filmed. Cunha and Jacobs had given themselves a two-day jump on the union by telling everyone they were going to be shooting at Paradise Cove. That way, they could pay the extras $5 a day instead of $25. Noise from the local repair shop disrupted several scenes, so Jacobs asked the owner if he would be kind enough to keep still while they were filming, but the man blew him off. So Ewing Brown, one of the supporting players, went back to the shop with Baer and made the same request. The owner spun around in his chair and told him to go to hell. Then he saw Baer standing the in the doorway, big and ominous. "We'd appreciate it,' Baer told him. Later that day, there was a sign in the window: GONE FISHING!

Viewed with low expectations, *Giant* from the Unknown is reasonably entertaining and the best of the four genre films that Cunha and Jacobs made. It's well photographed by director Cunha, and except for Sally Fraser the cast is good. Albert Glasser's score is, well, Albert Glasser's score.

Beast from Haunted Cave

Location shooting in Deadwood, South Dakota, helped take the low-budget sting out of *Beast from Haunted Cave* (1959), produced by Gene Corman, directed by Monte Hellman, and written by Chuck Griffith.

Charles Griffith said, "Roger was in South Dakota and he needed a horror script fast. It was always fast. So he wanted *Naked Paradise* (1957) again only with a monster, which I kept in a cave away from the rest of the people so he couldn't mess up the structure of the story. Everything was the same: the crooks were waiting to get away in an airplane, the gangster's moll falls for the rented hero, and there's the speech about security."

The movie deserves some credit for being richer in characterization than anyone would expect from such a low-budget effort. It's certainly better than *Naked Paradise*, and the actors Michael Forest, Sheila Carol, and Frank Wolff are good in their roles. The origin of the monster is never explained, it's just something that exists in an old cave. The sequences with the creature are creepy and effective, but when the monster is offscreen, the film is a bit of a bore.

1984

"Long live Big Brother!" Winston Smith (Edmond O'Brien) shouts at the end of *1984* (1956). He has embraced the totalitarian regime that he rebelled against. His love for Julia (Jan Sterling) has been quashed by the Thought Police in

Room 101. The state can't tolerate love because it's an emotion beyond its control, but it can control hate, and that's what it nurtures. In the end, Smith has joined the pod people: the sheep who follow orders without question. It's an ending so bleak that an alternate, bittersweet version was shown in some markets in which Smith shouts, "Down with Big Brother," before being gunned down by the police. Julia is shot as she approaches his corpse, but before she dies, she takes his hand.

Edmond O'Brien and Jan Sterling Photo courtesy of Bob Villard.

The most frightening thing about George Orwell's novel, on which this film is based, is how much of it has come to pass. Winston Smith's job at the Ministry of Truth is to constantly revise history to conform to whatever position the state chooses to take at that moment. Hate is one of the principal tools to divide and conquer the populace. It's no wonder that "Big Brother" has become a part of the popular culture.

1984 was produced by N. Peter Rathvon, written by William Templeton, and directed by Michael Anderson. It was the first big screen version of Orwell's novel. There had been a radio version in 1949 with David Niven and two television shows—one in America in 1953 on CBS's *Studio One* with Eddie Albert, and a British TV production the following year, adapted by Nigel Kneale and starring Peter Cushing.

"For several reasons," said Bill Warren, "*1984* can be considered a property best left unfilmed. The characters are ciphers—William Smith and Julia exist solely to demonstrate the total power of the state over the individual, and have almost no personalities otherwise; this is inextricably part of the story. Furthermore, if done faithfully, the storyline is so depressing as to indicate there is no hope for anyone once the state achieves the kind of power it has in *1984*.

Nonetheless, *1984* was filmed and although as a movie it's not too bad, several errors were made that make it look as though it was carved from gray soap and to be mostly undramatic, even dull."[7]

The Attack of the Puppet People

Bert Gordon was at a business meeting one afternoon when he happened to notice a man with an attaché case and wondered: "What if he has little people in there?" When the meeting was over, Gordon went home and wrote what has to be the most cockamamie story of his career. *The Attack of the Puppet People* (1958) was written by George Worthington Yates as *The Fantastic Puppet People*, which was an appropriate title as the puppet people attack no one; they're the victims of the piece.

Reynold Brown poster for Attack of the Puppet People *(1958). Photo from the author's collection.*

John Hoyt plays Franz, a puppeteer turned doll-maker. After his wife ran off with an acrobat when his marionettes were playing in Luxemburg, Franz invented a machine that can shrink people to the size of a doll, so he can keep them with him always and never be lonely again. His victims are kept in a state of suspended animation inside glass tubes. They include his former secretary Janet Hall (Jean Moorehead), mailman Ernie Larson (Hal Bogart), Mac the Marine (Scott Peters), Georgia Lane (Laurie Mitchell), Stan (Kenny Miller), Laurie (Marlene Willis), salesman Bob Wesley (John Agar), and Franz's most recent secretary, Sally Reynolds (June Kenney). Oh yes, and last but not least: Bert and Flora Gordon.

As the police begin to close in, Franz decides to commit suicide and take his puppet people with him. As he loads the glass tubes into his briefcase, he drops one of them. Sally crawls out of her tube and he tells her the police are getting uncomfortably close. "You'll free us, won't you? You'll make us our right size again," she says hopefully. "And be deprived of your company?" Franz replies. "Oh no, I couldn't let that happen. Can't you see it's better that we all bow out together? Can't you see

Marlene Willis, Scott Peters, June Kenney, Laurie Mitchell, Kenny Miller, and John Agar wonder if they should call their agents and give them a piece of their minds, small as they may be. Photo courtesy of Bob Villard.

it's better for all of us to meet death together than for any one of us to be left alone? There's nothing worse than loneliness."

Franz takes his little people to an empty theater for one last fling. Sally and Bob escape, return to Franz's office, and use the machine to restore themselves to normal size. As they shove Franz aside to phone the police, he pathetically calls after them, "Don't leave me. I'll be alone." This was a last-minute change on the set. In the script, Franz stops them before they can get to his machine and returns them to their glass tubes with the sound of a police siren growing louder in the background.

This movie is really more of a fairy tale than it is a sci-fi movie, and because of Hoyt's performance it has a touch of charm about it. I confess that I rode my bike fifteen miles in the rain on a tire that had a leak to see this film for the third time. In those days, there were gas stations everywhere, so I kept stopping to fill the tire with air. *The Puppet People* was, and still is, my favorite Bert Gordon movie, but it isn't very good. Gordon's direction is more leaden than usual and June Kenney and John Agar are pretty terrible. There's a scene between Agar and a Jekyll and Hyde marionette that's positively embarrassing and ultimately amusing. Franz changes the face from Jekyll to Hyde, which frightens Kenney. Agar yanks the head off of the marionette and tries to tear it apart, which is what he'd like to do to Franz. And while the other puppet people cheer him on, Agar gets all tangled up in the strings as he wrestles with the thing. It's quite a scene.

Bert's movie didn't exactly reflect the fears that gripped the nation in the fifties, but it did play a part in bringing about the downfall of President Richard M. Nixon. According to John Barrett—the undercover district cop who caught the Watergate burglars—they might have gotten away if their lookout, stationed across the street in the Howard Johnson Hotel, had been paying attention instead of watching the *Puppet People* on television.

Notes:

1. Mandell, Paul. "Careers," *Cinemagic*, vol. 8, no. 1, pg. 57.
2. Fultz, Jr. Lawrence. "The Last Words from the Last Woman on Earth," *Scarlet: the Film Magazine*, Number 5, pg. 53.
3. Weaver, Tom. *Attack of the Monster Movie Makers*, McFarland, Jefferson, NC, 1994, pg. 182.
4. Weaver, Tom. *Science Fiction Stars and Horror Heroes*, McFarland, Jefferson, NC, 1991, pgs. 404-405.
5. Ibid. Pg. 406.
6. Kaufman also wrote *Bad Day at Black Rock*.
7. Warren, Bill. *Keep Watching the Skies!* McFarland & Co., Jefferson, NC, 2010, pg. 633.

CHAPTER TEN
Tampering in God's Domain

*I will show the world that I can be its master. I will
perfect my own race of people... a race of atomic
supermen which will conquer the the world!*
—The Bride of the Monster

In the sci-fi films of the thirties and forties, Boris Karloff, Bela Lugosi, John Carradine, George Zucco, and Lionel Atwill would lock themselves away in some secret,
often isolated laboratory. It would be full of test tubes and Kenneth Strickfaden's
flashing, sparkling doo-dads. As the electricity danced from electrode to electrode
and smoke rose from beakers full of bubbling liquid, they would do the Devil's work.
In the fifties, a lot of the test tubes and electrodes were replaced by banks of blinking
lights and other electronic, computer-driven machinery. It didn't matter whether
these doctors were mad or simply driven, whether their intentions were well meaning or self-serving, the result was always the same: disaster! And it wasn't always
clear what it was that they were trying to accomplish.

The Magnetic Monster
Dying from a massive dose of radiation poisoning, Leonard Mudie tells Richard
Carlson that he bombarded serranium with alpha particles for 200 hours, creating
a new element which can turn energy into mass. With each meal, *The Magnetic
Monster* (1953) increases its size and its appetite. Mudie warns Carlson to "keep it
under constant electric charge. It has to be fed constantly or it will reach out its

*Harry Ellerbe, Richard Carlson, Michael Fox, Frank Gerstle, and King Donovan get their first look at
the magnetic monster. Photo courtesy of Bob Villard.*

magnetic arms and grab anything within its reach and kill it." Carlson wants to know how it can be stopped. "Other scientists will have to find the solution," Mudie says: "My contribution is finished." Some contribution! Thanks, Doc. Thanks a lot.

Curt Siodmak wrote *The Magnetic Monster* around the special effects footage from a 1934 German film called Das gelde. It may well be his best script—logical, tense, and ultimately exciting. It's certainly the best movie he directed, but it's not a kid's film. Maybe that's why the critics liked it. It's believable from start to finish, beginning as a mystery and ending with a desperate, last ditch effort to overload Mudie's newly created element with enough power to choke it before it throws the Earth off its axis.

Herbert Strock said, "*Magnetic Monster* was the first feature I directed. Ivar Tors didn't like what Siodmak was doing and after three days, he asked me to take over the picture. I've been a doctor of sick pictures all my life."

Asking a mediocre talent like Herb Strock to fix a troubled movie is rather like a drunk asking Stevie Wonder to drive him home. According to Michael Fox, who did double duty as an actor and a script supervisor on the film, Siodmak directed it from start to finish.

The Phantom from 10,000 Leagues

Mudie wasn't the only nitwit who created a menace for no apparent reason *The Phantom from 10,000 Leagues* (1956) was the handiwork of Michael Whalen, who got his paycheck from the Pacific College of Oceanography. Kent Taylor an oceanographer investigating the deaths caused by Whalen's monster, suspects that Whalen created the thing to guard a deposit of uranium ore on the ocean floor, but we never find out whether or not that's true. "I created such a mutant in my own laboratory," Taylor tells Whalen. "I destroyed it, just as this creature must be destroyed and the knowledge that went into creating it." Why these two men wanted to create such a creature in the first place is another piece of information that's withheld from the audience. At any rate, Whalen ultimately agrees with Taylor; he trashes his laboratory and burns his notes. The janitor (Pierce Lydon) walks in and sees a smaller version of the "phantom" dead on the floor. "You mean to say that's one of God's creatures, Professor?" he asks. Whalen replies: "No, Andy, that's one of man's follies and I pray God there'll never be another one." And so did everyone in the audience. Midway in this wheeze, the kids started throwing half-full boxes of popcorn and candy, and when they ran out of ammunition they started playing chase.

Boxoffice: "In describing a situation as this hodgepodge draws to a merciful close, a character intones: 'What a mess.' If it weren't for the fact that a prescribed amount of space has to be filled, that line of dialogue could aptly service as the beginning and the end of a critique of this offering."

The Unknown Terror

The Unknown Terror (1957) had a lot in common with *The Phantom from 10,000*
Leagues in that the story is so
entangled with plots and subplots that it never addresses
the one issue around which the
entire film revolves: the monster.

John Howard and Paul
Richards accompany Mala
Powers in her search for her
lost brother, who came to
South America looking for
the Cave of Death. They
never find her brother, but
they do find the Cave of
Death. They also find scientist Gerald Milton, who has

Mala Powers in menaced by a fungus-covered zombie in The
Unknown Terror *(1957). Photo courtesy of Bob Villard.*

developed a new kind of fungus. He's turned a lot of the natives into fungus-
covered zombies. Why? We don't know. Apparently the writer, Kenneth Higgins,
didn't know either and producer-director Charles Marquis Warren didn't care
to ask. Milton's fungus, oozing down the walls of the Cave of Death, looks suspiciously like massive globs of soapsuds. One could easily come away from this
film with the notion that Milton had retired to South America to do a huge load
of wash that got terribly out of hand.

The Neanderthal Man

Professor Clifford Groves (Robert Shayne) is ready to burst a blood vessel
as he attempts to explain to a handful of his contemptuous colleagues (and the
audience) that the brain of *The Neanderthal Man* (1953) was the same size as
the brain of modern man. "Are you advancing the astonishing concept that the
mentality of primitive man compares favorably with that organ that a million
years of revolutionary progress has developed in its modern counterpart?" one
of the scientists asks. "Let me assure you," Groves insists, "for want of your understanding, that modern man's boasting pride in alleged advancement is based
on one hollow precept and that is his ego." But everyone in the room agrees
that the size of the brain does not reflect the size of the mentality. "That you
should think so doesn't surprise me at all," Groves tells them angrily. "Whether
your skull is thicker or your intelligence thinner I can't determine. This is my
cross, the penalty of being born into an era of little men who are small even in

their spites. Hypocrisy is your bible! Stupidity is the cornerstone of your existence!" To prove his theory, this laughingstock of the scientific community turns himself into a prehistoric man, and he murders a few people before he's gunned down. As he returns to his normal self, someone remarks that he tampered with things beyond his province. Just before he dies, Groves says, "Its better this way." We couldn't agree more.

It takes a team effort to make a film as miserable as *The Neanderthal Man* and it begins with a terrible script—Aubrey Wisberg and Jack Pollexfen are the ones to blame for that. Like all of their scripts, it is full of awkward dialogue and foggy motivations and a story that makes no sense. The caveman mask, created by Harry Thomas, which doesn't look like any caveman you've ever seen, is as flexible as a block of cement and about as interesting. The director, Andre DuPont, must have been asleep in his chair. It's the only possible explanation for the film's one and only shining moment. In an effort to lure Groves away from the lab, his fiancée (Doris Merrick) playfully musses his hair and the actor is forced to play the rest of the scene looking as if he'd just stepped out of a wind tunnel. As if that wasn't enough, with his hair reaching for the ceiling, Groves tells the woman: "I will not be laughed at." Albert Glasser's score is exactly what this film deserved.

The Vampire

The Vampire (1957) was the result of Matt Campbell's regression pills. As he dies, he gives his friend Dr. Paul Beecher (John Beal) a bottle of these pills. Beecher, who suffers from migraine headaches, takes a couple of them by mistake, thinking they're aspirin. Throughout the picture, we get tidbits of information about these pills. All of Campbell's test animals, except for the vampire bats, have died of capillary disintegration. The pills may or may not hold the capillary disintegration in check and they drain blood from the brain. After all is said and done, there are only three things that we know for sure about the pills: they're addictive, they turn Beecher into a vampire, and his victims die of capillary disintegration. And maybe that's all we need to know since this Gardner-

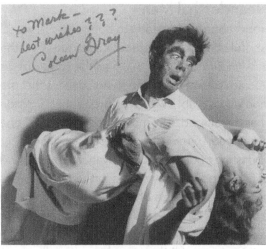

John Beal and Coleen Gray. Photo from the author's collection.

Laven-Levy production, directed by Paul Landres, does what it's supposed to do; it entertains and it frightens. Writer Pat Fielder admits she was influenced by other horror pictures when she wrote it. There's a lot of Val Lewton in this one. One sequence seems to have been inspired by *The Man with the Golden Arm* (1955). Beecher enlists the aid of an old friend (Dabbs Greer) to help him kick his addiction to the pills. It's a very intense sequence and a lot grittier than one would expect from a film like this.

Coleen Gray said, "I don't remember much about the movie. It was done so long ago and it was done so quickly. I do remember poor John Beal with that horrible makeup. He was such a good sport about it. I think he was glad to get the part. He hadn't done a picture in a while. I played his nurse and Ken Tobey was the police detective."

Paul Landres said, "It was a very successful combination of all of the elements necessary to make a successful show—producing, writing, directing, acting, editing, camera, etc. And the feeling on the set, from top to bottom, was one of great camaraderie, one of every person involved trying to do his best. It was a wonderful feeling and doesn't happen very often."[1]

The Werewolf

Doctors Morgan Chambers (George M. Lynn) and Emery Forrest (S. John Launer) believe that a nuclear war is inevitable. They believe that a series of inoculations—of a serum derived from a wolf that died from radiation poisoning—will save them and a chosen few from the radioactive fallout. "We'll be the only normal thinking people left," Chambers brags. For reasons that are never made clear, Chambers gave an overdose of the serum to Duncan Marsh (Steven

Steven Ritch as the werewolf. Photo from the author's collection.

Ritch), who is suffering from amnesia as a result of an auto accident. Marsh becomes *The Werewolf* (1956) and Chambers is afraid that if he gets his memory back, he'll lead the authorities straight to their door. "But you're not going to kill him?" Forrest exclaims. "You think he still wants to live after what he's become?" Chambers snaps. "It'll be an act of charity."

This expository sequence comes about a quarter of the way into the picture. It opens with Marsh—a frightened and confused man—wandering into a bar and restaurant in Big Bear called Chad's Place. Marsh asks the bartender (George Cisar) if he's ever seen him before but the bartender hasn't. One of the local barflies (Charles Horvath) follows Marsh out of the bar and tries to mug him. As the two men struggle in a dark alley, we hear the growl of an animal. The camera cuts to the outside of the alley as the two men fall to the pavement. We see two pairs of legs kicking until one of them goes limp. A woman (Jean Harvey) sees Marsh come out of the alley and screams. From this point on, it becomes a contest to see who will find Marsh first: the sheriff (Don Megowan) or the two scientists.

This movie is no classic by any stretch of the imagination, but it's scary and poignant, and it deserves more attention than it has received. As with most of Sam Katzman's efforts, the music is culled from the studio's A-pictures. The film's main title is a lift from *The Sniper* (1952) by George Antheil, which is used again in Katzman's *Zombies of Mora Tau*. Eddie Linden's moody photography strikes just the right chord and director Fred Sears seems to be going the extra mile to get the most out of every scene. His camera placement is exceptional and location shooting in Big Bear adds a lot to the production values. (A low-budget movie looks as good as a big-budget movie when you shoot outdoors.) For the most part, the script by Robert Kent and James B. Gordon is good and most of the performers are too, but it's Steven Ritch's performance as the beleaguered and tortured Marsh that everyone remembers. In spite of the efforts of the sheriff (Don Megowan) to bring him in alive, the audience knows that Marsh's fate has been sealed. The only thing they can hope for is that he'll get the two scientists before the sheriff gets him.

4-D Man

Add Tony Nelson (James Congdon) to the list of people at work on a project with questionable benefits. With the help of a force field to amplify the power of his brain, Nelson has successfully willed a pencil through a block of steel—a feat he's been unable to duplicate. He gets a job with his brother Scott (Robert Lansing), at the Fairview Research Center, owned by a selfish egomaniac named Theodore W. Carson (Edgar Stehli). Carson holds a press conference to announce Scott's newest discovery: Cargonite, an impenetrable metal. As the reporters shower

Carson with praise, he reminds them that a discovery of this magnitude takes a team effort, but he then trivializes his remark by having to consult his notes to give them the name of the team leader. Scott and his assistant Linda Davis (Lee Meriwether), leave the room in disgust.

Scott wants to marry Linda, but hasn't found the courage to ask her, so he passively watches as she falls in love with Tony. This is the second time that his brother has taken a woman away from him and he decides not to let it happen again. He proposes to Linda, but while she admires him, she doesn't love him. With his self-esteem circling the toilet, Scott returns to the lab, breaks into Tony's locker, grabs his notes and his force field, and successfully repeats Tony's experiment. But he gets his hand stuck in the process and while he struggles to free himself, one of his ambitious underlings, Roy Parker (Robert Strauss), steals Tony's notes and gives them to Carson as his own.

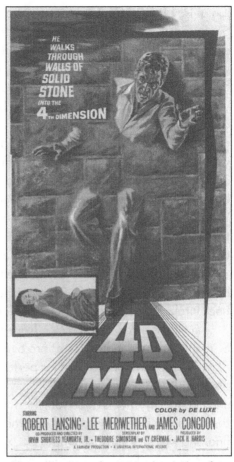

Three-sheet poster for 4D Man *(1959). Photo from the author's collection.*

Once Scott works his hand free, he calls Tony and together they perform the stunt again, only this time Scott does it without the aid of the force field. Working with radiation for so long has increased Scott's brain power, which is the cause of his blinding headaches. At this point of the story, Scott goes from being passive to dangerously aggressive as he becomes the *4-D Man* (1959). He strolls through the city streets exercising his new power, plucking a letter from a mailbox, an apple from a storefront display, and finally a large chunk of money from a bank vault. The next morning, to his horror, he finds that he's become an old man. Every time he entered the fourth dimension he was speeding up time and taking years off his life. He goes to his doctor (Dean Newman) for help, and he unintentionally passes his hands through the doctor's body. The doctor dies of old age in a matter of seconds while Scott becomes young again.

The next morning, Scott is called into Carson's office and asked for his opinion of Roy Parker. Carson suspects that the notes Parker gave him belong to Scott and, in a guarded conversation, asks Scott if he has anything new up his sleeve. Later that night, Scott confronts Carson in his home. As he casually walks through a chair, he tells his boss that from now on, he's the one who's going to be doing the taking. "You thought you had me in your pocket, didn't you, all tagged and classified?" he says bitterly. "Good old Scott. So what if we do pick his brains. Good old Scott. So what if his girl is a tramp. So what if he goes half blind with pain and fear as long as the world can have Cargonite Good old Scott, he won't care." The terrified Carson promises to put Scott's name on the project and offers him a more important position with more money but Scott kills him anyway. He also kills Parker and ultimately becomes a menace With tears streaming down his face, he promises Linda he'll stop his reign of terror if she'll go away with him. She doesn't even have to love him; he just wants to be with her. She agrees to his proposal and he comes out of 4-D long enough to kiss her, and long enough for her to shoot him. "Do you hate me that much?" he asks. "No," she replies. Dying from the wound and his broken heart, he slips back into 4-D and buries himself in a block of Cargonite.

4-D Man is a very good movie from producer Jack H. Harris, director Irwin S. Yeahworth, and writer Theodore Simonson—the same team that made The Blob. Oscars have been given for performances that didn't cover the range of emotions that Lansing successfully navigates in this film. He's truly remarkable and Lee Meriwether is good too; this was their film debut. James Congdon, on the other hand, is not so good. On the technical side, the special effects are fine, and while it's unusual to hear a jazz score in a picture like this, for the most part, composer Ralph Carmichael makes it work.

Indestructible Man

Two cancer research scientists (Robert Shayne and Joe Flynn) inadvertently bring Butcher Benton (Lon Chaney) back to life by sending 280,000 volts of electricity through his body. Ironically, Benton had just come from the electric chair for the murder of two guards during an armored car robbery. Maybe if he'd sat in the chair a little longer, he could have saved these two guys the trouble. Then again, maybe not, since another dose of electricity kills him at the end of the movie. It's most confusing. Anyway, the voltage that the scientists give him increases his cellular structure, turning his tissue into a solid mass of cells that can't be penetrated by bullets. As the Indestructible Man (1956), Benton is able to make good his prison house threat to kill his two hold-up partners, Joe Marcelli (Ken Terrell) and Squeamy Ellis (Marvin Ellis), whose testimony sent him to the chair. The only reason they turned on him was because Benton got greedy and ran off with the loot. Benton's lawyer, Paul Lowe (Ross Elliott), was the mastermind behind the robbery, and he knows he's next on Benton's hit list. He confesses to his part in the crime so the police will toss him into jail for protection. With Lieutenant Dick Chasen (Casey Adams) leading the charge, the police track Benton to the LA sewer system where he's hidden the money. The police drive Benton out of the sewer with flame throwers and bazookas.

This stinker was written, produced, and directed by Jack Pollexfen. For some reason, the climax in the sewer was added eighteen months after the film had been completed. In the first cut of the film, Benton broke into the police station and killed the lawyer in his cell. Benton's so-called girlfriend, Eva Martin (Marian Carr), is at the station at the time. She's injured when he carries her off to Bronson Caves, the location of the stolen money. (The reference to her being treated in the hospital is still in the film.) The cops drive Benton out of the cave with tear gas and chase him to the electrical plant, where he's killed by another massive dose of electricity. Why a film as cheap as this one would scrap what was probably ten minutes of footage is a real mystery. But, it explains a couple of things. There's a scene where the lawyer steals a map from Eva Martin that shows where Benton hid the money. The insert of the hastily drawn map, which the narrator tells the audience is a section of the LA sewer system, has no street names or numbers to indicate what section of the sewer system it's supposed to be. It's a map of precisely nothing. Also, during the chase through the sewer, the scenes of the police and the scenes of Benton were shot on separate days; they never appear in the same shot.

The Son of Dr. Jekyll

Pollexfen also wrote the story for *The Son of Dr. Jekyll* (1951), which writer Edward Huebsch turned into a screenplay. Huebsch was blacklisted shortly before the film went into release, and the studio removed his name from the credits. There's no producer's credit either, so either Huebsch was the producer too or whoever the producer was, he didn't care to take credit for the thing—which is understandable.

Jekyll's son Edward (Louis Heyward), wants to prove that his father was not a monster. He restores his father's lab and attempts to recreate the formula. It isn't long before the murdering monster is on the loose again and Edward is arrested and confined to a sanitarium run by Dr. Curtis Lanyon (Alexander Knox), the trustee of Jekyll's estate. Edward escapes just in time to see someone leaving his father's old Soho apartment. The woman living there has been murdered. Edward hurries to the lab and catches Lanyon in the process of burning his father's notes. In one of those "talking gun" sequences that the movies are so fond of, Lanyon admits that it was he masquerading as the fiend in order to discredit Edward so that he could keep the estate for himself.

One minor note of interest is the casting of Ottola Nesmith in a small role as a nurse. A few years later, the actress hosted a Los Angeles TV program called "Nightmare," which premiered the classic Universal horror library.

Daughter of Dr. Jekyll

Pollexfen wrote and produced *Daughter of Dr. Jekyll* (1957), a rehash of *Son of Dr. Jekyll*, which had been a rehash of *She Wolf of London* (1946)—one of Universal's worst horror pictures. Pollexfen dismissed Stevenson's story altogether. In his yarn, which he hired Edgar Ulmer to direct, he carelessly mixed vampire and werewolf legends.

"I had no intention of plagiarizing or re-using pre-existing elements," Edgar Ulmer told *Midi-Minuit* in 1965. "When I began the project, I insisted that a good part of the screenplay be rewritten. I thought that to follow the story of Dr. Jekyll and Mr. Hyde (which had already been brought to the screen a number of times) would lead us very far from our subject."

On her twenty-first birthday, Janet Smith (Gloria Talbott) is told by her guardian, Dr. Lomas (Arthur Shields), that she will inherit her father's estate. That's the good news. The bad news is that her father was the infamous Dr. Jekyll, a blood-drinking werewolf. "I still shudder when I recall that face, like some perverted mask of evil out of a legend of horror," Lomas tells Janet and her fiancé, Bob Hastings (John Agar). Janet is afraid that she may have inherited her father's dual personality. That very night, she has a dream about murdering Maggie the maid (Molly McCart) and wakes up with blood on her hands. Maggie's corpse is found by Jacob (John Dierkes). Her throat has been slit. Jacob believes that Janet is responsible, and after two more dreams and two more murders, Janet thinks so too. She begs Bob to drive a stake through her heart. "If you love me, please kill me!" But, Janet is innocent; Lomas is the werewolf. Using hypnosis, he planted the nightmares in Janet's head.

The movie was shot in an old mansion on Sixth Street near Hancock Park in Los Angeles. Talbott said there's a scene where she and Agar are having breakfast and through the window, you can see 1956 automobiles passing by the house in the distance. As the movie takes place sometime around the turn of the century, this might be some cause for concern if the movie was any good, but it isn't. Except for Miss Talbott's performance, it's a complete washout from beginning to end. The opening shot of a little toy car approaching Jack Rabin's tiny miniature house sets the stage for a film so short on story that, as Andrew Sarris points out, "it takes forty minutes to establish that the daughter of Dr. Jekyll is indeed the daughter of Dr. Jekyll." The plot is so flimsy that the characters are reluctant to give up what little information is needed to move it forward. It's like pulling teeth. And, for some reason, Talbott doesn't look anything like the woman in her nightmares and the woman in her nightmares doesn't look anything like a werewolf. She looks more like a vampire. The score, a mix of library music and cues from *Robot Monster*, is often in conflict with the action onscreen. And whoever signed off Agar's wardrobe should have his or her head examined; Agar's striped jacket makes him look like an ice cream vendor—all he needed was a straw hat. Champions of director Ulmer may find moments of brilliance in this dud, but we couldn't.

Abbott and Costello Meet Dr. Jekyll and Mr. Hyde

Abbott and Costello Meet Dr. Jekyll and Mr. Hyde (1953) is more frightening than either of Pollexfen's movies. The plot, what little there was of it, concerned Bud and Lou's efforts to catch "the monster" so they could get their jobs back as detectives assigned to Scotland Yard. In this show, Jekyll (Boris Karloff) is every bit as wicked as his alter ego Hyde (Eddie Parker). The film opens with Hyde killing his friend Dr. Stephen Poole (Herbert Deans). "Hyde did it; not me," he tells his mute assistant Batley (John Dierkes), who couldn't care less. Jekyll is in love with his ward, Vicky Edwards (Helen Westcott), but she's in love with newspaper reporter Bruce Adams (Craig Stevens). Hyde tries to kill him too. "Everything I've ever done has been for you," Jekyll tells Vicky after locking her in his office. He becomes enraged when she tries to get away and turns into Hyde without taking the drug. Her screams bring Bruce, Bud, and Lou to the rescue.

Boris Karloff behind the scenes from Abbott and Costello Meet Dr. Jekyll and Mr. Hyde. *Photo from the author's collection.*

In Abbott and Costello Meet the Invisible Man

In *Abbott and Costello Meet the Invisible Man* (1951), the police are after boxer Tommy Nelson (Arthur Franz) for the murder of his manager. To avoid arrest, Tommy injects himself with an invisibility serum that he is told will eventually drive him mad. But with the help of private detectives Abbott and Costello, Tommy hopes he can find the real killer (Sheldon Leonard) before that happens.

Arthur Franz said, "As soon as we'd finished a scene, Bud and Lou would disappear into one of their dressing rooms, close the door, and play cards until they were called back to the set. I never really got to know them. I did sense that there was tension between them."

The Bowery Boys Meet the Monsters

Taking a cue from Bud and Lou, Elwood Ullman and Edward Bernds wrote *The Bowery Boys Meet the Monsters* (1954). The plot, a lift from *Abbott and Costello Meet Frankenstein*, puts Horace Debussy Jones (Huntz Hall) in danger of losing his brain to a gorilla (Steve Calvert). Besides the gorilla in this house of horrors, there's a wolf man (Paul Wexler), a vampire (Laura Mason), a man-eating tree, and a robot (Norman Bishop). These were bread-and-butter movies for Allied Artists, made for small children and adults with low-watt brain power. In Los Angeles, it was used to support the Danny Kaye comedy *Knock on Wood* (1954).

Monkey Business

Producer-director Howard Hawks was up to some *Monkey Business* (1952) with one of his favorite actors, Cary Grant. Grant played Barnaby Fulton, an absent-minded professor who was working on a way to slow the aging process. His pet chimpanzee dumps a bunch of his chemicals into a water cooler and anyone who drinks the stuff feels and acts like a teenager again. Ginger Rodgers, Charles Coburn, Hugh Marlowe, and Marilyn Monroe are along for the ride. We don't recommend that you hop on board.

Written by Ben Hecht, Charles Lederer, and I.A.L. Diamond, this is a pretty "infantile" effort from Hawks, who didn't like it much himself. "Occasional scenes are briefly funny," wrote the critic for *Variety*, "but are not sustained and the joke wears thinner as it's spun out into further developments." Bosley Crowther agreed, "The trouble, we'd say—if trouble is what you'd call an extended barrage of whooping childish behavior by a film full of grown-up clowns—is that a screwball idea like this one can be kept funny just so long, which is maybe thirty-five or forty minutes and then it blows up and that's the end." Apparently audiences agreed as the film was anything but a howling success.

The Man in the White Suit

Ealing's *The Man in the White Suit* (1952) was a far better comedy effort—an even-handed assault on industrial capitalists, trade unions, and conservatism. Alec Guinness played chemist Sidney Stratton, whose stain-repelling, nearly indestructible fabric becomes a threat to the garment industry. Greedy manufacturer John Kierlaw (Ernest Thesiger) tries to bribe, suppress, and incarcerate Stratton. If he isn't stopped, factories will close and thousands of people will be thrown out of work. "Why can't you scientists leave things alone?" Stratton's landlady (Edie Martin) asks him. "What about my bit of washing when there's no washing to be done?" Joining forces, management and labor chase Stratton through the streets like the mob running after the Frankenstein monster. Written by Roger MacDougall, John Dighton, and director Alexander Mackendrick, this is a picture that's firing on all pistons. *Womaneater* (1959)—another British film—is running on four flat tires, however.

Womaneater

Dr. James Moran (George Coulouris) uses sap from a South American plant to bring the dead back to life. There's only one hitch: the plant has to eat a beautiful woman before it can produce the sap. Moran and his Inca buddy Tanga (Jimmy Vaughn), experience something akin to an orgasm as they watch the women Moran kidnaps being devoured by the plant. It's the sort of thing one would expect to see in a Herman Cohen movie. The whole business of killing people to bring the dead back to life seems thoroughly counter-productive to us, but then, we're not doctors.

Moran's housekeeper, Margaret (Joyce Gregg), suspects that he's up to something wicked, but she keeps her mouth shut because she's hopelessly in love with him. When Moran hires a younger woman (Vera Day) to help out around the house, Margaret gets her panties in a knot. "Why do you persist in these middle-aged jealousies? I'm very tired of them," Moran complains. "To be brutally frank, to me you're a thing of the past. You know very well I've only kept you on out of charity." Enraged, Margaret lunges at him with a knife. Moran strangles her, injects her with the sap, and she returns to life. But she's a zombie. She has no mind. Moran has been double-crossed. "The brain for us only," Tanga says with delight, "our secret not for you." And believe us, this movie not for you.

The Unearthly

John D. F. Black, well-known to fans of the original *Star Trek* TV series, was selling classified ads for *The Los Angeles Times* back in his salad days, hoping to break into the movies. He was sent to the office of low-end producer Boris Petroff to pick up the copy for an ad he wanted to run. Petroff, who often hid behind the name Brooke L. Peters, was looking for someone to write *The House of Monsters*, someone who wasn't a member of the Writer's Guild. Black told Petroff he could save the cost of the ad by hiring him. Since Black's job at the paper prohibited him from moonlighting, he wrote the script using the pseudonym Geoffrey Dennis. His handwritten script was turned over to Petroff's wife to type. She put her pen name on it, Jane Mann, and Petroff refused to pay Black for his work. Black turned to the Writer's Guild for help. Petroff claimed that his wife had written the script and that Black had only been hired as a typist. But Black told the Guild he couldn't type and he produced the contract he had with Petroff, who, at that point, was caught with his pants down. This was the genesis of the movie that came to be known as *The Unearthly* (1957).

Professor Charles Conway (John Carradine) has turned his home into a mental health clinic. All of his patients are screened by Dr. Loren Wright (Roy Gordon) to make sure they have no family ties because Conway uses all of his patients as guinea pigs. He's invented a seventeenth gland which he hopes will

Sally Todd. Photo from the author's collection.

prolong life indefinitely (Apparently he isn't concerned about the food shortage problem. He should talk to Professor Deemer.) So far, all that Conway has succeeded in doing is turning people into mindless monsters.

For someone who's supposed to know something about mental health, Conway puts on a lousy front. His cook and housekeeper is a 300-pound goon named Lobo (Tor Johnson). Lobo has the IQ of a rabbit; he's hardly the sort of a character who would put a nervous patient at ease. (A few shots of Lobo cooking dinner or dusting the furniture would have been delightful.) Conway's one and only prescription for what ails his patients is for them to get plenty of rest. Even the mentally deficient Lobo knows enough to tell them that. "Time for go to bed," he says, putting an end to Conway's organ recital of Bach's "Toccata and Fugue," which isn't likely to lift the spirits of his depressed patients, either.

Other than the presence of Allison Hayes and Sally Todd in the cast, the best thing about this picture is the climax. After Conway is killed by one of his victims, the police find a jail full of his mindless, hideous rejects in the cellar. Whether they will live forever or not is left up to question, but one thing is certain: the makers of this film succeeded in prolonging the life of the film's seventy-three-minute running time. It seems to go on forever.

The Man Who Turned to Stone

Like Conway's bogus health clinic, the LaSalle Detention Home for Girls provides Dr. Murdock (Victory Jory) and his 220-year-old staff with all of the victims they need in their quest for eternal life. These jokers were born in the mid-eighteenth century and were participants in an experiment to stop the aging process. By transferring bio-electricity from one person to another, which kills the donor, they have succeeded. But, from time to time, they need to renew their bio-electricity and the period of time between treatments is decreasing, especially for Eric (Frederick Ledebur). He needs them every day or he will become *The Man Who Turned to Stone* (1957).

The number of young, healthy women dying from heart attacks attracts the attention of the school's newly hired secretary and pseudo-psychiatrist, Carol

Adams (Charlotte Austin). When she attempts to look at the death records, she's told to mind her own business. But the state board is curious as well and they send Dr. Jess Rogers (William Hudson) to conduct an investigation of his own.

Eric is the closest thing this film has to a monster, but he's more irritating than he is frightening. With his mind all but gone, he impatiently slaps the arms of his chair like a spoiled child as he waits for his next treatment. You just want to spank him. Why Murdock and the rest of these selfish sociopaths keep him alive is a mystery because he's nothing but a liability. Yet, they choose instead to let Dr. Cooper (Paul Cavanagh) die because he's expressed some concern about their right to keep killing people. Earlier in the film, Cooper tells Dr. Rogers that 220 years is too long for any man to live, yet, as the others watch him petrify, Cooper wonders if he might be able to finish his research if he had just a few more years to live. It's the only decent moment in the entire film. You'll feel like your bio-electricity is being drained as you watch it.

She Demons

There's more transference going on in the cynically motivated *She Demons* (1958). Ex-Nazi scientist Karl Osler (Rudolph Andes), affectionately known as "The Butcher," transfers "Character X" from the beautiful native women on his remote island to his horribly disfigured wife (Leni Tana) in an attempt to restore her beauty. Richard Cunha referred to his cliché-ridden script as tongue-in-cheek,

Irish McCalla, Tod Griffin, and Victor Sen Young try to escape from the She Demons (1958). Photo courtesy of Bob Villard.

though head-up-ass is more like it. $15,000 of his $65,000 budget went to leading lady Irish McCalla, known to TV watchers as Sheena, Queen of the Jungle. Cunha wanted to shoot a topless scene for the foreign market, but McCalla wanted to keep her back to the camera. Cunha told the readers of a *Scarlet Street* interview that the actress had lost her bustline, but in a rebuttal letter, the actress insisted her bust never looked better and sent along some photographs to prove it. Frankly, if her performance was as good as her bosom, she would have been given an Oscar nomination, but acting was never Miss McCalla's strong suit. Her performance as one of the four castaways who wash ashore on Osler's island is probably the worst one in the film, though everyone but Victor Sen Yung is pretty lame. Some people think *She Demons* is a lot of fun. It has some laughs to be sure, but the last laugh is on the audience.

The Four-Sided Triangle

Equally boring, though better produced, Hammer's *The Four-Sided Triangle* (1953) has the ugliest and dumbest scientist of them all, a guy named Bill Legget (Stephen Murray). Leggett and his old pal, Robin Grant (John Van Eyssen), invent a machine that can duplicate anything and everything. Since childhood these two have been in love with the same woman, Lena Maitland (Barbara Payton). Bill is devastated when Lena marries Robin, but he gets what he thinks is a brilliant idea: he duplicates Lena. Of course, the duplicate is in love with Robin too, as anyone but this idiot could have predicted. Determined, Bill invents a device that can erase her memory, suffering under the egotistical delusion that with a clean slate, she'll naturally fall in love with him. Fortunately, a fire breaks out and kills them both.

Terence Fisher directed this hogwash and co-authored the script with Paul Tabori, adapted from William F. Temple's 1939 novel. Fisher attempts to add a little *Our Town* charm to the proceedings by having one of the characters (James Hayter) talking directly into the camera as he introduces the town and the people, but there's nothing charming about a film that gives its stamp of approval to snobbish notions of class structure. But, for a movie that's primarily about love and romance, there is nothing romantic about it. *The Monthly Film Bulletin* pretty well summed it up. "This is a tedious little melodrama, flatly directed, written, and played. Barbara Payton seems unlikely to achieve fame for her histrionic ability and Stephen Murray's performance is unadulterated ham."

The Fly

"THE FLY has opened—400 theaters never saw anything so big!" This was the bold-faced copy that appeared in a two-page spread in *The Motion Picture Herald*. The publicity boys at 20th Century-Fox got their hands slapped for this bit of sophomoric sniggering and were told not to do it again.

George Langelaan's novella *The Fly* was published in the June 1957 issue of *Playboy* magazine. Kurt Neumann read it and took it to Robert Lippert, who supplied 20th Century-Fox with $125,000 movies shot on independent lots and released through Fox as Regal Films. Lippert took an option on Langelaan's story and Neumann hired James Clavell to turn it into a screenplay. Lippert thought Clavell did such a fantastic job that he let Clavell write, produce, and direct *Five Gates to Hell* the following year. Clavell would later write such best-selling novels as *King Rat*, *Shogun*, and *Tai-Pan* and co-author the screenplay for *The Great Escape* (1963).

Buddy Adler, the head of production at Fox, thought that Clavell's script was the best first draft he'd ever seen, so he decided to increase the budget from $100,000 to $350,000 and release it as a Fox film in color and CinemaScope. Adler gave Lippert access to the studio and all of its resources; the gamble paid off. Shot in eighteen days, *The Fly* out grossed Fox's bigger pictures that year, taking in well over $3 million and making Lippert a minor celebrity on the lot.

Aside from the studio-imposed happy ending, Clavell stuck pretty close to Langelaan's flashback story structure. Helene Delambre (Patricia Owens) has murdered her scientist husband Andre (David Hedison), but she won't say why until Andre's brother, Francois (Vincent Price), tells her that he's captured the white-headed fly that she was looking for. With his promise to kill it, Helene tells him and police inspector Charas (Herbert Marshall) the whole story. Andre had invented a device that could disintegrate a solid object in one chamber and project it through space into another chamber where it was reintegrated again. But when Andre went through the process, he didn't notice the fly that was in the chamber with him until it was too late. Their atoms were mixed and Andre emerged with the claw and head of the fly. Helene unsuccessfully tried to capture the fly so Andre could go through the process again and maybe unscramble their atoms. Andre destroyed his machine and his notes, and he had Helene crush him with a steam press so there would be no trace of what had happened. Charas thinks Helene is crazy and orders her confinement to a mental institution. As she's being taken away, her son Philippe (Charles Herbert) tells Francois that he's seen the fly in a spider's web. Francois grabs Charas, and the two arrive in time to see the spider devour the fly with Andre's head.

Al (David) Hedison and Patricia Owens. Photo courtesy of Bob Villard.

Why the fly's head becomes as big as a man's head and the man's head as small as a fly's head defies all logic, but this is a film that has to be watched not with the head, but the heart. The filmmakers know this, so the story begins with its feet firmly planted in reality. The audience is presented with a mystery, the loving relationship between the Andre and Helene, and finally an incredible invention that, for a change, is a great idea. By the time they actually see the fly-headed human it's too late. They've been coerced into accepting just about anything.

Contract players David Hedison and Patricia Owens play the leads, and they're reasonably convincing as a happy couple who have been plunged into a nightmare. Hedison spends half of the film with his head covered by a cloth, no longer able to speak, and forced to communicate with Owens by hand or typewritten messages. "BRAIN SAYS STRANGE THINGS NOW," he types as he struggles to suppress the impulses of the fly. Owens insists that he go through the machine again without the fly, which he does to placate her, knowing it can't possibly work. She yanks the cloth from his head and sees what he has become for the first time. Through his eyes, we see multiple images of her screaming face. When she recovers, he scrawls LOVE YOU on a blackboard. It's a touching moment, and one that can't help but tug at the heart.

Vincent Price is fond of telling the story of how he and Herbert Marshall couldn't stop laughing when they were supposed to be looking at the human-headed fly in the spider's web. It may be silly, but no one who has ever seen the movie can forget that high-pitched little voice screaming, "Help me!" It's guaranteed to send a chill up your spine.

The New York Times called *The Fly* a "quiet, uncluttered, and even unpretentious picture, building up almost unbearable tension by simple suggestion." *Variety* said its strongest factor was "its unusual believability." Its weakest factor was its director. Neumann fumbles the ball on crucial moments and gets uneven performances from his actors; Price is often on the edge of being ridiculous and Herbert Marshall looks as if he's in danger of falling asleep. Charles Herbert is just plain awful. Still, it's a good film. Karl Struss's photography is clean, the score by Paul Sawtell is one of his best, and its character-driven story made it seem like an A-movie. The sequel is strictly a B-movie potboiler.

The Return of the Fly

Fox gave Lippert $225,000 to make *The Return of the Fly* (1959) in black and white. Bernard Glasser produced it, and Edward Bernds wrote and directed it. His script is full of plot holes, improbabilities, and forced expository dialog.

"When I wrote the picture," recalled Edward Bernds, "we were going to use some scenes from the original film as a lead-in. I don't remember why we didn't. We were going to have Herbert Marshall return as the police inspector, but that didn't work out either for one reason or another. The only actor we had from the previous film was Vincent Price. He told me he thought my script was better than the original."

Good God, can that be true?

It's fifteen years later when Bernds picks up the story, though you'd never know it. Except for the fact that Philippe is older, nothing else has changed. It doesn't look like 1973, that's for sure.

Brett Halsey turns in a decent performance as Philippe who, against the wishes of his uncle François (Price), continues his father's experiments. Working with him is Alan Hinds (David Frankham) who, unbeknownst to Philippe, is a murderer on the run from the police. Alan intends to sell the matter transmitter to the highest bidder, which is pretty stupid since he's Philippe's partner and would have made more money if he played by the rules for a change. Of course, Philippe begins to suspect that Alan is up to no good and the two get into a fight. Alan gets

David Frankham gets his just desserts. Photo from the author's collection.]

the best of Philippe, stuffs him into the chamber, tosses a fly in just for spite, and sends him on his way. As impossible as it may seem, Philippe's atoms and the fly's atoms mix in exactly the same way as in the previous film, only this time the fly's head is four times bigger—too big for stuntman Ed Wolff. The scene of him trying to negotiate his way through the woods is positively hysterical.

The Alligator People

Fox wanted a second horror feature to package with *The Return of the Fly* (1959). Lippert gave them *The Alligator People* (1959), written by Orville H. Hampton and Charles O'Neal (father of Ryan O'Neal). If the characters in their story were honest with one another, it would have taken half as long to tell. And yet, with all of the unnecessary secrecy and foot-dragging, the thing would have run at sixty-six minutes if Hampton and O'Neal hadn't added a pointless frame story.

A doctor (Douglass Kennedy) uses hypnotherapy on his nurse, Jane Marvin (Beverly Garland), to get to the bottom of her mental block. Jane is actually Joyce Webster, who was once married to Paul Webster (Richard Crane): a patient of Dr. Mark Sinclair (George Macready). However, the doc's well-meaning efforts to restore limbs and tissue to damaged people have gone haywire. His serum—extracted from alligators—ultimately turns the people he's cured into alligators. He warns Paul Webster of the impending danger in a cable, which Paul gets on his honeymoon. Paul abandons Joyce with no explanation. She tracks him down to a place called The Cypresses, where she learns the horrible truth. Sinclair is in the middle of his explanation when he's interrupted by one of his staff: there's trouble with one of the patients. Joyce follows Sinclair to a roomful of alligator people bandaged from head to toe.

"When I walked onto the set, they all looked like urinals to me," Miss Garland said. "I took one look at all these men with urinals on their heads and I just cracked up. I think they finally just cut and let me go back to my dressing room."

Lon Chaney is Manon, Sinclair's volatile, disgusting, drunken errand boy who hates alligators because one of them bit off his hand. In the only frightening moment of the film, Manon tries to rape Joyce. Paul comes to the rescue and the two men engage in a fight, which Paul wins. He carries Joyce back to the house. Enraged, Manon cries out, "I'll kill you, gator man, just like I would any four-legged gator!" Manon breaks into the lab during a crucial moment as Sinclair attempts to cure Paul with his new radioactively powered cobalt ray. Manon short circuits the machine and ends up electrocuting himself. Paul, now more of an alligator man than before, runs off into the swamp and sinks into a pit of quicksand as the house explodes behind him.

The Wasp Woman

A rejuvenation cream made from wasp enzymes turns cosmetics-firm owner Janice Starlin (Susan Cabot) into *The Wasp Woman* (1959). "A beautiful woman by day, a lusting queen wasp by night," promised the poster, which featured Miss Cabot's head on a giant wasp body, clutching a terrified man. Not exactly a case of what you see is what you get. Miss Cabot dons a pair of mittens and a fuzzy, bug-eyed head that's so dreadful the audience is never given a clear look at it.

"This was the first picture I made for The Filmgroup, which was my own company," said producer-director Roger Corman. "All of the pictures were budgeted at twenty to fifty thousand dollars. I believe *The Wasp Woman* was made for fifty thousand dollars. The idea occurred to me after I had read a magazine article about the use of bee jelly in women's cosmetics." The idea is credited to Kenta Zertuche, a chap who served as a production assistant, location manager, secretary, and whatever else Corman needed at the time. We suspect that *The Fly*, more than that magazine article, influenced Corman's decision to make the picture.

Some sources claim the film's original title was *The Bee Girl*, which would explain all of the bees buzzing about the opening credits. Whatever, this claustrophobic, counterfeit movie has no sting. It was too short for a television sale so Corman hired Jack Hill to shoot an additional seven minutes, which was added to the front of the picture. It was sixty-six minutes too long as it was.

She Devil

In 1935, *Astounding* magazine published a story called "The Adaptive Ulti-mate," written by John Jessel (Stanley G. Weinbaum), which proved to be a very popular story. In 1949, it was dramatized on radio's *Escape* and on TV's *Studio One*. Three years later, it was seen again on *Tales of Tomorrow* and again on *Science Fiction Theatre* in 1955. It hit the giant motion-picture screen in 1957 under the title She Devil, adapted by Carroll Young and producer-director Kurt Neumann.

In both Jessel's original story and in Neumann's version of it, a doctor (Albert Dekker) believes that a cure for any disease is simply a process of adaptation. Using a serum derived from a fruit fly, he is able to restore health to some tu-bercular pigs and mend a cat's broken spine. Kyra Selas (Mari Blanchard), dying from tuberculosis in a hospital charity ward, agrees to let the doctor test the serum on her. In no time, she's healthy again and up to no good.

In Jessel's story, Kyra is able to completely alter her appearance. After she kills an old man for his money, the skinny, drab brunette becomes a voluptuous white-haired woman, confounding the eyewitness to the murder. She is able to transform into the ideal of the men she hopes to seduce. In Neumann's film, her abilities are confined to changing the color of her hair. Big wow! Any woman with a wig or a bottle of hair dye could have done that. In short, Neumann took a potentially interesting story and squashed it. Paul Sawtell's sleazy main title is easily the best thing about the picture.

The Killer Shrews

The Killer Shrews (1959) has a lot working against it. Jay Simms' script has some pretty miserable dialogue and director Ray Kellogg's staging is unimagi-native. But, when it comes to the suspense sequences, Kellogg delivers enough shocks, shivers, and action to make it all worthwhile. There are some who criti-cize the movie's use of dogs with masks for the shrews, but how else would you do it? There was no other technique available at the time that would have been as effective.

James Best is the hero of the piece. He delivers some supplies to an island where a research team is trying to find an answer to the imposing threat of overpopulation. Best notices that everyone is on edge, but isn't curious enough to ask why. "Don't you wonder about the unusual things around here?" asks In-grid Goode (Miss Universe of 1957). But Best doesn't like to ask questions. "It's against my principals," he tells her; he'd rather drink instead. The characters in this movie do so much drinking it's a wonder they're able to keep on their feet.

Goode's father, Baruch Lumet, and his buddy Gordon McLendon (the film's executive producer) have been experimenting with shrews and trying to lower their metabolisms, which will increase their life spans. Exactly how this will solve the problem of overpopulation is never made clear. What is clear is that their experiments have put them all in jeopardy thanks to Ken Curtis (the film's producer) who carelessly left one of the cage doors open and let some of the shrews escape Now the island is teeming with giant shrews and they're very hungry.

Every decade had its share of scientists who wanted to create a master race and the fifties was no exception. Hiding in the *Mesa of Lost Women* (1953), Jackie Coogan thought he could do it by crossing female and tarantula genes. Who knows what Peter Cushing was hoping to accomplish by grafting all of those bodies together. Bela Lugosi thought atomic energy was the answer.

Bride of the Monster

Insert poster from Bride of the Monster *(1956). Photo from the author's collection.*

Lugosi was worn out and flat broke when he played Dr. Eric Vornoff in Ed Wood's *Bride of the Monster* (1956). It was his last speaking role and he gave it his all, bless his heart, and though his fans understandably hate this cheap and silly movie, it is a personal favorite of your authors We saw it twice at the Cozy, and for our money it's even better than Wood's more celebrated *Plan 9 from Outer Space*.

Vornoff was banished from his homeland for his unorthodox theories. For twenty years, he's been trying to create atomic supermen, and he's moved into the Old Willows' place, a two story house on the edge of Lake Marsh to continue his work. With the help of his bird-brained, overweight assistant Lobo (Tor Johnson)—whom he found in the wilderness of Tibet—he works feverishly to prove that his theory was correct One of his former colleagues, Professor Vladimir Strowski (George Becwar), having decided that Vornoff wasn't the idiot he thought he was, comes to take him home. One can only guess what made Strowski change his mind as Vornoff has nothing but dead bodies to show for his efforts. Regardless, Vornoff has no intention of going with Strowski. He feeds him to his pet octopus.

The film opens with two hunters (Bud Osborn and John Warren) caught in a storm. They seek shelter in Vornoff's home, but he sends them away. One of the hunters is killed by Vornoff's octopus, while the other is captured by Lobo and brought back to the lab. "You will soon be as big as a giant; the strength of twenty men," Vornoff tells him. "Or, like all the others, dead!" He says this with fiendish delight as he throws the switch. The man dies and Vornoff is surprised. It's a perfect Wood moment. Since Vornoff needed subjects for his experiments, one can only wonder why he didn't invite both of the hunters into his home in the first place. He could have had two guinea pigs instead of one.

The police are baffled by all of the missing people that disappear near the old Willows' place—twelve in all, yet they never question Vornoff about it. It's up to a feisty newspaper reporter, Janet Lawson (Loretta King), to do their job for them. She too winds up strapped to Vornoff's table, dressed in a wedding gown, which apparently he kept for just such an occasion. "You will soon be a woman of super strength and beauty," he tells her, "the bride of the atom!" But as Lobo gently strokes Janet's angora sweater, he decides he doesn't want Janet to fry. He releases Janet, straps Vornoff to the table, and turns on the juice. Only in an Ed Wood film could a frail old man survive the voltage that twelve younger men could not. Now a man of super strength, Vornoff kills Lobo and carries Janet into the woods. The police, who have been trying to find Janet since she disappeared, arrive in time to open fire on Vornoff, but the bullets have no effect. Janet's boyfriend, Lieutenant Dick Craig (Tony McCoy) pushes a boulder on Vornoff, knocking the superman into the pit with his octopus. A convenient bolt of lightning strikes them both and sets off an atomic explosion. (Don't ask how.) Captain Tom Robbins (Harvey B. Dunn), who hasn't the faintest idea what Vornoff has been up to, says to no one in particular, "He tampered in God's domain."

The Gamma People

Working behind the Iron Curtain in the quaint little town of Gudavia, where Walter Rilla uses gamma rays to make *The Gamma People* (1956): a race of genius children. Now and then, things don't work out and he produces a moron instead, but even they come in handy as a Gestapo-like police force. It's up to journalist Paul Douglas, his photographer Leslie Phillips, and one of Rilla's little geniuses, Michael Caridia, to bring an end to his totalitarian reign of terror.

This is one of the oddest sci-fi films of the decade: a political comedy thriller that never quite gels, but deserves a nod of respect for trying something a little different. It was produced by John Cossage for Irving Allen and Albert R. Broccoli's Warwick Films. John Gilling directed and, unfortunately, can't seem to get the lead out of his pants; the film is sluggish. Story credit goes to Louis Pollock, though it's based on something Robert Aldrich wrote in 1951 for a movie he wanted to make with John Garfield—another actor who ended up on the Hollywood blacklist.

The presence of Paul Douglas in the cast (who is very good as usual) suggests that this may have been a U.S./British co-production, whereby an American company would take advantage of Eady funds. These funds were a pool of production money garnered from a tax on cinema tickets sold in the United Kingdom—money intended to aid in the production of British commercial films for the domestic and international market.

Terror is a Man

Equally interesting and unusual is *Terror is a Man* (1959); a Filipino horror film written by Harry Paul Harber, and based—without acknowledgement—on H.G. Wells's *The Island of Dr. Moreau*. Charles Girard (Francis Lederer), a successful New York surgeon, has come to the secluded Isla de Sandre (Blood Island) with his wife Frances (Greta Thyssen), in the hope of surgically turning a panther into a man. William Fitzgerald (Richard Derr), the sole survivor of a downed freighter, washes ashore in a lifeboat and Girard quickly takes him into his confidence. With chemicals and surgery, Girard has successfully altered the function and the size of the brain, thereby speeding up the process of evolution. "Changes in evolution have come about through a process of natural selection, haven't they?" Fitzgerald asks. "But, in your work, the selection isn't nature's: it's your choice." Girard can't help but notice Fitzgerald's concern. "I am a scientist, not a philosopher," he casually replies. "I cannot worry about the moral implications of my work. There'll be enough people who are only too eager to take care of that when the time comes." Girard believes that by starting fresh, he can create a man who won't be hampered by thousands of years of preconceptions that the human race carries with it. Girard isn't interested in creating a super race, just a rational one. His wife, however, no longer shares his dream. She knows the panther man is dangerous as it's already murdered a couple of the natives, and the rest of the natives have moved to another island. Francis is afraid of the panther man, but feels sorry for him. When she tells Fitzgerald she's frightened and wants to leave the island, he makes a pass at her. She pulls away. "I'm not lonely," she tells him. "I'm frightened." But she is lonely and the sexual tension between her and Fitzgerald becomes thick enough to slice with one of Girard's surgical instruments. Eventually they make love, an act she immediately regrets. Girard had neglected her for so long that she couldn't help herself any more than the panther man can repress his jungle instincts.

Before the credits roll on *Terror is a Man*, the audience is warned that the picture they are about to see has a scene so shocking that the management suggests the squeamish and faint-hearted close their eyes at the sound of the bell and reopen them when the bell rings again. This gimmick was highlighted on all of the advertising, which also claimed that the picture was more horrifying than *Frankenstein* and more terrifying than *Dracula*. The scene in question was nothing more than a scalpel cutting into the flesh of some animal—probably a pig. The audience that this sort of ballyhoo would attract could only have been disappointed by what they saw. For that audience, the film's strengths work against it. There are no villains or heroes, just people. Even the panther man is sympathetic. It's a thoughtful, sober movie, and although Gerry de Leon's direction could use a little goosing now and then, he has nothing to be ashamed of. Predictably, the film lost money the first time around, but when it was re-released as *Blood Creature* a few years later, it did all right and kicked off a series of Blood Island movies that wallowed in gore and nudity—a gold mine for producers Kane W. Lynn and Eddie Romero.

T.H. Huxley once posed the question: "If a little knowledge is dangerous, where is the man who has so much as to be out of danger?" We don't know the answer to his question, but one thing we do know is you won't find such a person in any of these films. The fate of these seekers of truth is sealed from the start and the message is clear: *Leave well enough alone.* A few of these scientists seem to know it. Didn't one of them say that the only hope for mankind was to hurl it back to its primitive dawn? No knowledge. That's the only thing that can save us. The perfect science is the one that ends all science. That's what George Lynn said in *The Werewolf*. So if knowledge is the real villain, then movies such as *Donovan's Brain* (1953), *The Colossus of New York* (1958), *The Invisible Boy* (1957), and *Fiend Without a Face* (1958) get right to the heart of the matter by dealing with the power of the mind divorced from all other considerations.

Donovan's Brain

W.H. Donovan, a ruthless and vindictive tycoon, crashes his private plane near the home of Dr. Patrick Cory (Lew Ayres). Cory can't save him, but he keeps Donovan's brain alive, floating in a tank. It grows larger and more powerful, imposing its will on Cory and proving that Professor Clifford Groves was right all along: the size of the brain does have something to do with its mental prowess. Donovan forces Cory to carry out his income tax evasion scheme. Cory makes a list of the names[2] under which Donovan has money stashed in various accounts across the country. Cory's assistant, Dr. Frank Schratt (Gene Evans), realizes the experiment has gotten out of control and attempts to shoot the brain. But the brain forces him to turn the gun on himself. Ultimately, Donovan concludes that anyone who knows of his existence poses a threat. Cory is

Lew Ayres, Gene Evans, and Nancy Davis stare at Donovan's brain. Photo courtesy of Bob Villard.

ready to kill his wife (Nancy Reagan), but God intervenes in the nick of time and strikes the brain with a bolt of lightning.

This is not exactly the sort of a movie that will set anyone's pants on fire, but it's a well-made adaptation of Curt Siodmak's 1942 novel. Producer Tom Gries wanted the writer to direct the picture, but things didn't work out for one reason or another and it's probably just as well. Siodmak proved to be a pretty lousy director. Writer-director Felix Feist was a better choice even if he wasn't the most innovative guy around. He's competent and he gets remarkably nuanced performances from Lew Ayres and Gene Evans. It was the only time Evans was asked to wear his glasses. "I'd made fifteen pictures or so before *Donovan's Brain* and, my God, all of a sudden I could see everything—there were people around and talking to each other and whispering and all that," the actor told Tom Weaver. "When I didn't wear my glasses, I didn't have those distractions. So it kind of blew me away at the start!"

The Colossus of New York

Unlike W.H. Donovan, who continued to be a son of a bitch with or without his body, International Peace Prize winner Jeremy Spensser (Ross Martin)— once an altruistic, socially conscious human being—becomes a hardcore Republican as *The Colossus of New York* (1958), a film produced by William Alland and directed by Eugene Lourie.

Jeremy is the victim of an auto mishap. His father (Otto Kruger) transfers his brain to the body of an eight-foot-tall Frankenstein-like automaton—with clothes—designed by his other son, Henry (John Baragrey). Every time Jeremy takes a step, it sounds like someone dropped a sack of potatoes from the top of the Empire State Building. (Producer Alland must have hired the guy who supplied the sound effects for the Three Stooges shorts.) With no explanation offered, Jeremy develops extrasensory perception and hypnotic abilities. And though it may not be standard equipment on most robots, Henry gave Jeremy death-ray eyes. Henry is the first person Jeremy zaps for trying to put the make on his wife (Mala Powers).

John Goodman, Charles Gemora, and Ralph Jester were the ones responsible for the cool-looking, but completely ridiculous robot. Their

Mala Powers and the Colossus of New York. Photo from the author's collection.

cumbersome 160-pound creation was worn by Ed Wolff. When he wasn't able to move as fast as the director wanted, the film editor simply removed frames to speed up the action. The editor got a little carried away in one sequence though; as the giant advances on John Baragrey and Mala Powers, the editor cut frames from two scenes of the couple reacting to it—it's pretty jarring. Later, during the film's climax, the robot breaks into the United Nations building and starts zapping people. As he's poised to strike, the editor cut to a shot of the crowd reacting. There's a woman already dead on the floor. The camera cuts back to the robot. His very first victim is the same woman. Not that it matters much; it's a stupid sequence. Otto Kruger strikes a ridiculous pose and holds it as people drop like flies. Nobody runs for the exit. They just stand there, waiting to be zapped.

Jeremy's father should have listened to a family friend (Robert Hutton), who believed that a brain divorced from human experience—hunger, cold, pleasure, pain, love, and hate—would become dehumanized to the point of monstrousness. In less than a year's time, Jeremy questions the need to create food for the lame and the useless. "Why should we work to preserve slum people of the world when it's simpler and wiser to get rid of them instead?" Jeremy berates himself for once having been a so-called humanitarian scientist who tried to keep human trash alive. His new plan is to kill all of the idealists.

William Alland said, "*That* could have been a hell of a movie, I think. The inspiration for that was a famous old legend, the Golem—that was what inspired me to develop that idea... It was a far more poignant story, and had far more meaning, than Lourie put into it... The relationship with his father, the relation ship with his own son, it was blown through the nose, it was not done with the sense of timing and feeling that it could have had. Details in that film were lost key elements that would have made it better. But, look, everything is relative and you get what you pay for. I paid for a fast shuffle and that's what I got."[3]

Alland—who had a history of throwing people under the bus—is being rather disingenuous when he tries to blame the director for all of the film's shortcom ings. Alland was the one who signed off on Thelma Schnee's screenplay and that's where the problems begin. It's a collection of ideas that never come to gether. Her dialogue is stilted and full of pomposity, and she makes Charles Herbert—one of the worst of the child actors—sound as if he'd suffered brain damage. What was Lourie supposed to do, rewrite the script? And who signed off on Van Cleave's inappropriate piano score? Why, we believe that would have been Alland as well. He should have been grateful his eight-day picture came off as well as it did. Anyone interested to see what happened when Alland sat in the director's chair should watch Look in Any Window (1961). He really blew that one through the nose.

The Invisible Boy

The Invisible Boy (1957) was the first movie about a renegade computer, and it contained a potpourri of sci-fi concepts: space travel, time travel, mind control and, of course, invisibility. It was conceived as a vehicle for Robby the Robot, al though there was no robot in the short story by Edmund Cooper, which was the basis for Cyril Hume's scenario. We are grateful that producer Nicholas Nayfack chose Richard Eyer to play the title character and not Charles Herbert.

By cleverly suggesting changes in its own feedback system over a twenty nine-year period, the computer—designed by Dr. Tom Merrinoe (Philip Abbott)— is ready to take over the world. "I will seek out organic life wherever it may exist down even to the littlest virus which in time might evolve mentality, so, at last all of the universe will be cleansed. All will be sterile. All will be myself!" it tells its creator. Using Robby the Robot to plant control transmitters into the skulls of several key personnel, it puts its plan into action. "It's never at conflict with itself over such human considerations such as honor, or love, or pity," Merrinoe tells a room full of its controlled victims, who look like refugees from an episode of The Untouchables. "Like every living creature, it's motivated, as some of you are now aware, by an instinct for survival. And in obeying this basic urge, it can tolerate no interference on the part of the human race. This, gentlemen, and we ought to have foreseen it, is the revolt of the machine. And the thing we left out of it was sanity."

The computer orders Robby to kidnap Merrinoe's son Timmie (Eyer), to force Merrinoe to disclose the numerical combination built into the machine to prevent it from being moved. Any such attempt would set off a minor atomic blowout that would wreck the basic unit. The computer's plan is to put itself—section by section—into orbit around the Earth, making the planet its slave. But, it can't risk wiring Merrinoe's skull to get the combination, because one of the controlled victims died. "One out of eight," Merrinoe snarls. "You don't even dare take a twelve point five risk. *Me* helpless? Why, if you had knees, you'd be down on both of them begging me."

Your authors were ten years old when we saw *The Invisible Boy*: exactly the right age for it, yet the film was a bit of a disappointment. As far as we were concerned, too much time was spent with Timmie and his problems with his parents. Some of the bits are funny, others confusing. As an example, after having his brain overhauled by the computer, Timmie is able to put Robby the Robot together, which none of the other scientists working for his father were able to do. Yet when they see Timmie's remarkable accomplishment, they react with boredom and indifference. It's supposed to be funny, but it isn't. It isn't rational. The reaction of Timmie's mother to the robot is equally confusing. Instead of being astounded, she's annoyed.

Herman Hoffman's direction is pedestrian, the special effects by Jack Rabin and Irving Block are ragged, and the score by Les Baxter is cheesy. It could have been a good movie if it hadn't been made for children. As it stands, it's just okay.

Fiend Without a Face

In March of 1930, *Weird Tales* published a short story called "The Thought Monster" by Amelia Reynolds Long. Her agent, Forrest Ackerman, was a friend of Jim Nicholson, who was the president of American International Pictures at the time. Ackerman thought Nicholson might be interested in the property, but he wasn't. Alex Gordon, who was working at AIP at the time, sent the magazine to his brother, Richard.

Richard Gordon said, "I read the story and liked it very much and I thought it'd be a great idea for a low-budget science fiction movie... Herbert Leder, who later went on to write and direct a few low-budget horror films on his own, did a screenplay for us which became *Fiend Without a Face* [1958]."[4]

In a farming community on the Canadian/American border, the citizens are being killed by some invisible force. An autopsy reveals that the brains and spinal cords have been sucked out of their bodies through two punctures in their necks. "It's as if some mental vampire were at work," declares Major Jeff Cummings (Marshall Thompson), the military man investigating the mysterious crimes. By the time Cummings gets to the bottom of things, the movie is in serious danger of wearing out its welcome when its makers pull out all of the stops and deliver a climax that's well worth waiting for.

Professor R.E. Walgate (Kynaston Reeves) invites Cummings, some of the top brass, and some of the town officials to his home to confess that he is responsible for the gruesome deaths. Using atomic energy from the radar base to amplify his brain waves, Walgate was able to create a being. "But like thought itself, it was invisible," he tells them. The thing escaped from his lab and has been able to survive and multiply by feeding on the brains and nerve centers of the people it killed. "We're facing a new form of life that nobody understands," he tells them. He turns to Cummings's superior officer, Colonel Butler (Stanley Maxsted), and ads, "I believe it feeds on the radiation from your atomic plant and that it's evil." At this point, Walgate's doctor (Peter Madden) arrives and the Colonel says, "Doctor, I'm glad you're here. This man has become a raving lunatic." The colonel has to eat his words when, seconds later, one of the invisible fiends smashes a window and kills one of the military men (Michael Balfour). A power surge at the plant makes Walgate's thought-monsters visible, and there are dozens of them. They look like brains with antennae and use their spinal cords to propel themselves along. Everyone frantically begins shoring up the house, pounding nails into boards across the windows, and shoving tables against the doors. The monsters pull the boards apart and come flying through the gaps. They float down the chimney. The soldiers can't kill them fast enough. Their only hope is to shut down the atomic plant. Cummings makes a run for it. After a while, the leading lady (Kim Parker, who is as cute as she can be) expresses her concern for his welfare. "It's been so long since..." And for just a moment, she can't remember his name. If this hadn't been such a rush job, they would have done a second take.

Florenz von Nordhoff and Karl-Ludwig Ruppel created the fabulous special effects for the climax. Combining stop-motion animation with motor-controlled rubber props, they managed to give their creatures more personality than most of the characters in the film. A tip of the hat goes to the sound-effects people, who supplied the delightfully repulsive gurgling and belching noises that accompanied the globs of blood that burbled from the brains when they were shot. According to producer John Croydon, he had to step in and direct a lot of these scenes because Arthur Crabtree didn't understand how to match his live action with the special effects.

The picture was shot in three weeks, and back-to-back with *The Haunted Strangler* for a combined budget of $300,000. Less money was allocated to *Fiend*, but the special effects drove the cost over budget.

Easily the goriest and most revolting sci-fi film of the decade—the newspapers said the film was a disgrace to the British film industry. The film had its U.S.

premier at Detroit's Adams Theater, much to the dismay of its manager, who was forced to show the movie after a successful engagement of MGM's Academy-Award winning *Gigi* (1958). Amelia Reynolds Long caught up with it when it came to Harrisburg, Pennsylvania. She told author Chet Williamson it "was on a double bill they had here—mine and a Boris Karloff movie, the title of which can't remember, but it wasn't one of his best. But then, if it has been one of his best, mine would have looked so much worse!"

The Creature with the Atom Brain

The Creature with the Atom Brain (1955) is a remote-controlled atomic zombie. Crime boss Frank Buchanon (Michael Granger) uses them to kill the men responsible for deporting him to Italy. "If I'd only known when you first offered to help me financially," says his partner in crime, Professor Wilhelm Steigg (Gregory Gaye). "Dr. Steigg, if it weren't for my money, you'd still be experimenting with cats and dogs in that flea-sized lab of yours in Europe. I made it possible to prove your theory with human beings," Buchanon reminds him. "But my theory was to use these creatures to help people live by doing everything that was difficult and dangerous," Steigg replies. "You just want to kill people."

Indeed he does, and the first one on his list is Jim Hennessey. One of Steigg's zombies (Carl Davis, looking a little like Ed Asner) breaks his neck and spine. He's shot by some of Hennessey's boys, but the bullets have no effect. Dr. Chet Walker (Richard Denning) analyzes its so-called blood and finds that it's some kind of radioactive chemical compound. Captain David Harris (S. John Launer) tells Walker that the killer's fingerprints belonged to Willard Pierce. As Walker reads Pierce's rap sheet, he's taken aback. "How could a tubercular man have strength enough to break those bars like that?!" Harris replies: "You think that's something? Answer this one. How could a dead man have strength enough to do it?"

Written by our old pal Curt Siodmak, this film is as silly as its title, but it's a lot of fun and would have been even better if Siodmak hadn't put all of his cards on the table in the first five minutes of the picture. It would have been much more interesting if it had been played like a mystery, following Chet Walker as he put all of the pieces of the puzzle together. As it stands, it plays like an old serial. Still, in spite of producer Sam Katzman and director Edward L. Cahn, it's creepy and more than a little gruesome.

The Man Without a Body

Last on our list of madmen, and perhaps the maddest of them all, is Karl Brussard (George Coulouris)—a tyrant tycoon who has a fatal brain tumor. He steals the head of Nostradamus (Michael Golden) from its crypt and takes it to Dr. Phil Merritt (Robert Hutton), who has had a lot of success keeping disembodied monkey heads alive. Merritt brings Nostradamus's head back to life and Brussard spends the bulk of the film trying to convince *The Man Without a Body* (1957) that he *is* Karl Brussard so the two men can switch brains and Brussard can continue to rule his empire. "You are Karl Brussard!" Brussard tells the head. "I am Nostradamus," it insists. This standoff goes on for hours. Perhaps hypnosis would have helped.

Robert Hutton said, "It was ridiculous—it was stupid, really stupid. And we felt stupid talking to that head—we would almost break up! The actor was un derneath the table, and you felt like a damn fool talking to him."[5]

Equally ridiculous is Hutton's claim that he was forced to appear in junk like this because his right-wing politics kept him out of better movies and ultimately torpedoed his career. Everyone knows that it was the left-wing people who had their careers destroyed during this period, and for Hutton to believe otherwise suggests an extreme case of denial—the same sort of hallucinatory thinking that created this movie. As it draws to a close, we see Brussard chasing after Merritt's assistant (Sheldon Lewis) with the head of Nostradamus grafted onto his shoulders, encased in what appears to be a bandaged trashcan—one might wonder if the management was spiking their Coca-Cola mix with acid.

"This remarkable shocker piles its horrors up with such extravagant bathos it finally achieves an almost surrealistic quality of absurdity," said the *Monthly Film Bulletin*. It was produced by Guido Coen and directed by W. Lee Wilder. Charles Saunders shares directing credit, but he was there to satisfy the British quota requirements; he had nothing to do with it and shouldn't be held ac countable. The screenplay was written by William Grote, who took his ten-year old son to see the movie. There were two sailors sitting in front of them, and making jokes about it. His son was furious until he saw that his father was laugh ing so hard there were tears in his eyes.

Footnotes:
1. Weaver, Tom. *Science Fiction Stars and Horror Heroes*, McFarland, Jefferson, NC, 1991, pg. 93.
2. The first four names on the list are the names of the crew: production designer H.B. Chapman, assistant director Boris Levin, assistant director Jack Berne, and set decorator Edward Boyle. Fred Russell, the fifth name on the list, was a popular sports writer.
3. Weaver, Tom. *Monsters, Mutants and Heavenly Creatures*, Midnight Marquee Press, Baltimore, MD, 1996, pg. 70.
4. Weaver, Tom. *Interviews with B Science Fiction and Horror Movie Makers*, McFarland, North Carolina, 1988, pg. 177.
5. Weaver, Tom. *Science Fiction Stars and Horror Heroes*, McFarland, North Carolina, 1991, pg. 227.

CHAPTER ELEVEN
The End of the World

Who would ever have believed that human beings
would be stupid enough to blow themselves off the
face of the Earth?

—On the Beach

Rocketship X-M was the first movie to warn of the possible consequences of a nuclear war, by showing what had happened to the once highly advanced Marian civilization. Producer-writer-director Arch Obler took the devastation on a far-off planet and set it in our own backyards—or rather *his* own backyard—in the independently made *Five* (1951). It was filmed almost entirely on Obler's ranch along California's coastline in the Santa Monica Mountains, sixty miles from Los Angeles. In his film, a cloud of radioactive dust kills everyone in the world except for five people and a few birds; Obler was forced to add a reason why the birds survived when he couldn't keep them from flying through his scenes.

Obler's crew consisted of five USC film students who stayed in a tent on Obler's ranch. Susan Douglas, the only woman in the cast, slept in Obler's guest house while the rest of the actors—William Phipps, James Anderson, Charles Lampkin, and Earl Lee—stayed in Obler's house. One afternoon, a fight broke out between Obler and crew member Art Swerdloff on the balcony of the guest house. The two men exchanged punches and bloodied noses before they were pulled apart. This behind-the-camera incident was more exciting than anything that took place in front of it. At best, Obler's film is only mildly engaging and doesn't seem, with all of its moralizing and postulating, to be getting at much other than to say that an atomic war is a bad idea.

Variety: "Principal criticism lies in its dearth of action."

The New York Times: "The five people whom [Obler] had selected to forward the race of man are so cheerless, banal, and generally static, they stir little interest in their fate."

Time: "...tries to imagine what life would be like for the last five survivors of a worldwide atomic catastrophe. Life, it seems, would be pretty dull."

Captive Women

A recurring theme in these apocalyptic prophecies is the segregation of the survivors into conflicting societies, like the Morlocks and the Eloi in H. G. Wells's *The Time Machine*. There are three societies in *Captive Women* (1952): the

Norms, the Mutates, and the Up-river people. Over shots of everything from atomic explosions to Boy Scouts on the march, a narrator warns us that World War III could return man to the kind of lawless, primitive society we're about to see depicted, living in the rubble of what was once New York City.

The Norms and the Up-river people hate the Mutates because they're scarred from radiation. Every now and then, the Mutates kidnap some of the Norm women in the hope of breeding a race of normal-looking people. The Up-river people want to rule what's left of the world. After a while, you forget that you're watching a story that's supposed to be set in the future. It seems more like a low-rent version of *Robin Hood*.

Robert Clarke is Rob, the son of the leader of the Norms. On the eve of his wedding, his father is killed by the Up-river people. His would-be bride (Gloria Saunders) willingly gives herself to Gordon (Stuart Randall), the leader of the Up-river people. Fleeing for his life, Rob and his buddy Bram (Robert Bice) are captured by the Mutates. Rob and Riddon (Ron Randell)—the leader of the Mutates—join forces to defeat the nasty Up-river people. In the end, Riddon marries Ruth (Margaret Field), who is the first Norm to willingly give herself to a Mutate.

This was the first of a three-picture deal that Aubrey Wisberg and Jack Pollexfen had with Howard Hughes at RKO, and while we'd like to say they came out strong, we simply can't. *Captive Women*—re-released a few years later as *1000 Years from Now*—is a tedious bore directed by Stuart Gilmore.

Robert Clarke said, "He'd been an editor and I think Hughes felt he owed him a favor. I don't believe it was the first picture he'd directed, but he seemed to be in over his head. I don't know what his trouble was. One afternoon, as he was getting ready to shoot a scene in this underground tunnel, somebody got trigger happy and released this landslide. Gilmore was buried by all of these rocks. I don't think he ever directed another picture."

Terror from the Year 5000

Salome Jens travels through time to mate with John Stratton in Robert J. Gurney's *Terror from the Year 5000* (1958), an American International picture. Apparently, that marriage between Riddon and Ruth didn't make a lick of difference. In the year 5000, every fifth child is still a mutant.

Gurney's movie was originally announced as *The Girl from 2,000,000 A.D.* and was based on Henry Slesar's short story "Bottle Baby." By the time it reached the screen, it bore so little resemblance to Slesar's story that he received no screen credit and very little money. The film is noteworthy for three reasons: It's the first movie to feature a time machine, and it's the unofficial debuts of actress Jens and film editor Dede Allen.[1] Allen said that Gurney cut an entire reel out of the picture because he wasn't happy with Joyce Holden's performance. AIP didn't think he'd cut enough and trimmed some more out of it. "I'll never work for you again," Gurney told Arkoff and Nicholson. Arkoff said, "Don't be a dilettante." On his way out the door, Gurney said, "Sam, you don't even know what the word means."

The critic for the *Monthly Film Bulletin* wrote, "The woman of the future is an unimaginative creation and whatever horrific possibilities she has are soon expended." We couldn't agree more. As far as we're concerned, Dede Allen should have cut a few more reels out of the picture.

Teenage Caveman

Filmed as *Prehistoric World*, the climax of Roger Corman's *Teenage Caveman* (1958) was

One sheet poster from Terror from the Year 5,000 (1958). Photo from the author's collection.

supposed to be such a surprise that it would negate every boring moment the audience had suffered. Robert Vaughn is "The Boy" who questions the laws of his tribe and dares to explore forbidden territory in his quest for truth. After braving a few outtakes from *One Million B.C.*, he discovers that this is not our prehistoric past at all, but is instead our prehistoric future. As with *Rocketship X-M*, we've bombed ourselves back to the Stone Age, dinosaurs and all.

"And here is mankind trying to struggle out of it, building all the myths, the taboos, doing all the things that were supposed to preserve the remnants of the race long enough for it to survive," writer Bobby Campbell told W.C. Stroby in *Fangoria*. "And when Vaughn's character goes stumbling off into the lush forest, when he goes daringly out there—which is also allegorical, that somebody sooner or later is going to turn their back on the teaching of the elders and find out that what was said was not true—he was supposed to come upon this spaceman in what I envisioned as a marvelous, elaborate spacesuit, you know, Victorian, sort of like the kind of stuff Disney did in *20,000 Leagues Under the Sea*. Well (and this is why I say that Roger really had no artistic intent about most of what he did), instead of this, he came up with this lizard-man suit he'd found."

Half sheet poster from Teenage Caveman *(1958). Photo from the author's collection.*

Beach Dickerson said, "I was supposed to fall off a log into this water that was so filthy it almost made me throw up. So I held my breath and jumped in and started flailing around. Roger kneels beside me and says, 'I don't believe you're drowning. You're not convincing me.' Well, of course I didn't want to stick my face in this gunk, but I figured I might as well get it over with, so I finally gave him what he wanted. I kicked and screamed and sank and floated to the stop like a dead man. Then we went to Bronson Canyon and shot my funeral sequence. Everybody was sitting in a half circle and I was sitting in the wardrobe truck watching. Roger comes over to me and says, 'What are you doing here?' And I said, 'Well, I can't be out there. It's my funeral.' And he said, 'Bullshit. Who would recognize you anyway?' If you see the picture, I'm in the front row in a bearskin and a fright-wig, beating a tom-tom."

Ed Nelson, one of the villains in the picture, was supposed to be attacked by a pack of wild dogs. The animal trainer told Nelson he'd better ditch the spear he was holding because if his animals saw it, they'd get aggressive. Nelson told the trainer it wouldn't make much sense for him to toss the spear as he was being attacked. "I'm just tellin' ya fer yer own protection," the trainer said, "you figger out the rest."

Ed Nelson: "This is a true story, as God is my witness! I said, 'Roger, look, before I hear the dogs, I get tired or something and I lay the spear down. Or something

ke that. I can't throw the spear away!' I mean, it's tough enough I had to fight
hese dogs! Roger said okay, okay. And you know Roger, we gotta get it on the
irst take—we were losin' the light, or he only had the dogs for ten minutes, or
ome damn thing. So I put the spear down, I hear the dogs coming, I brace my-
elf and I go, AAAARRRRGGGGHHHH! like that. The dogs stop—stare at me—
nd they take off... in the opposite direction!"[2]

World Without End

In the year 2508, we learn that H.G.
Wells was mistaken. The good guys don't
ive on the surface of the Earth, the bad
guys do. The good guys are the ones who
ive underground in Allied Artists' *World
Without End* (1956), in color and CinemaS-
cope, and directed by Edward Bernds.

"I put a lot of thought into that picture,"
said Bernds, producing a notebook full of
andom ideas he'd jotted down during pre-
production for my inspection. "Richard
Heermance was the one who got the ball
olling. He wanted to make a science fiction
picture using the rocket ship footage from
Flight to Mars which wasn't all that great. I
was told I could have Hugh Marlowe or
Frank Lovejoy for the lead. Lovejoy wanted
our times the amount of money that Mar-
owe wanted, so we went with Marlowe. I
wish I'd gone with Frank Lovejoy. Hugh
Marlowe was a pain in the ass. He was lazy.
He was unprepared. He'd wander off between takes to find some shade and forget
where he put his backpack. He'd been in
bigger pictures at Fox. Maybe he felt work-
ng at Allied Artists was a comedown.
Maybe he was right, but that's no excuse
for behaving the way he did."

Marlowe, Rod Taylor, Nelson Leigh, and
Christopher Dark are the four astronauts
sent to Mars on a reconnaissance mission.
Returning home, they experience a sudden

3-sheet poster for World Without End *(1956).
"It finally took a small company like AA to
make a movie of this type with some sense to
it," wrote exhibitor Harold Bell. "This has been
the best for us since* War of the Worlds.*"
Photo from the author's collection.*

burst in acceleration and break the time barrier. They crash on Earth and find that an atomic war has destroyed everything and divided the human race into two cultures. The ones who live above ground are mutants who have become savages—much like the Martians in *Rocketship X-M*. The ones who live under ground are normal, but the race is dying for want of sunlight—although Nancy Gates and Lisa Montell look healthy enough. It's up to our boys to persuade them to come out of their hole.

Toward the end of the picture, Hugh Marlowe has to fight the leader of the mutants. If he's victorious, and we know he will be, the rest of the tribe will take order from him. Rod Taylor's name in the film is Herb. Christopher Dark's is Hank. As Marlowe prepares to do battle, he refers to Taylor as both Hank and Herb in the same shot. Once Marlow ensures the big cheese has been defeated, the mutants and the underground people work together for their mutual benefit.

Edward Bernds said, "I struggled for a living, literally, my whole God damn career. Everybody needs some 'screw you' money. I never had any. I scrambled for every job and I took everything that came along. In retrospect, I might have gone a lot farther if I'd been more selective. Looking back on it, I should have insisted on more time and money on *World Without End*. I wanted that closing sequence to be bigger. I wanted to show the beginning of a new world, the construction of new buildings with workers all around. We didn't have any of that thanks to Heermance. He was a funny guy. He'd splurge for some things and cut costs for other things. I should have said, 'I want to do it right or get another boy!' Allied Artists wouldn't have replaced me halfway through *World Without End*. They might have hated me, though."

Day the World Ended

In Roger Corman's *Day the World Ended* (1956), narrator Chet Huntley tells us that mankind has done what it can to wipe itself out, but God, in his infinite wisdom, has spared a few. Retired Navy captain Jim Maddison (Paul Birch) has built a home in a valley surrounded by mountains with high lead content. He's got his own gas generator and enough food and supplies for himself, his daughter Louise (Lori Nelson), and her fiancé, who they assume was killed in the nuclear blast. Against his better judgment, Maddison offers shelter to Rick (Richard Denning), Tony (Michael Connors), Ruby (Adele Jergens), Pete (Raymond Hatton), and Radek (Paul Dubov). Only Denning and Nelson make it to the end of the picture. Tony kills Ruby, Jim kills Tony, Louise's fiancé (Paul Blaisdell)—who has become a three-eyed, four-armed crusty mutant—kills Radek, pure rainwater kills the mutant, and Pete and Jim die from radiation poisoning. All of these characters, like the movie, are black and white. Writer Lou Rusoff was a hack. Still, the movie is entertaining if your expectations are set accordingly.

Paul Blaisdell and Lori Nelson. Photo from the author's collection.

Roger Corman said, "*Day the World Ended* was my first science fiction film and AIP's first financial success. It was the first time there was a line around the block of people waiting to get into the theater. Needless to say, we are all very happy about that."

Just before he dies, Dr. G. E. Soberin (Albert Dekker) says to the woman who just shot him, "Listen to me, as if I were Cerberus barking with all his heads at the gates of hell. I will tell you where to take it, but don't... don't open the box!" But Gabrielle (Gaby Rodgers) isn't going to heed his warning, and we don't want her to. Just as she's about to lift the lid, Mike Hammer (Ralph Meeker) bursts in. He's looking for kidnapped secretary Velda (Maxine Cooper). Gabrielle shoots him too, and then... she opens the box. What's in it? "The head of Medusa," Soberin told her just before she shot him. "That's what's in the box and whoever looks on her will be changed not into stone, but into brimstone and ashes." But it isn't really Medusa's head: it's something atomic. Velda called it The Great Whatzit. One thing is for sure, it isn't the heroin that the Mafia was after in Mickey Spillane's novel, *Kiss Me Deadly* (1955), on which this film is based.

Spillane was one of the most popular writers in America at the time. He saw his Private Eye as an Angel of Vengeance: the guy who didn't have his hands tied by the rules that prevented the police from bringing criminals to justice. To Spillane, he was a hero, but to us, Mike Hammer was a Neanderthal: a sadistic

Albert Dekker and Gaby Rodgers. Photo courtesy of Bob Villard.

bully with no heart, and that's the way he is portrayed by Ralph Meeker in Robert Aldrich's film. Screenwriter A. I. Bezzerides said that Spillane hated what he and Aldrich did to his character and novel, and no wonder. Spillane's the end-justifies-the-means philosophy is turned on its head. Hammer's meddling causes the end of the world.

The plot of the movie is elusive, not so much because it's convoluted or confusing, but because there are so many questions left unanswered. Christina Bailey (Cloris Leachman) escapes from a mental institution and is picked up by Mike Hammer. If he can get her to a bus, she tells him to forget about her. If he can't, "Remember me." A car pulls in front of them and the two are taken to a beach house, where Christina is tortured to death. She and Hammer are put back into his car and pushed over the side of the road. Mike survives and is questioned by Federal Agents. His policeman pal, Lieutenant Pat Murphy (Wesley Addy), revokes his P.I. license and someone gives him a new car with a couple of bombs in it. Hammer knows the woman he picked up must have been involved in something big. "And a cut of something big could be something... big," Velda remarks. Hammer tells her to find out all she can about Christina. Velda muses, "First, you find a little thread, the little thread leads you to a string, and the string leads you to a rope, and from the rope you hang by the neck."

This is more of a detective thriller than it is a science fiction movie: an uncompromising piece of cynicism peopled with sleazy, nihilistic characters and gritty locations. It was condemned by the Catholic Legion of Decency and was called the number one menace to American youth by the Kefauver committee. There's even a wonderfully sleazy song during the main credits, sung by Nat "King" Cole, "I'd Rather Have the Blues."

The World, the Flesh and the Devil

Matthew Phipps Shiel's 1902 novel, *The Purple Cloud*, was the basis for *The World, the Flesh and the Devil* (1959). A sodium-isotope attack replaced the cyanide gas eruption that featured in the novel, which had been purchased for filming in 1927. But, it remained unfilmed because the concept of a catastrophe extinguishing all life on Earth seemed too far-fetched. Director-writer Ranald MacDougall updated the novel by adding a second male survivor and a well-meaning, but poorly executed, plea for racial understanding.

Many critics at the time divided the film into three parts, indicating that each part was less satisfying than the one that had preceded it. The first part dealt with Ralph Burton (Harry Belafonte), a coal miner trapped in a mineshaft. After several days, he is able to unearth himself only to find that everyone has disappeared. Burton travels to New York, which is a completely deserted town. Radio station recordings tell him about the atomic war.

In the second part, he meets Sarah Crandall (Inger Stevens). The two of them still cling to the racial distinctions which had previously separated them, but after some initial awkwardness, Burton allows her to stay in his well-supplied apartment while he sleeps in a separate room. When Sarah suggests that they share the apartment, he replies: "Move in? People will talk." She tells him she's "free, white, and twenty-one."

The last part deals with the entrance of Benson Thacker (Mel Ferrer). He sails into New York harbor, bringing the racism and hate that further divides the characters and inevitably leads to violence. The two men engage in their own war, hunting each other through the empty canyons of the city until better judgment prevails. The final shot shows the last three people on Earth walking arm in arm into the future—an endorsement of brotherly love and a possible interracial ménage à trois. Bosley Crowther thought the ending was "such an obvious contrivance and so cozily theatrical you wouldn't be surprised to see the windows of the buildings suddenly crowded with reintegrated people, cheering happily and flinging ticker tape."

The logistics of making a film on location in New York created numerous problems. With the aid of the city and local police, the film's producers were able to shut down sections of New York for the limited time needed to film. The George Washington Bridge was closed, and eighty parked cars were added to give the illusion that the bridge had been choked with traffic prior to the apocalypse.

Preliminary production studies proved that 6:45 on a Friday morning was ideal for shooting, on the basis of traffic and lighting conditions. The police preferred Sunday morning, but finally agreed with the production analyst that Friday was more opportune. Permits were obtained to stop all traffic entering Times Square for six periods of six minutes each and for all traffic lights to be blacked out on cue. A complex set of arrangements were made for all stores, restaurants, and businesses in the area to put out their signs and lights during shooting. An elaborate signal system was set up for a distance of twenty blocks to guarantee simultaneous cues for all involved. At 7:20, the cue was given to stop all incoming traffic. The camera rolled at 7:25 and by 7:28 shooting was completed. All this trouble was for a scene of Belafonte walking through Times Square, which on the screen ran for exactly forty-five seconds. This was only one of thirty-seven different location set-ups.

On the Beach

John Paxton and James Lee Barrett wrote the screenplay for Stanley Kramer's production of Nevil Shute's best-selling novel, On the Beach (1959). It starred Gregory Peck, Ava Gardner, Fred Astaire, and Anthony Perkins. Nuclear war has made quick work of everyone in the northern hemisphere. Alone, Australia has not yet been affected. However, this refuge is only temporary as the deadly radioactive clouds, which cover the rest of the world, are slowly moving south. Suicide pills are dispensed to spare everyone the agony of radiation sickness. Among the survivors are Dwight Towers (Peck)—commander of the last operational U.S. submarine—and Moira Davidson (Gardner)—a world-weary divorcee. Defenses lowered, the couple allow themselves one last chance at happiness. As the end draws near, Towers's crew decides that they want to die closer to home. Reluctantly, Towers commandeers the submarine on its last voyage, and Moira, having found fulfillment, watches from the shore.

The last scene of the film is a view of the deserted streets. The radioactive cloud has finally killed all life and the silent city stands as a monument to a civilization whose technical advances outdistanced its capacity to control them. Blowing in the wind is a tattered banner from an earlier revival meeting which reads: There is still time, brother.

If the ending seemed a trifle heavy-handed, it is in keeping with the polemic attitude of producer-director Kramer. During the fifties and sixties, he functioned as America's liberal conscience, dealing with a myriad of controversial subjects including racism, the disabled, isolationism, mob violence, the mentally ill, the separation of church and state, war crimes, Nazism, mental retardation, and miscegenation. During much of this time, Kramer was one of the few outspoken liberal voices working within the largely conservative major studio struc-

ure. It is not at all surprising that he would take up the banner of nuclear dis-
rmament. Whatever reservations one might have concerning the excesses of
On the Beach and Kramer's ham-fisted direction, he was able to employ a big-
name cast in a major motion picture, making the subject acceptable to a mainstream audience who wouldn't be caught dead watching any of the other films
in this chapter.

Footnotes:

Dede Allen edited a number of important movies including *The Hustler* (1961), *Bonnie and Clyde* (1967), *Little Big Man* (1970), and *Serpico* (1973).

. Weaver, Tom. *Attack of the Monster Movie Makers*, McFarland & Co. Jefferson, NC, 1994, pg. 236.

EPILOGUE

They said *The Curse of Frankenstein* would haunt me forever, but I didn't believe them. It does, in fact, still haunt me. All of these movies haunt me. They've become so much a part of my life that I wouldn't know what to do without them. I was at an outdoor concert with some friends recently and, after having a little too much wine, Ace Mask pointed to the crystal-clear mountains and began talking as if he had just become at one with nature. Everything was beautiful, serene, and wonderful, and the air was crisp and clean. I let him wax on for a few minutes before I said, "But look at that cloud on the mountain. The Crawling Eye could be in that cloud." His expression changed from bliss to one of disgust and disappointment, the same expression I often wore while watching these movies.

Writing this book has been a lot of fun for me. I know I may have tickled a painful memory or two of an ill-spent afternoon watching *Curucu or Daughter of Dr. Jekyll*, but take some solace in the knowledge that between Randy and I, we saw every one of these movies, usually more than once.

Mark Thomas McGee

Appendix
Double Feature Packages
1955
Revenge of the Creature / Cult of the Cobra
It Came from Beneath the Sea / Creature with the Atom Brain
1956
Day the World Ended / Phantom from 10,000 Leagues
Invasion of the Body Snatchers / The Atomic Man
(in some areas, The Body Snatchers was paired with Indestructible Man)
World Without End / Indestructible Man
The Black Sleep / The Creeping Unknown
Earth vs. the Flying Saucers / The Werewolf
The She-Creature / It Conquered the World
1984 / The Gamma People
Man Beast / Prehistoric Women
Curucu, Beast of the Amazon / The Mole People
1957
Voodoo Island / Pharaoh's Curse
Voodoo Woman / The Undead
Attack of the Crab Monsters / Not of This Earth
Kronos / She Devil
Beginning of the End / The Unearthly
The Curse of Frankenstein / X... the Unknown
The Giant Claw / The Night the World Exploded
I Was a Teenage Werewolf / Invasion of the Saucer-Men
The Monster That Challenged the World / The Vampire
20 Million Miles to Earth / The 27th Day
The Cyclops / Daughter of Dr. Jekyll
Back from the Dead / The Unknown Terror
From Hell It Came / The Disembodied
The Amazing Colossal Man / The Cat Girl
I Was a Teenage Frankenstein / Blood of Dracula
1958
The Brain from Planet Arous / Teenage Monster
Bride and the Beast / The Beast of Budapest
Giant from the Unknown / She Demons
Viking Women and the Sea Serpent / The Astounding She-Monster
The Return of Dracula / The Flame Barrier
Attack of the 50ft Woman / War of the Satellites

The Revenge of Frankenstein / Curse of the Demon
Horror of Dracula / The Thing That Couldn't Die
The Space Children / The Colossus of New York
(in some areas, Colossus was paired with From the Earth to the Moon)
Cosmic Monsters / The Crawling Eye
Fiend Without a Face / The Haunted Strangler
The Fly / Space Master X-7
How to Make a Monster / Teenage Caveman
The Hideous Sun Demon / A Date with Death
Attack of the Puppet People / War of the Colossal Beast
It! The Terror from Beyond Space / Curse of the Faceless Man
Queen of Outer Space / Frankenstein 1970
The Blob / I Married a Monster from Outer Space
The Screaming Skull / The Brain Eaters
(in some areas, Brain Eaters was paired with Terror from the Year 5000)
Blood of the Vampire / Monster on the Campus
The Spider / Terror from the Year 5000
Missile Monsters / Satan's Satellites
Monster from Green Hell / Half Human
Frankenstein's Daughter / Missile to the Moon
The 7th Voyage of Sinbad / Ghost of the China Sea
1959
House on Haunted Hill / The Cosmic Man
The Four Skulls of Jonathan Drake / Invisible Invaders
(in some areas, Jonathan Drake was paired with The Hound of the Baskervilles;
Invaders with The Wonderful Country)
Horrors of the Black Museum / The Headless Ghost
The Mummy / Curse of the Undead
The Mysterians / The First Man into Space
The Killer Shrews / The Giant Gila Monster
Gigantis the Fire Monster / Teenagers from Outer Space
The H-Man / The Woman Eater
The Return of the Fly / The Alligator People
The Wasp Woman / Beast from Haunted Cave
A Bucket of Blood / Attack of the Giant Leeches
(in some locations, Bucket was paired with Circus of Horrors; Leeches with
House of Usher)
The Incredible Petrified World / Teenage Zombies
The Mummy / Curse of the Undead

Index

CPSIA information can be obtained at www.ICGtesting.com
Printed in the USA
LVOW04s0707240814

400621LV00004B/401/P